File for Divorce in California

Sixth Edition

File for Divorce in California

Sixth Edition

John J. Talamo

and

Edward A. Haman
Attorneys at Law

SPHINX® PUBLISHING
AN IMPRINT OF SOURCEBOOKS, INC.®
NAPERVILLE, ILLINOIS
www.SphinxLegal.com

Sixth Edition, 2008

Published by: **Sphinx® Publishing, An Imprint of Sourcebooks, Inc.®**

Naperville Office
P.O. Box 4410
Naperville, Illinois 60567-4410
630-961-3900
Fax: 630-961-2168
www.sourcebooks.com
www.SphinxLegal.com

This publication is designed to provide accurate and authoritative information in regard to the subject matter covered. It is sold with the understanding that the publisher is not engaged in rendering legal, accounting, or other professional service. If legal advice or other expert assistance is required, the services of a competent professional person should be sought.

From a Declaration of Principles Jointly Adopted by a Committee of the American Bar Association and a Committee of Publishers and Associations

This product is not a substitute for legal advice.

Disclaimer required by Texas statutes

Library of Congress Cataloging-in-Publication Data

Talamo, John.
  File for divorce in California / by John J. Talamo and Edward A.
Haman.-- 6th ed.
    p. cm.
  Includes index.
  ISBN-13: 978-1-57248-619-5 (pbk. : alk. paper)
  ISBN-10: 1-57248-619-8 (pbk. : alk. paper)
  1. Divorce--Law and legislation--California--Popular works. 2. Divorce
suits--California--Popular works. I. Haman, Edward A. II. Title.

  KFC126.Z9T35 2005
  346.79401'66--dc22
                                                            2005027010

Printed and bound in the United States of America.
SB — 10 9 8 7 6 5 4 3 2 1

Contents

Request for Judgment, Judgment of Dissolution of Marriage,
   and Notice of Entry of Judgment
Notice of Revocation of Petition for Summary Dissolution

Using Self-Help Law Books

Before using a self-help law book, you should realize the advantages and disadvantages of doing your own legal work and understand the challenges and diligence that this requires.

The Growing Trend

Rest assured that you will not be the first or only person handling your own legal matter. For example, in some states, more than 75% of the people in divorces and other cases represent themselves. Because of the high cost of legal services, this is a major trend, and many courts are struggling to make it easier for people to represent themselves. However, some courts are not happy with people who do not use attorneys and refuse to help them in any way. For some, the attitude is, "Go to the law library and figure it out for yourself."

We write and publish self-help law books to give people an alternative to the often complicated and confusing legal books found in most law libraries. We have made the explanations of the law as simple and easy to understand as possible. Of course, unlike an attorney advising an individual client, we cannot cover every conceivable possibility.

Cost/Value Analysis Whenever you shop for a product or service, you are faced with various levels of quality and price. In deciding what product or service to buy, you make a cost/value analysis on the basis of your willingness to pay and the quality you desire.

When buying a car, you decide whether you want transportation, comfort, status, or sex appeal. Accordingly, you decide among choices such as a Camry, a Lincoln, a Rolls Royce, or a Porsche. Before making a decision, you usually weigh the merits of each option against the cost.

When you get a headache, you can take a pain reliever (such as aspirin) or visit a medical specialist for a neurological examination. Given this choice, most people, of course, take a pain reliever, since it costs only pennies; whereas a medical examination may cost thousands of dollars and take a lot of time. This is usually a logical choice because it is rare to need anything more than a pain reliever for a headache. But in some cases, a headache may indicate a brain tumor, and failing to see a specialist right away can result in complications. Should everyone with a headache go to a specialist? Of course not, but people treating their own illnesses must realize that they are betting, on the basis of their cost/value analysis of the situation, that they are taking the most logical option.

The same cost/value analysis must be made when deciding to do one's own legal work. Many legal situations are very straightforward, requiring a simple form and no complicated analysis. Anyone with a little intelligence and a book of instructions can handle the matter without outside help.

But there is always the chance that complications are involved that only an attorney would notice. To simplify the law into a book like this, several legal cases often must be condensed into a single sentence or paragraph. Otherwise, the book would be several hundred pages longer and too complicated for most people. However, this simplification necessarily leaves out many details and nuances that would apply to special or unusual situations. Also, there are many ways to interpret most legal questions. Your case may come before a judge who disagrees with the analysis of our authors.

Therefore, in deciding to use a self-help law book and to do your own legal work, you must realize that you are making a cost/value analysis. You have decided that the money you will save in doing it yourself outweighs the chance that your case will not turn out to your satisfaction. Most people handling their own simple legal matters never have a problem, but occasionally people find that it ended up costing them more to have an attorney straighten out the situation than it would have if they had hired an attorney in the beginning. Keep this in mind while handling your case, and be sure to consult an attorney if you feel you might need further guidance.

Local Rules   The next thing to remember is that a book which covers the law for the entire nation, or even for an entire state, cannot possibly include every procedural difference of every jurisdiction. Whenever possible, we provide the exact form needed; however, in some areas, each county, or even each judge, may require unique forms and procedures. In our state books, our forms usually cover the majority of counties in the state or provide examples of the type of form that will be required. In our national books, our forms are sometimes even more general in nature but are designed to give a good idea of the type of form that will be needed in most locations. Nonetheless, keep in mind that your state, county, or judge may have a requirement, or use a form, that is not included in this book.

You should not necessarily expect to be able to get all of the information and resources you need solely from within the pages of this book. This book will serve as your guide, giving you specific information whenever possible and helping you to find out what else you will need to know. This is just as if you decided to build your own backyard deck. You might purchase a book on how to build decks. However, such a book would not include the building codes and permit requirements of every city, town, county, and township in the nation; nor would it include the lumber, nails, saws, hammers, and other materials and tools you would need to actually build the deck. You would use the book as your guide, and then do some work and research involving such matters as whether you need a permit of some kind, what type and grade of wood is available in your area, whether to use hand tools or power tools, and how to use those tools.

Before using the forms in a book like this, you should check with your court clerk to see if there are any local rules of which you should be aware or local forms you will need to use. Often, such forms will require the same information as the forms in the book but are merely laid out differently or use slightly different language. They will sometimes require additional information.

Changes in the Law
Besides being subject to local rules and practices, the law is subject to change at any time. The courts and the legislatures of all fifty states are constantly revising the laws. It is possible that while you are reading this book, some aspect of the law is being changed.

In most cases, the change will be of minimal significance. A form will be redesigned, additional information will be required, or a waiting period will be extended. As a result, you might need to revise a form, file an extra form, or wait out a longer time period. These types of changes will not usually affect the outcome of your case. On the other hand, sometimes a major part of the law is changed, the entire law in a particular area is rewritten, or a case that was the basis of a central legal point is overruled. In such instances, your entire ability to pursue your case may be impaired.

Introduction

Going through a divorce is one of the most common, and most traumatic, encounters with the legal system. At a time when you are least likely to have extra funds, paying a divorce lawyer can be one of the most expensive bills to pay. In a contested divorce case, it is not uncommon for the parties to run up legal bills of over $10,000. Horror stories abound of lawyers charging substantial fees with little progress to show for it. This book will enable those of you without high-risk issues to obtain a divorce without hiring a lawyer. Even if you do hire a lawyer, this book will help you to work with him or her more effectively, which can also reduce the legal fee.

This is not a law school course, but a practical guide to get you through the system as easily as possible. Legal jargon has been nearly eliminated. For ease of understanding, this book uses the term *spouse* to refer to your husband or wife (whichever applies), and the terms *child* and *children* are used interchangeably.

Please keep in mind that different judges, and courts in different counties, may have their own particular (if not peculiar) procedures, forms, and ways of doing things. The court clerk's office can often tell you if it has any special forms or requirements, but court clerks will not give you legal advice.

The first two chapters of this book give you an overview of the law and the legal system. Chapter 3 helps you decide if you want an attorney. Chapter 4 helps you evaluate your situation and gives you an idea of what to expect if you decide to go through with a divorce. The remaining chapters show you what forms you need, how to fill out the forms, and what procedures to follow.

You will also find two appendices in the back of the book. Appendix A contains selected portions of the California law and court rules dealing with property division, alimony, and child support. Although these provisions are discussed in the book, it is sometimes helpful to read the law exactly as it is written.

Appendix B contains the forms you will complete. You will not need to use all of the forms. This book tells you which forms you need, depending upon your situation. Most of the forms in Appendix B are California Judicial Council forms, which are found in the Family Code, and which must be used according to the local rules of almost all courts. The California Judicial Council forms are updated periodically, and courts will not accept the old version of a form. Therefore, you should check with the court clerk's office to be sure you use the most current version of a form.

Be sure to read "An Introduction to Legal Forms" in Chapter 5 before you use any of the forms in this book.

Marriage Ins and Outs

Several years (or maybe only months) ago you made a decision to get married. This chapter discusses, in a general way, what you got yourself into, how to get out, and whether you really want to do so.

MARRIAGE

Marriage is frequently referred to as a contract. It is a legal contract, and for many, it is also a religious contract. This book deals only with the legal aspects. The wedding ceremony involves the bride and groom reciting certain vows, which are actually mutual promises about how they will treat each other. There are legal papers signed, such as a marriage license and a marriage certificate. These formalities create certain rights and obligations for the husband and wife. Although the focus at the ceremony is on the emotional aspects of the relationship, the legal reality is that financial and property rights are being created. It is these financial and property rights and obligations that cannot be altered without a legal proceeding.

Marriage gives each party certain rights in property. It also creates certain obligations of support for the spouse and any children they have together (or adopt). Unfortunately, most people do not fully realize that these rights and obligations are being created until it comes time for a divorce.

California does not recognize common law marriage, which is a marriage without a marriage ceremony or certificate. Some states confer the benefits and responsibilities of marriage on couples who have lived together and acted as a married couple for a certain time period.

California does, as a practical matter, recognize same-sex marriage. It is not called marriage, but *domestic partnership*. Ending a registered domestic partnership requires much the same procedure as ending a marriage.

This book uses the term "marriage" to refer to both married couples and domestic partners. The legal and procedural differences for divorce are addressed in Chapter 2. If you are in a domestic partnership and have no children, own no real estate together, have few assets and debts, want no support and agree on all aspects of ending the relationship, go directly to Chapter 8 to see if you qualify for a simple termination procedure not available to married couples. If you do not qualify, you will use the same procedures as a married couple.

DIVORCE

A divorce is the most common method of terminating or breaking the marriage contract. In California, a divorce is officially called a *dissolution of marriage*. In this book, the terms *divorce* and *dissolution of marriage* are used interchangeably and have the same meaning. In a divorce, the court declares the marriage contract broken, divides the parties' property and debts, decides if either party should receive support, and determines the custody, support, and visitation with respect to any children the parties may have.

Traditionally, a divorce could only be granted under certain specific circumstances, such as for *adultery* or *mental cruelty*. Today, a divorce is granted simply because one or both of the parties want one. The wording used is that *irreconcilable differences* have arisen in the marriage, and those such irreconcilable differences are *irremediable*.

NULLITY (ANNULMENT)

Nullity is the legal name for an annulment. It differs from divorce in that the marriage itself becomes invalid. The result is as if the marriage never occurred.

There are two types of marriages subject to nullity. The first is a marriage that is *void*. This means that there never was a marriage as far as the law is concerned. There are only two grounds for a void marriage—incest and bigamy. *Incest* is marriage to a close relative. (Family Code Section 2200 lists the relationships.) *Bigamy* is when one of the parties is already married to someone else. (Family Code, Section 2201.)

A void marriage can happen even if the parties *never go to court*, although having a court determination removes any uncertainty about the marital status. Also, even though there legally was never a marriage, support and property rights may be asserted as if a marriage existed.

The second type of marriage subject to nullity is the *voidable marriage*. The grounds are minority, unsound mind, fraud, force, physical incapacity, and two exceptions to the bigamy rule discussed above under void marriages. The party seeking the nullity must prove the allegations or the marriage remains valid.

The grounds for nullity are set forth in Family Code Sections 2210 and 2211. There is no reason to go through each one here. There are, however, some things you should know.

- ✪ Unlike *no fault* divorce, the grounds for nullity must be proved. This makes it more difficult to obtain.

- ✪ There is a time limit for bringing the action, except for bigamy and unsound mind. The limitation is four years from the marriage date for force and physical incapacity; in the case of fraud, four years from the date of learning of the fraud; and in the case of minority, four years from the date the minor turns 18 years old.

✪   A spouse changing after marriage, no matter how radical or disappointing the change may be, is not grounds for nullity. Grounds for nullity must exist at the time of the marriage.

Voidable marriages are valid unless the court grants a nullity. Unlike the void marriage, there must be a court action. An attorney should be consulted if you are seeking a nullity.

LEGAL SEPARATION

California permits a *legal separation*. This procedure is used to divide the property and provide for child custody and support in cases in which the husband and wife live separately, but remain married. This is usually used to break the financial rights and obligations of a couple whose religion does not permit divorce. It may also be advantageous when a divorce would cause one of the parties to lose Social Security, veteran's, or other benefits, or cause a spouse with a serious illness or disability to lose medical insurance.

The term *legal separation* is used in two contexts in California:

1.   when a spouse physically separates (*e.g.*, leaves the house) with the intent to obtain a divorce, the parties are said to be legally separated; and,

2.   when a spouse obtains a formal legal separation in court.

In both instances, the sweep of the *community property laws* stop (see Chapter 4) and the assets and debts obtained by a spouse after such legal separation are that spouse's separate assets and debts. A spouse does not have to leave the house to be legally separated. The decision to divorce without the intent to reconcile is what is important. When a spouse obtains a court legal separation, the grounds are the same as for a dissolution of marriage. So unless you are seeking a legal separation for one of the specific reasons stated previously, there is usually little reason to get a legal separation instead of a dissolution of marriage.

NOTE: *See an attorney if you believe you might need a legal separation instead of a divorce.*

– Caution –

If you are moving out of the house with the intent to seek a divorce, tell your spouse. If you say you just need some time alone or something similar, what you earn before you begin the divorce proceedings may be community property (half belonging to your spouse). Something in writing or before a witness is better since verbal communication is difficult to prove.

DO YOU REALLY WANT A DIVORCE?

Getting a divorce is one of the most emotionally stressful events in a person's life. So, before beginning the process of getting a divorce, you should think about its effects on your life. This section discusses these effects and offers alternatives if you want to try to save your relationship. Even if you feel absolutely sure that you want a divorce, you should still read this section so that you are prepared for what may follow.

Divorce is the breaking of your matrimonial bonds—the termination of your marriage contract and partnership. Going through the court system and dealing with your spouse creates a lot of stress. Divorce can be confrontational and emotionally explosive. There are generally five matters to be resolved through divorce:

1. the divorce of two people (basically, this gives each the legal right to marry someone else);

2. the division of their property (and responsibility for debts);

3. the care and custody of their children;

4. spousal support; and,

5. child support.

Although it is theoretically possible for a legal divorce to be granted after a few months, the legalities often continue for years. This is most often caused by emotional aspects leading to battles over the children.

Divorce will have a tremendous impact on your social and emotional lives that will continue long after you are legally divorced. These impacts include the following.

Lack of companionship. Even if your marriage is quite stormy, you are still accustomed to having your spouse around. As a result, you may notice emptiness or loneliness after the divorce. It may not be that you miss your spouse in particular, but just miss another person being around.

Grief. Divorce may be viewed as the death of a marriage, or maybe the funeral ceremony for the death of a marriage. Like the death of anyone you have been close to, you might feel a sense of loss. This can take you through all of the normal feelings associated with grief, such as guilt, anger, denial, and acceptance. You might feel angry and frustrated over the years you have "wasted." You might feel guilty because you failed to make the marriage work. You might find yourself saying, *I can't believe this is happening to me.* For months or even years, you might spend a lot of time thinking about your marriage. It can be extremely difficult to put it all behind you and get on with your life.

Dating. After divorce, your social life will change. If you want to avoid solitary evenings before the TV, you will find yourself trying to get back into the *singles' scene.* This will probably involve a change in friends, as well as a change in lifestyle. This can be very difficult, especially if you have custody of the children. On the other hand, it can be an exciting adventure.

Divorce has a significant financial impact in just about every case. Many married couples are just able to make ends meet. After getting divorced, there are suddenly two rent payments, two electric bills, etc. For the spouse without custody, there is also child support to be paid. For at least one spouse, and often for both, money becomes even tighter than it was before the divorce. Also, once you have divided your property, each of you may need to replace the items the other person got to keep.

The effect upon your children, and your relationship with them, can often be the most painful and long-lasting aspect of divorce. Your relationship with your children may become strained as they work through their feelings of blame, guilt, disappointment, and anger. This strain may continue for years. Your children may even need professional counseling. Also, as long as child support and visitation are involved, you will be forced to have at least some contact with your ex-spouse.

By the time you have purchased this book and read this far, you may have already decided that you want a divorce. However, if what you have just read has made you want to make a last effort to save your marriage, there are a few things you can try. These are only very basic suggestions. Details and other suggestions can be offered by professional marriage counselors.

Talk to your spouse. Choose the right time (not when your spouse is trying to unwind after a day at work or is trying to quiet a screaming baby) to talk about your problems. Try to establish a few ground rules for the discussion.

- ✪   Talk about how you feel instead of making accusations that may start an argument.

- ✪   Each person listens while the other speaks (no interrupting).

- ✪   Each person must say something that he or she likes about the other and about the relationship.

As you talk, you may want to discuss such things as where you would like your relationship to go, how it has changed since you got married, and what can be done to bring you closer together.

Change your thinking. Many people get divorced because they will not change something about their outlook or their lifestyle. Then, once they get divorced, they find they have made that same change they resisted for so long.

Example:
George and Wendy were unhappy in their marriage. They did not seem to share the same lifestyle. George felt overburdened with responsibility and bored. He wanted Wendy to be more independent and outgoing, meet new people, handle the

household budget, and go out with him more often. However, Wendy was more shy and reserved, was not confident in her ability to find a job and succeed in the business world, and preferred to stay at home. Wendy wanted George to give up some of his frequent nights out with the guys, help with the cooking and laundry, stop leaving messes for her to clean up, and stop bothering her about going out all the time. But neither would try change, and eventually all of the little things built up into a divorce.

After the divorce, Wendy was forced to get a job to support herself. Now she has made friends at work and goes out with them two or three nights a week. She is successful and happy at her job, and she is quite competent at managing her own budget. George now has his own apartment, cooks his own meals (something he finds he enjoys), and does his own laundry. He has also found it necessary to clean up his own messes and keep the place neat, especially if he is going to entertain guests.

Both George and Wendy have changed in exactly the way the other had wanted. It is just too bad they did not make these changes before they got divorced! If you think some change may help, give it a try. You can always go back to a divorce if things do not work.

Counseling. Counseling is not the same as giving advice. A counselor should not be telling you what to do. A counselor's job is to assist you in figuring out what you really want to do. A counselor's job is mostly to ask questions that will get you thinking.

Just talking things out with your spouse is a form of self-counseling. The only problem is that it is difficult to remain objective and non-judgmental. You both need to be able to calmly analyze what the problems are and discuss possible solutions.

Very few couples seem to be able to do this successfully, which is why there are professional marriage counselors. As with doctors and lawyers, good marriage counselors are best discovered by word of mouth. You may have friends who can direct you to someone who helped them. You can also check with your family doctor or your clergyman for a referral, or even check the Yellow Pages under "Marriage and Family Counselors" or a similar category. You can see a counselor either alone or with your spouse. It may be a good idea for you to see a counselor even if you decide to go through with the divorce.

Another form of individual counseling is talking to a close friend. Just remember the difference between counseling and advice giving. Do not let your friend tell you what you should do.

Trial separation. Before going through the time, expense, and trouble of getting a divorce, you and your spouse may want to try just getting away from each other for awhile. This can be as simple as taking separate vacations, or as complex as actually separating into separate households for an indefinite period of time. This may give each of you a chance to think about how you will like living alone, how important or trivial your problems are, and how you really feel about each other.

NOTE: *Your immigration status in the United States could be jeopardized by a divorce. If you are not a citizen of the United States, consult an immigration attorney before filing any court papers.*

chapter 2

The Legal System

This chapter gives you a general introduction to the legal system. There are things you need to know in order to obtain a divorce (or help your lawyer get the job done) and to get through the legal system with minimum stress. These are some of the realities of our system. If you do not learn to accept these realities, you will experience much stress and frustration.

THEORY VS. REALITY

Our legal system is a system of rules. There are basically three types of rules.

1. *Rules of Law.* These provide the basic substance of the law, such as a law telling a judge how to go about dividing your property.

2. *Rules of Procedure.* These tell how matters are to be handled in the courts, such as requiring court papers to be in a certain form, delivered to the other party in a certain manner, or filed within a certain time.

3. *Rules of Evidence.* These require facts to be proven in a certain way.

The theory is that these rules allow each side to present evidence most favorable to that side, and an independent person or persons (the judge or jury) will be able to figure out the true facts (*i.e.*, which evidence is more reliable). Legal principles will be applied to those facts, which will give a fair resolution of the dispute between the parties. These legal principles are supposed to be relatively constant so that we can all know what will happen in any given situation and can plan our lives accordingly. This provides order and predictability to our society. Any change in the legal principles is supposed to occur slowly, so that the expected behavior in our society is not confused day to day.

The System is Not Perfect

Contrary to how it may seem, legal rules are not made just to complicate things and confuse everyone. They are attempts to make the system fair and just. They have been developed over hundreds of years, and in most cases, they do make sense. Unfortunately, our efforts to find fairness and justice have resulted in complex rules. The legal system affects our lives in important ways, and it is not a game. However, it can be compared to a game in some ways. The rules are designed to apply to all people and in all cases. Sometimes the rules do not seem to give a fair result in a certain situation, but the rules are still followed. Just as a referee can make a bad call, so can a judge.

The System is Often Slow

Even lawyers get frustrated at how long it can take to get a case completed. Whatever your situation, things will take longer than you expect. Patience is required to get through the system with minimum stress. Do not let your impatience or frustration show. No matter what happens, keep calm and be courteous and polite to the judge, to the court clerks, to any lawyers involved, and even to your spouse.

No Two Cases are Alike

Just because your friend's case went a certain way does not mean that yours will have the same result. The judge can make a difference, and more often than not, the circumstances will make a difference. Just because your co-worker makes the same income as you and has the same number of children, you cannot assume you will be ordered to pay the same amount of child support. There are usually other circumstances involved that account for differences.

Half of the People Lose

Remember, there are two sides to every legal issue, and there is only one winner. Do not expect to have every detail go your way. If you leave anything to the judge to decide, you can expect to have some things go your spouse's way.

THE PLAYERS

The law and the legal system are often compared to games, and just like games, it is important to know the players.

The Judge   Getting the divorce itself (what lawyers call *status*) is usually automatic. How your property will be divided, which of you will get custody of the children, and how much the other will pay for child support and spousal support is the province of the judge. The more you and your spouse can agree on and the more complete your paperwork is, the more you will please the judge.

The judge is the last person you want to make angry with you. In general, judges have large caseloads and like it best when your case can be concluded quickly and without hassle.

The Judge's Secretary   The judge's secretary sets the hearings for the judge. He or she can frequently answer many of your questions about the procedure and what the judge will require.

The Court Clerk   The court clerk handles the files for all of the judges. The clerk's office is the central place where all of the court files are kept. The clerk files your court papers and keeps the official records of your divorce.

Most people who work in the clerk's office are friendly and helpful. While they cannot give you legal advice (such as telling you what to say in your court papers), they can help explain the system and the procedures (such as telling you what type of papers must be filed).

The clerk has the power to accept or reject your papers, so you do not want to anger the clerk. If the clerk tells you to change something in your papers, just change it. Do not argue or complain.

Lawyers   Lawyers serve as guides through the legal system. They try to guide their own clients and be advocates for them. (Chapter 3 discusses lawyers in more detail.)

Family Law Facilitator   In 1996, California created the *Family Law Facilitator Act*. The family law facilitator is available to anyone who does not have a lawyer. Your ability to see a family law facilitator is not dependent on how much or how little money you make. The California Court website at **www.courtinfo.ca.gov** provides information about family law facilitators.

What is a family law facilitator? A family law facilitator is a lawyer with experience in family law who works for the superior court in your county to help parents and children involved in family law cases with child, spousal, and partner support problems.

What does the family law facilitator do? The family law facilitator gives you educational materials that explain how to:

✪   establish parentage and

✪   get, change, or enforce child, spousal, or partner support orders.

The family law facilitator can also:

✪   give you the court forms you need;

✪   help you fill out your forms;

✪   help you figure out support amounts; and,

✪   refer you to your local child support agency, family court services, and other community agencies that help parents and children.

The family law facilitator in your county may be able to help you in other ways as well.

The family law facilitator is not *your* lawyer. He or she is an independent lawyer who can help parents or children who do not have their own lawyer.

Both parties can get help from the same family law facilitator. You do not have attorney-client privilege, so what you say to the family law facilitator is not confidential.

Your local office. Not all Family Law Facilitator offices are able to assist with dissolution (divorce) and custody issues. Some counties limit services to child support, spousal support, partner support, and health insurance in ongoing cases. Contact your legal office for further information. Type "California family law facilitator" into any search engine to find the office in your county. In areas where there is not enough staffing to handle one-on-one sessions, there may be group meetings to explain rights and answer questions.

NOTE: *Domestic partners have the same right to the facilitator as married couples.*

This Book This book will serve as your map through the legal system. If you start getting lost or the dangers seem to be getting worse, hire a lawyer to come to your aid.

DIVORCE LAW

The law of divorce, as well as any other area of law, comes from two sources:

1. California statutes, which are laws passed by the California Legislature, and

2. past decisions of the California appeal courts.

A portion of the California statutes relating to property division, spousal support, and child support can be found in Appendix A of this book.

Residency Requirement: One basic law of which you need to be aware is that either you or your spouse must have lived in California for at least six months, and in the county where the divorce case is being filed for at least three months, immediately before filing your Petition with the court.

NOTE: *If you do not meet these residency requirements and need to file immediately, an attorney may be able to guide you around this obstacle.*

The other source of law, which is the past decisions of the California appeal courts, is more difficult to locate and follow. However, if you wish to learn more about how to find these court decisions, see the section on "Legal Research" later in this chapter.

You will need to show the following in a divorce:

❂ a statement that your marriage has differences that are *irreconcilable* and *irremediable* (this is done simply by stating as much, which means that your marriage cannot be saved);

❂ how your property should be divided between you and your spouse;

❂ if spousal support should be awarded, and in what amount; and,

❂ how custody of your children is divided and how they should be supported.

DIVORCE PROCEDURE

The procedural requirements come from the California statutes, the California Rules of Court, and the local rules of court. The basic uncontested divorce process may be viewed as a five-step process.

1. File court papers asking the judge to grant a divorce (which includes dividing property, deciding how the children will be taken care of, as well as determining child and spousal support).

2. Notify your spouse that you are filing for divorce.

3. File papers explaining your financial situation, and upon what you and your spouse have agreed.

4. Obtain a hearing date.

5. Attend a hearing before the judge, and have the judge sign a judgment to finalize the divorce.

There is a *Summary Dissolution* procedure that some people can use that allows them to skip some of these steps. (see Chapter 6.) Each of the five steps are looked at here in a little more detail, and then later chapters tell you how to carry out these steps.

Preparing and Filing a Petition

A **Petition** (form 3, form 3A, or form 22) is simply a written request for the judge to grant you a divorce and divide your property. Instructions for completing the forms are provided in later chapters. Once the **Petition** is completed, it is taken to the court clerk to be filed.

Notifying Your Spouse

After you have prepared the **Petition**, you need to officially notify your spouse. Even though your spouse may already know that you are filing for divorce, you still need to have him or her *officially* notified. This is done by having a copy of your **Petition** delivered to your spouse. This must be done in a specific manner that is explained in detail later.

Obtaining a Hearing Date

Once all of your paperwork has been filed, you need to set a date for a hearing for the granting of the divorce. This is done by filing a request for an uncontested or a contested hearing with the court clerk.

The Hearing

The judge will review the papers you have submitted and any additional information you have. The judge will then make a decision about whether to grant the divorce, how your property should be divided, whether spousal support is payable, how custody of your children will be divided, and how the children are to be supported. If you and your spouse agree on these matters, the judge may simply approve your agreement if he or she finds the agreement is in the best interests of the children.

Conciliation

If you live in a county with a Conciliation Court and have any disagreements about child custody or visitation, the judge will order you and your spouse to participate in a *mediation process* called *conciliation*. You will not be allowed to present your case to the judge before the court *mediator* speaks with you about the children. Often, the mediator can resolve the dispute by dispelling any misinformation that you or your spouse may have regarding your children.

Local Variations and Rules

Unfortunately, each county superior court has its own multitude of policies called *local court rules*. Additionally, be aware that an individual judge may have particular policies for his or her courtroom, that court rules are not always followed, and that rules can change frequently. In order to get your divorce through the system with minimum hassle, determine the local policy on major matters. The clerk's office or family law facilitator each know local requirements.

LEGAL RESEARCH

If you need or want to find out more about divorce law in California, this section gives you some guidance on how to go about doing this.

The Internet

Almost everything you can find in a law library can be found from your home or office on the Internet. The difference is that, unlike the library, much of it requires payment. One of the best free sites is **www.courtinfo.ca.gov/selfhelp/family/divorce**. An easy way to access it is to type "California court self-help center" into any search engine. It is a good idea to access this site even if you do not think you need it because they have the latest forms and information.

> **NOTE:** *Out-of-date forms will not be accepted and will delay your filing. The forms in this book are the latest forms available at the time of publication. While some forms rarely change, it is up to you to verify that you are using the latest court mandated form.*

California Codes

The main source of California divorce law is the portion of the California statutes called the *Family Code*. This is a set of laws passed by the California Legislature. A set can usually be found at the public library, although be sure they have the most recent set. The *Family Code* is also available on the Internet and at law libraries in *West's Annotated California Codes* or *Deerings California Annotated Codes*. These are volumes that contain the California statutes, followed by summaries (or *annotations*) of court cases that discuss each section of the statutes. Both of these sets contain all of the California statutes—not just those relating to divorce (*e.g.*, *Probate Code* and *Criminal Code*). They are divided into various subjects, so look for the volumes marked "Family Code."

Case Law

In addition to the laws passed by the legislature, law is also made by the decisions of the appeal courts. This *case law* will be found at a law library. Each county has a law library connected with the court, so ask the court clerk where the law library is located. Also, law schools have libraries that may be open to the public. Case law may be found in the annotations in the code books as well as the specific references listed below.

California Digest

West's California Digest, 2d gives short summaries of cases and is the place where you can find the court's full written opinion. The information in the digest is arranged alphabetically by subject.

Case Reporters

Case reporters are books containing written opinions of appellate courts on cases that have been appealed to them. California has two versions of appellate cases—the official version published by statutory authority and the unofficial version published by West Publishing as part of its National Reporter System.

The case citations in both are similar. A case in the official reports will be referred to as, for example, *Smith v. Jones*, 19 Cal. App. 4th 198 (1988). This tells you that the case titled *Smith v. Jones* may be found in volume 19 of the set of books called *California Appellate Reports, Fourth Series*, on page 198. The number in parentheses (1988) is the year in which the case was decided. The same case in the unofficial reports would be referred to as, for example, *Smith v. Jones*, 48 Cal. Rptr. 483 (1988), which tells you the case titled *Smith v. Jones* is found in volume 48 of the set of books called *California Reporter*, on page 483.

California Jurisprudence

California Jurisprudence (Cal. Jur.) is a legal encyclopedia. You simply look up the subject you want (*e.g.*, Dissolution of Marriage), in alphabetical order, and it gives you a summary of the law on that subject. It will also refer to specific court cases.

California Rules of Court

The *California Rules of Court* are the rules that are applied in the various courts in California. They also contain approved forms. You will primarily be concerned with the *Family Law Rules* beginning with Rule 1200.

Other Sources

Other sources at the law library include the following.

- ✪ *California Practice Guide, Family Law*, published by the Rutter Group, a West Group affiliate.

- ✪ *California Family Law Practice and Procedure, 2d ed.,* published by Matthew Bender Company.

- ✪ *Practice Under the California Family Code,* published by the California Continuing Education of the Bar.

- ✪ *California Domestic Partnerships*, published by the California Continuing Education of the Bar.

Lawyers

Whether or not you need an attorney will depend upon many factors, such as how comfortable you feel handling the matter yourself, whether your situation is more complicated than usual, and how much opposition you get from your spouse or from your spouse's attorney. It may also be advisable to hire an attorney if you encounter a judge with a hostile attitude. A very general rule is that you should consider hiring an attorney whenever you reach a point in which you no longer feel comfortable representing yourself. This point will vary greatly with each person, so there is no easy way to be more definite. Other situations in which you might need an attorney are discussed in later chapters of this book.

THE NEED FOR A LAWYER

Although this book is about going it alone, you may want to hire an attorney for several reasons. One of the most important things you can do in any legal action is to think clearly and objectively. Divorce is probably the most difficult area of the law to do this. You are dealing with someone you believed you would stay with for a lifetime. You now either feel guilty because you are breaking up the marriage or bitter because your spouse is breaking up the marriage. You might be trying to save the marriage. Any of these feelings can cloud your judgment, which can cost you money.

A lawyer has no feelings, good or bad, about your spouse. This, coupled with experience, can save later regret as to the outcome. If you find yourself in a situation similar to the ones discussed below, hiring an attorney may be in your best interest.

✪   You do not want the marriage to end and believe by giving in to your spouse's demands he or she will change his or her mind.

Example:

A woman wrote to a legal advice column in a newspaper. She wrote that her husband wanted a divorce. She did not. Her strategy was to agree to everything he wanted. He would then see what a good person she was and how much she still loved him. He would change his mind and they would get back together again.

It is not hard to predict that she will later regret this strategy. Not only will she lose her husband, she will lose many financial benefits that might make her life alone a little, or maybe a lot, easier. This may seem like a ludicrous example, but it happens more often than you would expect.

✪   You know little about the family finances. In most marriages, one of the spouses writes the checks and keeps track of their financial status. There are many couples in which not only is one unaware of day-to-day bills and expenses but is also unaware of the major commitments like how much is owed on the mortgage.

If this is your situation, you need someone such as a lawyer or accountant to tell you exactly what you own, what you owe, and what might be a fair division of these assets and liabilities. Even though you may simply want to be fair, do not count on your spouse feeling the same way. People who are normally honest and fair minded can become, to put it plainly, mean and sneaky in a divorce proceeding.

✪   You always give in to your spouse or are intimidated by him or her. If your spouse could always talk you into things you really did not want to do, or you feel threatened by him or her, you need a buffer. You do not want direct negotiations.

✪   If your spouse has a lawyer, you will most likely be at a disadvantage without one.

DECIDING TO USE A LAWYER

In deciding to use a lawyer, one of the first questions you want to consider is, *How much will an attorney cost?* Attorneys come in all ages, shapes, sizes, sexes, races, and ethnicities—and price ranges. For a very rough estimate, you can expect an attorney to charge from $1,500 to $2,000 for an uncontested divorce, and $2,500 and up for a contested divorce.

Lawyers usually charge an hourly rate for contested divorces, ranging from about $150 to $350 per hour. Most new (and less expensive) attorneys are capable of handling a simple divorce, but if your situation became complicated, you would probably prefer an experienced lawyer. As a general rule, your legal bill will be more than what you thought it would cost at the beginning.

The following are some of the advantages to hiring a lawyer.

✪   Judges and other attorneys will take you more seriously. Most judges prefer both parties to have attorneys. They feel this helps the case move in a more orderly fashion because both sides will know the procedures and relevant issues. Persons representing themselves often waste time on matters that have no bearing on the case.

✪   You can let your lawyer worry about the details. By having an attorney you need only become generally familiar with the contents of this book, as it will be your attorney's job to file the proper papers in the correct form and to deal with the court clerks, the judge, the process server, your spouse, and your spouse's attorney.

✪ Lawyers provide professional assistance with problems. In the event your case is complicated or suddenly becomes complicated, it is an advantage to have an attorney who is familiar with your case. It can also be comforting to have a lawyer to turn to for advice and to answer your questions.

The following are some advantages to representing yourself.

✪ You save the cost of a lawyer.

✪ Sometimes judges permit the unrepresented person a certain amount of leeway with the procedure.

✪ The procedure may be faster. Two of the most frequent complaints received by the bar association about lawyers involve delay in completing the case and failure to return phone calls. Most lawyers have a heavy caseload, which sometimes results in cases being neglected for periods of time. If you are following the progress of your own case, you will be able to push it along the system diligently.

✪ Selecting an attorney is not easy. As the next section shows, it is difficult to know whether you are selecting an attorney that will make you happy.

You may want to look for an attorney who will be willing to accept an hourly fee to answer your questions and give you help as you need it. This way, you will save some legal costs but still get some professional assistance. Not all attorneys are willing to do this. Some insist on handling your case completely.

There are law firms that specialize in doing everything except the contested divorce trial. They want to mediate, negotiate, fill out forms, and give advice. Check the firms in your area and ask what they are willing to do.

Also, consider making all your settlement arrangements. Tentatively agree to them. Then take them to a lawyer and get an opinion as to whether this is a fair settlement. Be sure to let your spouse know that your agreement is tentative. You might even want to write a note to your spouse that you will make a final decision by a certain date. Then see the lawyer.

NOTE: *If possible, agree to the settlement. Do not squabble over minor things. Once you try to change the agreement, your spouse will most likely start picking at it also. Naturally, if you discover that the settlement is basically unfair, you have no choice but to renegotiate.*

SELECTING A LAWYER

Selecting a lawyer is a two-step process. First, you need to decide with which attorney to make an appointment. Then you need to decide if you want to hire that attorney. California has a good system for finding a lawyer. Lawyers can be certified as *specialists* by practicing for a specified number of hours in a certain area of the law and passing tests displaying their knowledge.

Finding a Lawyer

The following are some suggestions to help you locate lawyers.

✪ Contact your local bar association or the State Bar of California. Either can be contacted by phone or on the Internet. Type the words "California Bar Association" into any search engine to get the website. You can find the specialists in your area and start contacting them to pick one. The State Bar also has listings for legal help that is either free or at a low cost.

> **NOTE:** *Use a search engine as Web addresses change. The search engine will give you the current site and related sites that may be helpful.*

✪ Check the Internet. Many attorneys now advertise on the Internet, and attorney referral services operated by a host of private organizations provide names, locations, and specialties of attorneys in your area.

✪ Ask a friend. A common, and frequently the best, way to find a lawyer is to ask someone you know. This is especially helpful if the lawyer represented your friend in a divorce or other family law matter.

✪ Find a lawyer referral service. You can find a referral service by looking in the Yellow Pages phone directory under "Attorney Referral Services" or "Attorneys." This is a service, usually operated by a bar association, designed to match a client with an attorney handling cases in the area of law the client needs. The referral service does not guarantee the quality of work nor the level of experience or ability of the attorney. Finding a lawyer this way will at least connect you with one who is interested in divorce and family law matters and probably has some experience in this area.

✪ Check under the heading for "Attorneys—Divorce" in the Yellow Pages phone directory. Many of the lawyers and law firms place display ads indicating their experience and educational backgrounds. Look for firms or lawyers that indicate they practice in areas such as "divorce," "family law," or "domestic relations."

✪ Ask another lawyer. If you have used the services of an attorney in the past for some other matter (for example, a real estate closing, traffic ticket, or a will), you may want to call and ask if he or she could refer you to an attorney whose ability in the area of family law is respected.

Evaluating a Lawyer

Select three to five lawyers worthy of further consideration. Your first step will be to call each attorney's office, explain that you are interested in seeking a divorce, and ask the following questions.

✪ Does the attorney (or firm) handle divorces?

✪ How much will it cost? (Do not expect to get a definite answer, but they may be able to give you a range or an hourly rate. You will probably need to talk to the lawyer for anything more detailed.)

✪ How soon can you get an appointment?

If you like the answers you get, ask if you can speak to the attorney. Some offices will permit this, but others will require you to make an appointment. Make the appointment if that is what is required, but be sure to ask first what this appointment will cost. (Some attorneys will not charge for the first appointment, others will charge a nominal fee such as $20, and others will start the meter running at their regular hourly rate the moment you step into their office.)

Once you get in contact with the attorney (either on the phone or at the appointment), ask the following questions.

- ✪ How much will it cost?

- ✪ Is there a lower fee for work done by a paralegal in the office? (Some attorneys separate the work they do and work done by a paralegal and charge accordingly.)

- ✪ How will the fee be paid?

- ✪ How long has the attorney been in practice?

- ✪ How long has the attorney been in practice in California?

- ✪ What percentage of the attorney's cases involve divorce cases or other family law matters? (Do not expect an exact answer, but you should get a rough estimate that is at least 20%.)

- ✪ How long will it take? (Do not expect an exact answer, but the attorney should be able to give you an average range and discuss things that may make a difference.)

- ✪ Is he or she a certified specialist in family law? (Using a specialist has two major advantages. First, a specialist will know what he or she is doing without a lot of research. This will give you a good idea of your position in your first meeting with the lawyer. Second, even though a specialist will usually charge more per hour, he or she will do the work faster and may be cheaper in the long run.)

If you get acceptable answers to these questions, it is time to ask yourself the following questions about the lawyer.

- ✪ Do you feel comfortable talking to the lawyer?

✪   Is the lawyer friendly toward you?

✪   Does the lawyer seem confident?

✪   Does the lawyer seem to be straightforward with you and able to explain things so that you understand?

If you get satisfactory answers to all of these questions, you probably have a lawyer with whom you will be able to work. Most clients are happiest if they feel comfortable with their attorney.

WORKING WITH A LAWYER

You and your attorney will work best with each other if you both keep an open, honest, and friendly attitude. You should also consider the following suggestions.

Ask Questions

If you want to know something or if you do not understand something, ask your attorney. If you do not understand the answer, say so and ask him or her to explain it again. There are many points of law that many lawyers do not fully understand, so you should not be embarrassed to ask questions. Many people who say they had a bad experience with a lawyer either did not ask enough questions or had a lawyer who would not take the time to explain things to them. If your lawyer is not taking the time to explain what he or she is doing, it may be time to look for a new lawyer.

Give Complete Information

Give your lawyer complete information. Anything you tell your attorney is confidential. An attorney can lose his or her license to practice if he or she reveals information without your permission. So do not hold back. Tell your lawyer everything, even if it does not seem important to you. There are many things that seem unimportant to a nonattorney, but actually can change the outcome of a case.

Also, do not hold something back because you are afraid it will hurt your case. It will definitely hurt your case if your lawyer does not find out about it until he or she hears it in court from your spouse's attorney. By knowing information in advance, plans can be made to eliminate or reduce damage to your case.

Accept Reality

Listen to what your lawyer tells you about the law and the system, and accept it. It is not your lawyer's fault that the law or the legal system does not work the way you think it should. For example, if your lawyer tells you that the judge cannot hear your case for two months, do not demand that a hearing be set for tomorrow. By refusing to accept reality, you are setting yourself up for disappointment.

Be Patient

Be patient with the system (which is often slow) and with your attorney. Do not expect your lawyer to return your phone call within an hour. He or she may not be able to return it the same day either. Most lawyers are very busy and overworked. It is rare that an attorney can maintain a full caseload and still make each client feel like the attorney's only client.

Talk to the Secretary

Your lawyer's secretary can be a valuable source of information. The secretary will often be able to answer your questions, and you may not get a bill for his or her time. Some small firms have a paralegal who doubles as a secretary. If you find this situation, he or she may be especially helpful.

Dealing with Your Spouse

Let your attorney deal with your spouse. It is your lawyer's job to communicate with your spouse or with your spouse's lawyer. Many lawyers have had clients lose or damage their cases when the client decides to say or do something on his or her own.

Be on Time

Be on time to appointments with your lawyer and to court hearings. While you may have to spend some time waiting (especially for court hearings), you are expected to be there and ready when called.

Keeping Your Case Moving

Many lawyers operate on the old principle of the squeaky wheel gets the grease. Your task is to become the squeaking wheel that does not squeak *too* much. Whenever you talk to your lawyer ask the following questions.

- ✪ What is the next step?

- ✪ When do you expect it to be done?

- ✪ When should I talk to you next?

If you do not hear from the lawyer when you expect, call again the following day. Do not remind your lawyer that he or she did not call—just ask how things are going. If you have multiple questions, write them down and cover them all in one phone conversation. This will save you money over multiple phone calls and keep a better relationship with your attorney.

Paying Your Attorney

Have a clear understanding with your lawyer. Make sure you and your lawyer both understand what is expected. You should always get a written fee agreement that states the flat or hourly rate, how payment is to be made, and how often you will receive a statement. This is standard with all reputable attorneys.

Many attorneys will ask for initial deposits of $1,500 to $5,000, or more, depending upon the complexity of the case, plus court filing fees, process server fees, and other anticipated costs for obtaining financial or personal information. Be wary if your attorney calls you or sends you a statement asking for more money before the initial papers are prepared or filed, or if you notice that most of the deposit is used before the initial papers are filed. Although courts favor settlements, numerous phone calls and letter writing by your attorney discussing possible settlement with your spouse or your spouse's attorney may not necessarily be the best use of your limited funds.

NOTE: *Always require that your attorney send you copies of all court documents and correspondence.*

Firing Your Lawyer

If you can no longer work with your lawyer, it is time to either go at it alone or get a new attorney. You will need to send your lawyer a letter stating that you no longer desire his or her services and are discharging him or her from your case. Also state that you will be coming by the office the following day to pick up your file. The attorney does not have to give you his or her own notes but must give you the essential contents of your file (such as copies of papers already filed or prepared, and any documents that you provided). If he or she refuses to give your file to you for any reason, contact the California State Bar about filing a complaint (*grievance*) against the lawyer. Of course, you will need to settle any remaining fees charged for work that has already been done by the lawyer. However, you do not have to pay your bill in order to get your file.

There are certain rules an attorney must follow before the court will officially allow him or her to *withdraw* from your case. Sometimes a hearing may even be required that will lengthen the time to complete your case. Discuss your concerns fully with your attorney to try and resolve the situation first. Remember, you will be responsible for the case until the court accepts any new attorney you hire.

Evaluating Your Situation

You should carefully consider the following matters before you file for divorce.

YOUR SPOUSE

Unless you and your spouse have already decided to get a divorce, you may not want your spouse to know you are thinking about divorce. This is a defense tactic, although it may not seem that way at first. If your spouse thinks you are planning a divorce, he or she may do things to prevent you from getting a fair result. These things include withdrawing money from bank accounts, hiding information about income, and hiding assets. Collect all of the information you will need before you file.

In an ideal world, the system would prefer you keep evidence of the assets (such as photographs, sales receipts, or bank statements) to present to the judge if your spouse hides them. However, once your spouse has taken assets and hidden them, or sold them and spent the money, even a contempt order may not get the money or assets back.

If you determine that you need to get the assets in order to keep your spouse from hiding or disposing of them, be sure you keep them in a safe place and disclose them on your SCHEDULE OF ASSETS AND DEBTS. (see form 7, p.211.) Do not dispose of them. If your spouse claims you took them, you can explain to the judge why you were afraid that your spouse would dispose of them, and that you merely got them out of his or her reach.

If you are dealing with cash, do not take too much. Remember, if it is community property, only half is yours. Taking all of it because you think that your spouse or partner will spend it foolishly may seem like a good idea to you, but it will make you look overly controlling to the court.

FINANCIAL INFORMATION

It is important that you collect all pertinent financial information. Make copies of as many of these papers as possible and keep them safe in a private place. This information should include originals or copies of the following:

- ✪ your most recent income tax return (and your spouse's if you filed separately) and the past two years' returns;

- ✪ the most recent W-2 tax forms for yourself and your spouse;

- ✪ any other income reporting papers (such as interest, stock dividends, etc.);

- ✪ your spouse's three most recent pay stubs, hopefully showing year-to-date earnings (otherwise, try to get copies of all pay stubs since the beginning of the year);

- ✪ deeds to all real estate;

- ✪ titles to cars, boats, or other vehicles;

- ✪ your and your spouse's will;

- ✪ life insurance policies;

✪   stocks, bonds, or other investment papers—including stock options—whether exercised or exercisable;

✪   pension or retirement fund papers and statements;

✪   health insurance card and papers;

✪   bank account or credit union statements;

✪   your spouse's Social Security number and driver's license number;

✪   names, addresses, and phone numbers of your spouse's employer, close friends, and family members;

✪   credit card statements, mortgage documents, and other credit and debt papers;

✪   a list of vehicles, furniture, appliances, tools, etc., owned by you and your spouse (see the following sections in this chapter on "Property" and "Debts" for forms and a detailed discussion of what to include);

✪   copies of bills or receipts for recurring, regular expenses, such as electric, gas, or other utilities, car insurance, etc.;

✪   copies of bills, receipts, insurance forms, or medical records for unusual medical expenses (including those for recurring or continuous medical conditions) for yourself, your spouse, or your children;

✪   any other papers showing what you and your spouse earn, own, or owe; and,

✪   any documentation showing property to be separate property. This could be a will or court order showing that you inherited the money or item or even a letter or card that came with a gift, evidencing that it was a gift to you only and not to both you and your spouse or partner.

PROPERTY

This section is designed to help you get a rough idea of where things stand regarding the division of your property and to prepare you for completing the court papers you will need to file. The following sections deal with your debts, child support, custody, and visitation. If you are still not sure whether you want a divorce, these sections may help you to decide.

This section will assist you in completing the **SCHEDULE OF ASSETS AND DEBTS**. (see form 7, p.211.) Chapter 7 discusses how this form fits into the overall scheme. If you do not qualify for the summary dissolution procedure, you must use form 8, which provides a list of, and key information about, all of your property and debts.

First, you need to understand how property is divided. Trying to determine how to divide assets and debts can be difficult. Under California law, assets and debts are separated into two categories—*community property* (meaning it is half yours and half your spouse's) and *separate property* (meaning it is yours or your spouse's alone).

Community Property   California is a community property state. What is community property? The easiest way to explain it is that for financial purposes, two people become one (the *community*) when they marry. When you go to work and get a paycheck, the community is going to work and get that paycheck. It does not matter if your spouse stays at home and produces no income.

Most people do not understand this. The *breadwinner* feels that he or she has earned the money. Why should your spouse be entitled to half, especially the retirement plan money from the job? The simple answer is, that is the law.

If you are reading this book in anticipation of marriage instead of divorce (a smart thing to do), consult an attorney about an *antenuptial agreement* (pre-nup) if this worries you.

Separate Property   *Separate property* is your property alone. It is property acquired before marriage and property acquired during marriage either as a gift to you alone or because someone died and left it to you alone.

The most important thing about separate property is record keeping. While that may seem easy enough, look at this example.

Example:

You are single and own a small condo in which you live. You marry, sell the condo, and buy a house to have more room to raise a family. You use $25,000, the proceeds from the sale of your condo, as your down payment on the house. You acquire the house in both your and your spouse's names.

Now you are getting a divorce. The house is worth $75,000 more than you paid for it. Can you trace the money from the sale of the condo (separate property) to the house (community property)? If so, you can recover the $25,000 in addition to half the increase in value of the house. However, just because you sold the condo does not mean you used that money to buy the house.

When you sold the condo, did you put the money in a separate bank account or mix it with other funds in a joint account with your spouse? Suppose the joint account already had $25,000 of community property in it. Was your $25,000 from the condo used to buy the house or was the other $25,000, the community property, used as the down payment?

Let us make it more difficult and say that since the sale of the condo, you have bought and sold three houses, making a profit on each. Can you trace your original money from the first sale? You can see the problem.

Keeping separate property *separate* keeps it separate property. What you intended to do, or which funds you intended to use, matters little compared to the records you have kept and what you can prove. Mixing your separate property with community property makes it difficult to identify.

If you have kept good records, you should be able to trace your separate property and get it back, even if there has been some commingling of the funds with community property. If there is a lot of money involved, it is certainly worth a consultation with a lawyer.

Gifts during the marriage are separate property if given only to one of the parties. Did that expensive dining room set your parents gave you come with a card that said "for our daughter on her wedding day" or "for the happy couple?" Did you save the card? Probably not, as most people do not constantly plan for the eventuality of divorce. Therefore, you must realize that more of "your" property will probably be considered community property than you think.

There is a third category of property that, generally speaking, is treated the same as community property.

Quasi-Community Property

Quasi-community property is property acquired in another state that would have been community property if acquired in California.

Example:
You buy your retirement condominium in Florida. Florida is not a community property state. Even if the condo is in your name only, it would have been community property if acquired in California, unless your spouse specifically gave up his or her interest.

Domestic partners may have a problem with this situation. Although domestic partners agree to be governed by California law even if one or both leaves the state, it is not clear whether other states will honor this and whether they must honor the contract to use California law as they would in other types of contracts.

Your Own Business

If you are in business for yourself (or your spouse is), you will likely encounter additional considerations in classifying and dividing its value. If you owned the business before marriage, and it increased in value during the marriage, the increased value is community property. This is because the time and effort you used to grow the business was legally done by the community. This is true even if your spouse never even visited the business.

If the business has increased substantially in value during the marriage or was started during the marriage, you may not be financially able to buy out your spouse's interest. If you borrow to buy him or her out, you may not be able to borrow again if you need money to keep the business going, such as if you need to buy new equipment or survive a temporary slowdown.

If you have a business, you are also going to be dealing with accountants and appraisers to determine its value. Hiring a lawyer to guide you through the process is strongly advised.

If you own a home and have children, your spouse may have a strong incentive to keep the house, especially if he or she has physical custody of the children. A trade for his or her interest in the business is a possibility. If you are going to pay alimony or child support, your spouse will benefit from your success in business.

Investments   Unlike a business that requires maximum time and effort, investments are treated differently. If you buy stock, for example, with community funds and the value increases, the increase is obviously community. This is true even if you are the stock expert, did all the research, and handled the purchase.

Suppose you bought the stock before marriage. It would be separate property and the increase would be separate property (yours alone). This is because the community put no time and effort into the increased value. In other words you did not do anything to cause the stock price to rise.

Real estate is slightly different. If you bought rental property before marriage and it increased in value during marriage, you most likely didn't cause the increase. Real estate prices simply went up. However, unlike stocks, real estate must be managed. How much time and effort did you put into managing the property? Did you manage it yourself or did you hire a management company? Whatever you (the community) did required compensation. Were some or all of the rents turned over to the community or did you keep all the rents in a separate account for yourself?

If you kept all the rents, the court would attempt to estimate the value of your total time spent managing the property and award half that amount to your spouse. If you owned the property for several years during the marriage, the amount could be considerable.

If you put community money into your property, the court could also award half of any increased value to your spouse.

The Checkbook

If you write the checks, you take the risks. If you write a check from community funds to improve your separate property, the community will recover that money, possibly more. If you write a check to improve your spouse's separate property, it can be considered a gift. If it is considered a gift, the community cannot recover it.

Courts have used the gift concept to achieve what it considered fairness between the parties. If you write all the checks, you need to be aware of this possibility.

Distinguishing Community and Separate Property

From the above examples, you can see how simple everyday acts can change your legal status in property upon divorce. To assist in making the distinction between community and separate property, the following rules apply.

- ✪ If the asset or debt was acquired after the date you were married, it is presumed to be a community asset or debt. It is up to you or your spouse to prove otherwise.

- ✪ A separate asset or debt is one that was acquired before the date of your marriage or acquired by gift or inheritance at any time. Income from separate property is also separate property (if kept separate). If you exchange one of these assets or debts after your marriage, it is still separate.

Example:
You had a $6,000 car before you got married. After the marriage, you traded it for a different $6,000 car. The new car is still separate property.

It is also possible for one spouse to make a gift of separate property to the other spouse, such as by commingling separate property with community property, thereby making it all community property. Property acquired after the date of separation, even though you are not yet divorced, is separate property.

✪ You and your spouse may sign a written agreement that certain assets and debts are to be considered community or separate.

– Caution –

Be careful on this one. It looks simple, but it is not. In order for spouses to validly transfer any property between themselves (called *transmutation*) (at least as to transfers as of January 1, 1985), the transfer must:

✪ be in writing;

✪ have the signed intelligent consent of the spouse giving up the property interest;

✪ specifically describe the property interest involved;

✪ specifically describe the consenting spouse's interest in the property; and,

✪ express that the interest in the property is changing from the current interest (community or separate) to the new interest.

NOTE: *If the property was transferred orally or in a writing that does not meet the above requirements, the transfer may or may not be valid, depending upon the proof.*

✪ Community assets and debts are those that were acquired during your marriage, even if they were acquired by you or your spouse individually. This also includes the increase in value of a community asset during the marriage due to the use of community funds to pay for or improve the property or through appreciation. All rights accrued during the marriage in pension, retirement, profit-sharing, insurance, and similar plans are community assets.

✪ Real estate held jointly in both names is considered community property, and the spouse claiming otherwise must prove it.

✪ The value of any asset, community or separate, is determined as of the trial date, or as near to it as possible.

✪ Joint tenancy property of any kind is considered community property for divorce purposes.

SCHEDULE OF ASSETS AND DEBTS

To determine your position as to you and your spouse's or domestic partner's community property and its value as well as what you believe to be separate property, you fill out the **Schedule of Assets and Debts**. Your spouse or domestic partner may dispute any items on the list, either as to classification, value, or both. You also list debts and who is responsible for each. These may also be disputed. Agreements can either be negotiated or imposed by the court.

The **Schedule of Assets and Debts** and the instructions that follow call for a specific listing of property and debt. (see form 7, p.211.) The **Petition** calls for only a general listing. (see form 3 or form 3A.) You will notice that form 7 is divided into five columns, designated as follows.

Column 1) "Assets—Description." This is the listing of all your property. Note that certain attachments are required, such as copies of deeds, account numbers, and so on.

Column 2) "Sep. Prop" This refers to whether you consider the property in Column 1 separate or community. If you consider it separate, place either an "H" for husband or a "W" for wife in this column.

Column 3) "Date Acquired." This is self-explanatory and requires at least a month and year date.

Column 4) "Current Gross Fair Market Value." This refers to the price at which you could sell the item.

Column 5) "Amount of Money Owed or Encumbrance." This refers to the debt owed on the property or any encumbrance, like a mortgage or deed of trust. Attach to the form the latest statement showing such debt.

Use items 1 through 16 in Column 1 to list all of your property.

NOTE: *You will not need to list your clothing and other personal effects. Pots, pans, dishes, and cooking utensils ordinarily do not need to be listed.*

Property   The following guidelines for each of the listed categories may help.

1. Real Estate. List each piece of property in which you have any interest. The description should include a street address for the property as well as the legal description found on the deed. You might also use the county assessor's parcel number. Real estate (or any other property) may be in both of your names, in your spouse's name alone, or in your name alone. The only way to know for sure is to look at the deed to the property. (If you cannot find your deed, ask a local realtor to get you a copy.)

If you do not know a realtor, you can get a copy of your deed in three ways. Many counties now offer the ability to search records online. Type the name of the county where the property is located and follow directions. You can sometimes use an address. If the *Assessor's Parcel number* is required, you can get it from your tax bill. The second way is to walk into the county recorder's office. Someone will show you how to search the records and will charge a few dollars for a copy. The third way is to contact a title company and ask for a copy. You can find a title company in the yellow pages. Call first, as they may be able to complete the transaction over the phone and mail you a copy. If there is a charge, they will probably want you to come in. The charge should be under $20.

You should also get some idea of the value of the property. Type "property appraisal" into a search engine and many choices will come up. Most likely, you will be directed to a local real estate company for a "Broker's Price Option." It is not necessarily as accurate as hiring an appraiser but it is free and close enough for purposes of negotiation with your spouse.

The owners of property are usually referred to on the deed as the *grantees*. In assigning a value to the property, consider the market value, which is the amount you could probably get for the property. This might be what similar houses in your neighborhood have sold for recently. In dividing real estate and other appreciated assets, check out any potential tax consequences.

If there are children, you may want one spouse to continue living in the home and defer the division of the equity (the difference between the fair market value and the debt) until the children reach a certain age. At that time, the house could be sold with the profit divided. In the meantime, the spouse living in the home with the children would pay the maintenance, mortgage, tax, and insurance, but capital improvements, such as a new roof, would be shared, unless otherwise agreed. Remember, it's all negotiable. Of course, you could exchange the equity in the home for the equity in another asset of approximately the same value. This also applies if you own a business, but determining the value is more difficult and will require the work of an accountant. Whatever is best for the children is the rule here.

NOTE: *If there is substantial equity, consult with an attorney for this issue. In transferring real estate, get a professional's help to make sure the deed is prepared properly.*

2. Household Furniture, Furnishings, and Appliances. List all furniture generally. You should include the type of piece (such as sofa, coffee table, etc.) and then just estimate a value, unless you know what it is worth. Other than antiques, use garage sale prices. This category also includes such things as refrigerators, lawn mowers, and power tools. Again, estimate a value, unless you are familiar enough with them to simply know what they are worth. More importantly, try to dispose of this issue informally with your spouse. The judge will not be happy using court time to decide who should get the arm chair.

3. Jewelry, Antiques, Art, Coin Collections, etc. You do not need to list inexpensive costume jewelry. You can plan on keeping your own personal watches, rings, etc. However, if you own an expensive piece, you should include it in your list, along with an estimated value. Be sure to include silverware, original art, gold, coin collections, other collectibles, etc. Again, be as detailed and specific as possible.

4. Vehicles, boats, and trailers. This category includes cars, trucks, motor homes, recreational vehicles (RVs), motorcycles, boats, trailers, airplanes, and any other means of transportation for which the state requires a title and registration. Your description should include the following (which can usually be found on the title or on the vehicle itself).

- ✪ *Year.* The year the vehicle was made.

- ✪ *Make.* The name of the manufacturer, such as "Ford," "Honda," "Chris Craft," etc.

- ✪ *Model.* The model may be a name, a number, a series of letters, or a combination of these.

- ✪ *Serial Number/Vehicle Identification Number (VIN).* This is most likely found on the vehicle, as well as on the title or registration.

Make a copy of the title or registration. Regarding a value, you can go to the public library and ask to look at the *blue book* for cars, trucks, etc. A blue book (which may actually be yellow, black, or any other color) gives the average values for used vehicles. Your librarian can help you find what you need. This can also be done on a computer. Type "blue book" into any search engine. Another source is the classified advertising section of a newspaper to see how similar vehicles are priced. You might also try calling a dealer to see if he or she can give you a rough idea of the value. Be sure you take into consideration the condition of the vehicle.

5. Savings Accounts. List all accounts in which you have any interest. State the name on the account, the account number, and the bank and branch. Attach a copy of the latest statement if you have it.

6. Checking Accounts. List these the same as savings accounts.

7. Credit Union and Other Deposit Accounts. List these the same as savings and checking accounts.

8. Cash. This refers to cash you have available, not to money you have in accounts.

9. Tax Refund. Any expected tax refund or unspent tax refund should be listed here.

10. Life Insurance with Cash Surrender or Loan Value. This is any life insurance policy that you may cash in or borrow against, and therefore has value. Attach a copy of the declaration page for each policy. If you cannot find a cash value or declaration page in your papers, call the insurance company or agent and ask.

11. Stocks, Bonds, Secured Notes, and Mutual Funds. All stocks, bonds, or other *paper investments* should be listed, including stock options whether exercised or exercisable. Write down the number of shares and the name of the company or other organization that issued them. Also, copy any notation such as *common* or *preferred* stock or shares. This information can be obtained from the stock certificate itself, or from a statement from the stockbroker. Make a copy of the certificate or the statement.

In dealing with corporations that are not publicly traded, the type of distribution (in kind or cash out) is complex. You should consult an attorney.

12. Retirement and Pensions. The division of pensions, military pensions, and retirement benefits can be complicated. Whenever these types of benefits are involved, and you cannot agree on how to divide them, you will need to consult an attorney or an actuary to determine the value of the benefits and how they should be divided. Unless you both agree to keep your own retirement benefit, or agree to cash out the benefits, you will need a QDRO (*Qualified Domestic Relations Order*) and an attorney. (QDROs are beyond the scope of this book.)

A general overview of this area will be helpful. The first principle is that separate property and community property interests in the asset should be determined, unless all the benefits were accrued during the time of marriage and before separation. The community property portion is half yours and half your spouse's, regardless of which spouse was the employee. This method of calculation, in terms of time, however, is not applied if the benefit is not substantially related to the time of the employee's service.

Some pension plans need actuarial evaluation. The value of other benefits such as IRAs, 401(k)s and 403(b)s, deferred compensation, profit sharing, SEPs, and Keogh plans (listed in the next section) might be on the latest statement, but again, if the amount is substantial, consult with an attorney to be safe. This asset may be the largest in the marriage. The plan will often have a death benefit payable to the survivor spouse and offer options regarding the benefit.

The two main methods of distributing these assets are *in kind* or *cash out*. A *distribution in kind* means that you and your spouse are each awarded one-half the community interest. A *cash out* means that the asset is exchanged for another asset of approximately equal worth. For example, if the house equity is about the same value as the actuarial value of the pension, one spouse would get the full house equity and the other the full pension. As you can surmise, the cash out method makes sense when one spouse would not realize any benefit for many years, when the valuation would be complex, or when the marriage is of short duration.

But if the amount is significant and the marriage is of long duration, the in kind division may be appropriate. If so, the in kind division is made a subject of a separate judgment that binds the pension plan.

A military pension is also treated as community property subject to division. Some restrictions apply, such as the portion subject to division can only be the disposable retired pay, which is the net monthly amount payable after certain required deductions, including any portion that is for disability. Some other restrictions are that the marriage must have a duration of at least ten years and that only active duty time is included.

NOTE: *Social Security is not community property. However, a spouse's right to Social Security benefits arising from the working spouse's Social Security accrual is not affected by the divorce, provided the marriage lasted at least ten years.*

13. Profit-Sharing, Annuities, IRAs, and Deferred Compensation. Attach a copy of the latest statement. If you do not have it, you will need to contact the company or financial institution involved. You may need an actuary to determine the present community value.

14. Accounts Receivable and Unsecured Notes. Attach copies if you have them. This category mostly refers to businesses; however, if you have loaned money to anyone, you need to show this with details.

15. Partnerships and Other Business Interests. If you or your spouse are in business, whether the form of the business be a partnership, corporation, limited liability company, or sole proprietorship, you will probably need a CPA's help to determine the community value. This is a complicated area of the law and beyond the scope of this book.

16. Other Assets. This is simply a general reference to anything of significant value that does not fit in one of the categories already discussed. Examples might be a portable spa, an above-ground swimming pool, golf clubs, guns, pool tables, camping or fishing equipment, farm animals, or machinery.

17. Total Assets from Continuation Sheet. If there is not enough space to list all of your items of property in any category, you will need to use other sheets of paper. Here you will indicate the total of your assets from any such continuation sheet.

18. Total Assets. Add all of your figures in the market value and money owed columns, and write in the total here.

Debts   Items 19 through 24 of the **Schedule of Assets and Debts** are for listing your debts. Included is a column to check if the debt is a separate debt. State the total amount that is owed, and fill in the date the debt was incurred. The following guidelines may be of some help in completing this section of form 7.

19. Student Loans. State the name and address of the institution to whom the loan is owed and the loan number.

20. Taxes. State the type of tax owed (*e.g.*, federal income tax, state personal property tax, or county property tax) and the tax year.

21. Support Arrearages. If you or your spouse are behind on money that was ordered to be paid to a previous spouse for spousal or child support, list such amounts here, as well as providing a copy of the support order.

22. Loans—Unsecured. List all *unsecured debts*, except credit card debt which is listed separately as the next item. Unsecured debt means the lender has no legal interest in any of your property to safeguard the loan. A secured debt is one in which the lender takes back an interest in your property, such as when the lender can foreclose on your home or repossess your car if you do not make your payments.

23. Credit Cards. List all of your credit card debts with copies of the latest statement.

24. Other Debts. List here any other debt of yours or your spouse that is not listed elsewhere on this form.

Dividing Property and Debts

Once you have completed the SCHEDULE OF ASSETS AND DEBTS (see form 7, p.211), make a copy of it, and then go back through it and try to determine who should end up with each item. The ideal situation is for both you and your spouse to go through the list together and divide things fairly. However, if this is not possible, you will need to offer a reasonable settlement to the judge.

On a copy of this list, consider each item and make a check mark to designate whether that item should go to the husband or wife. You may make the following assumptions:

- ✪ your separate property will go to you;

- ✪ your spouse's separate property will go to your spouse;

- ✪ you should get the items that only you use;

○ your spouse should get the items only used by him or her; and,

○ the remaining items should be divided, evening out the total value of all the community property, and taking into consideration who would really want that item.

To equally divide your property (this only applies to community property), you first need to know the total value of your property. Do not count the value of the separate property items. Add all the remaining community property amounts to get an approximate value of all community property.

When it comes time for the hearing, you and your spouse may be arguing over some or all of the items on your list. This is when you will be glad that you made copies of the documents relating to the property on your list. Arguments over the value of property may need to be resolved by hiring appraisers to set a value. However, you will have to pay the appraiser a fee. Dividing your property will be discussed further in later chapters.

Generally, whoever gets the property also gets the debt owed on that property. This seems to be a fair arrangement in most cases. It also usually alleviates the problem of your spouse not making the payment on the car you were awarded in the divorce.

As with separate property, there is also *separate debt*. This is any debt incurred before you were married. You will be responsible for your separate debts, and your spouse will be responsible for his or hers.

CHILD CUSTODY AND VISITATION

As with everything else in divorce, things are ideal when both parties can agree on the question of custody of the children. Generally, the judge will accept any agreement you reach, provided it does not appear your agreement will cause harm to your children. With respect to child custody, the California Family Code, Section 3020, makes the following significant statement:

The Legislature finds and declares that it is the public policy of this state to assure minor children frequent and continuing

*contact with both parents after the parents have separated or dis-
solved their marriage, and to encourage parents to share the
rights and responsibilities of child rearing in order to effect this
policy, except where the contact would not be in the best interest
of the child...*

California statutory and case law state there is no preference or presumption as to custody, and that the paramount rule is the *best interest*
of the child. Most custody plans award *joint legal custody* to both parents and *primary physical custody* to one parent. *Legal custody* refers
to parenting decisions involving schooling, medical care, religion, and
the like. *Physical custody* refers to the child's primary residence with
one parent and visitation rights to the other parent. An exceptional situation must exist to have *sole legal custody*.

Joint legal custody and joint physical custody are becoming more popular so that neither parent feels like he or she is a *visitor* to the child. This
happens even when the physical custody is not equal periods of time.

If you and your spouse cannot agree on these matters, you will be
ordered to see a court mediator if you are in one of the counties that
have conciliation departments. Only then will the judge hear your custody or visitation dispute. The judge cannot possibly know your child as
well as you and your spouse, so it make sense for you to work this out
yourselves. Otherwise, you are leaving the decision to a stranger.

If the judge must decide the question, he or she is required by law to
have the health, safety, and welfare of the child as the primary concern. Other factors are:

✪   any abuse allegations;

✪   which parent is most likely to allow the other to visit with the
     child and to develop and maintain a close and continuing par-
     ent-child relationship;

✪   the love, affection, and other emotional ties existing between
     the child and each parent;

- ✪   the ability and willingness of each parent to provide the child with food, clothing, medical care, and other material needs;

- ✪   the length of time the child has lived with either parent in a stable environment;

- ✪   the permanence, as a family unit, of the proposed custodial home;

- ✪   the moral fitness of each parent;

- ✪   the mental and physical health of each parent;

- ✪   the home, school, and community record of the child;

- ✪   the preference of the child (providing the child is of sufficient intelligence and understanding); and,

- ✪   any other fact the judge decides is relevant.

There are too many factors and individual circumstances to predict the outcome of a custody battle. The exception is a situation in which one parent is clearly unfit *and* the other can prove it. Drug abuse is the most common charge, but unless there has been an arrest and conviction, it is difficult to prove to a judge. In general, do not charge your spouse with being unfit unless you can prove it. Unfounded allegations can do your cause more harm than good, and judges are not impressed with them.

If your children are older, consider their preference even if it is to live with the other parent. Your fairness and respect for their wishes may benefit you in the long run. Just be sure that no matter what they decide, you keep in close contact with them and visit them often.

Custody battles and visitation skirmishes are always lose-lose-lose situations—for mother, father, and children—unless an obvious problem is present, for example, physical abuse or drug abuse. Judges have a distaste for the revengeful mothers and whining fathers (or vice versa) who verbally spit at each other in front of them. As soon as one dispute is resolved, there is sure to be another tomorrow, or next week, or next month. An immature father or mother will doom any parenting plan.

Nevertheless, a parenting plan must be included in every judgment or **Marital Settlement Agreement (MSA)**. A parenting plan can be as simple as:

Joint legal and physical custody with reasonable visitation by one spouse when the child is with the other spouse.

Unfortunately, such a plan has high risk for problems, especially in the first few traumatic years after the divorce, because it does not provide specific guidelines. The child's age, maturity, extracurricular activities, distance between the parents' homes, school location, and many other concerns must be considered.

Legal custody will always be joint unless there are exceptional circumstances. You may want to designate primary physical custody with one parent and give the other parent visitation for designated periods. You may want the children to live alternately with each parent for certain periods of time. You may want to spell out the visitation days and times, including provisions for holidays and summer vacations, mid-week and weekend visitations, and include at the end a provision that visitation *shall be reasonable, but in the event of disagreement, the above schedule shall become effective.* That way you have a fall-back position if your spouse starts taking advantage.

Ultimately any parenting plan is up to you and your spouse, and no matter what parenting plan you devise, you can count on a monkey wrench being thrown in it by guess who? That's right—your child, who is completely oblivious to your schedule. Some sample parenting plans are included in the **Marital Settlement Agreement (MSA)**. (see form 16, p.235.)

The California Family Code also provides for grandparents' visitation rights. Section 3013 applies during dissolution proceedings and has only the standard of the *best interest of the child.* Section 3104 applies when the parent awarded sole legal and physical custody of the child objects to visitation. There must be a *preexisting relationship* and *bond* between the child and grandparent(s). Under both sections there is a rebuttable presumption against the grandparent(s) if there is a parental objection to the visits.

POTENTIAL PROBLEMS

Custody battles are frequent and can be nasty. Child abuse is frequently alleged both to get back at the spouse and to gain an advantage in court. The usual allegations range from drug use in the child's presence to neglect to inappropriate sexual behavior with the child or with a third party in the child's presence.

Obviously refrain from any abusive or neglectful behavior. Any personal problems you are experiencing or resentments against your spouse should never be directed toward your children.

If your spouse makes unfounded allegations or you expect him or her to, be prepared. Keep detailed records, especially regarding injuries. Children have accidents and get sick. If your child becomes ill or has an accident, it's a good idea to visit a doctor even if it is not serious. You may also want to call your spouse and explain what happened. Putting the children first and keeping the lines of communication open regarding them is the best manner to avoid these potential problems.

If you have a girlfriend or boyfriend, it is a good idea to keep this person away from your child until the custody issue is settled. While your new love interest may be anxious to meet your child, keep in mind that both your spouse and child may resent this person. Plus, any show of affection may be exaggerated by your child and reported as inappropriate behavior.

If a social worker comes to your door, get a lawyer even if you have done nothing wrong. Do this before you answer any questions from the social worker. If the social worker comes alone, refuse entry to your home and give the lawyer's name to the worker. Then call the lawyer immediately. If the social worker comes with the police and a warrant, you will not be able to refuse entry. Call the lawyer immediately.

If this happens to you, you will be shocked and completely unprepared, unless you have done some homework. Since these charges go into the state Department of Justice data bank, even if not substantiated, you could have problems with later employment. This is especially true if you apply for a job dealing with children. Find a lawyer with experience in this area before a problem arises and keep his or her phone number handy. The situation may never come up, but if it does, you will be glad that you took the time to prepare yourself.

CHILD SUPPORT

Because child support stems from the child's right to support from parents, parents cannot waive this obligation between themselves, nor can they avoid it through voluntary unemployment or by voluntarily reducing income. If the judge thinks the paying parent has voluntarily reduced his or her income, the support amount will be based on ability to earn, not actual earnings.

Example:

Around the time of the dissolution, the paying parent was making $20 per hour. He then voluntarily takes a position that only pays $10 per hour. Other circumstances being equal, the support amount can be based on the $20 per hour earnings.

Child support continues until the child reaches the age of majority (18 years). It can continue until the child completes the twelfth grade or reaches 19 years (whichever occurs first), provided the child is unmarried, not self-supporting, and in high school full time. Because child support is a continuing obligation, either party, at any time, can ask the court to increase or decrease the amount based on changed circumstances.

Sometimes parents have arguments regarding visitation. This is a separate issue from support, and the support check is still due. Many of these problems, however, have been solved by the **ORDER/NOTICE TO WITHHOLD INCOME FOR CHILD SUPPORT**. (see form 46, p.323.) This is an order that is sent to the paying parent's employer, directing the employer to take the support amount directly from the paycheck of its employee and send it to the recipient spouse.

Any problems in receiving support should be referred to the Child Support Services in your county, an attorney, or the Family Law Facilitator.

Determining Child Support

The amount of child support is established by a statewide uniform guideline found in the Family Code, Sections 4000 to 4253. The guideline is mandatory—a specific amount that must be ordered unless the judge puts on the record the reasons for the variance. The amount is primarily the result of two factors—the income of each parent and the custody time each has with the child. Reasons for not adhearing to the guideline could be such things as delaying the sale of the family residence for the benefit of the children or an extraordinary financial hardship.

The following principles upon which the guidelines are based are found in Family Code Section 4053 (see Appendix A):

- a parent's primary obligation is support of his or her minor children according to the parent's circumstances and station in life;

- both parents are mutually responsible for support;

- each parent's actual income and level of responsibility;

- each parent's ability to pay support;

- California's top priority is the interests of children;

- children should share in the standard of living of both parents; and,

- the children's financial needs should be met through private financial resources as much as possible.

If you and your spouse can agree on the amount of support, the judge will probably go along with it as long as the child's provisions are adequate. Even so, your proposed **JUDGMENT** (see form 17, p.247) must have specific language that:

❂ the parents are fully informed of their rights regarding child support;

❂ the agreement was made freely without duress, coercion, or threat; and,

❂ the agreement is in the best interest of the child and the amount will adequately meet the needs of the child.

Child support also includes mandatory additional amounts for child care in order to enable the custodial or part-custodial parent to work. This also includes health insurance for the child. These amounts are the actual amounts spent and are usually shared equally between the parents.

Calculating Child Support

The amount of child support is calculated by a formula set forth in Family Code Section 4055. However, because of the formula's complexity, most judges and attorneys use a computer program. Two popular programs are Dissomaster and SupporTax. Type either of these names into a search engine and they will give you current information. You can purchase the calculator. You can get the numbers from your local Child Support Services or Family Law Facilitator. You can also ask the judge to assess the guideline amount at your hearing. Although the courts have a computer program, most judges prefer to have a computer printout presented to them initially, even though they will still calculate the amount on their own.

It is not recommended that you try to figure the amount by means of the formula. However, if you are interested in getting an *idea* of the amount, Family Code Section 4055 (see Appendix A) and the following example explain the steps to take. Following are some specific terms in the formula that need clarification.

Gross income. Your overall income from all sources before any deductions. It includes your wages or salary before any deductions, and other forms of income such as rent checks, commissions, royalties, interest, pensions, bonuses, overtime, workers' compensation benefits, spousal support from another marriage, and the like. If you or your spouse are self-employed, gross income is total receipts less expenses of the business, such as inventory, salaries, supplies, etc.

NOTE: *Child support you receive from a previous marriage is not income, but spousal support is.*

Net income. This is gross income minus federal and state taxes, state disability insurance, mandatory deductions such as union dues and in some cases retirement contributions, and child and spousal support being paid to a former spouse by court order.

Annual net disposable income. This is explained in Family Code Section 4059, which is reprinted in Appendix A. Generally, it is the money left over after mandatory payroll deductions.

Example:

A husband and wife have a total net disposable monthly income of $1,000 (generally, this is the money left over after mandatory payroll deductions). They have two minor children. The husband is the higher earning spouse with a $600 monthly income. He has 20% physical custody time with both children.

Now apply the formula:

CS = K [HN - (H%)(TN)]

Where:

CS is the child support amount.

HN is the net monthly disposable income of the higher earning parent.

H% is the percentage of custody time the parent with the higher income has. (If you have several children with different times, use the average.)

TN is the total net monthly disposable income of both parents.

K is the amount of both parents' income set aside for child support, arrived at by the following computation:

> K = One plus H% (1 + H%) if the higher earning parent has fifty percent or less custody time,

OR

> K = Two minus H% (2 - H%) if the higher earning parent has more than fifty percent custody time.

Depending upon which case is applicable, you then multiply the result by one of the following fractions, depending upon the net disposable income range.

If total net disposable income per month is:	Use the applicable fraction:
$0 to $800:	0.20 + TN/16,000
$801 to $6,666:	0.25
$6,667 to $10,000:	0.10 + 1,000/TN
Over $10,000:	0.12 + 800/TN

In this example, the .25 fraction applies because the total net is between $801 and $6,666.

A value is obtained for K:

> K = (1 + 0.20) x 0.25
> K = 0.30

Because this couple has two children, multiply the final result by 1.6 (as show in the table from Family Code Section 4055).

Our couple has two children and the husband is the higher-earning spouse with $600. He has twenty percent custody of the two children. The couple's total net disposable income is $1,000 per month. So—

$$CS = K [HN - (H\%)(TN)]$$

Where:

HN	=	$600
H%	=	20%
TN	=	$1,000
K	=	$(1 + 0.20) \times 0.25 = .30$

Then:

CS	=	K [HN - (H%)(TN)]
CS	=	.30 [$600 - (20%)($1,000)]
CS	=	.30 [$600 - $200]
CS	=	.30 ($400)
CS	=	$120

Because the couple has two children, multiply CS ($120) by 1.6. CS then equals $192 (CS = $120 x 1.6 = $192). The result is the child support is $192, which the husband must pay to the wife.

(If the resulting figure, in our example $192, were a negative number instead of a positive number, the low-earner spouse would pay that amount to the high-earner spouse.)

NOTE: *When you have more than one child, child support must be allocated so that the support amount for the youngest child is the amount of support for one child. The amount for the next youngest child is the difference between that amount and the amount for two children. There are similar allocations for additional children.*

Child care costs and medical insurance are added to the child support after you have calculated it using the statutory formula. Uninsured medical expenses are usually divided between the parties half-and-half, unless their income gap is unusually wide. If your disposable income is under $1000 per month, Section 4055 (7) allows for a reduction from the formula amount. If you qualify, the court will calculate the deduction.

SPOUSAL SUPPORT (ALIMONY)

Spousal support can be given to either husband or wife. If you and your spouse agree on the amount, the judge will probably go along with it. Spousal support is not mandatory and there is no specific amount the court must use if it does award it. However, judges must consider all of the factors in Family Code Section 4320 (see Appendix A), without emphasizing one factor over another, even though they have wide discretion. (Refer to Chapter 8 for a more complete discussion of the factors the judge must consider.)

Sometimes, the parties will separate their divorce into two phases. The first phase declares them divorced. The second phase, which resolves property and support issues, is reserved for a later hearing.

Spousal support is based on actual earnings; however, if a spouse has voluntarily reduced earnings to lessen support, the judge can use an *ability to earn test*. Also, *new mate income* (income earned by an ex-spouse's new wife or husband) is not considered in determining spousal support.

Life insurance is a way to make sure support payments continue, or to pay off the mortgage on the home where the kids are living if the paying spouse dies. The law gives the court discretion to order the paying spouse to purchase an annuity or life insurance to protect the supported spouse's needs. The court may also order the paying spouse to include the children as beneficiaries of his or her life insurance.

Generally, the cost of insurance premiums will be part of the support award. In making such an order, the court must look at the entire circumstances. In many cases, the parties have barely enough to pay for shelter and food, and insurance or the setting up of a trust is a luxury. On the other hand, if the parties are young, term life insurance is relatively cheap.

POTENTIAL PROBLEMS

Both alimony and child support are subject to future modification. Do not count on either to remain the same if you are the payer.

Alimony

Child support cannot be waived. Alimony can. If at all possible, make a settlement that waives alimony, even if the alimony is only a nominal sum. Future financial setbacks by your spouse will have you back in court.

A paying spouse's increased earnings alone are theoretically not enough to increase support, provided support was adequate when granted and the receiving ex-spouse's expenses have not increased. Also, a paying spouse's subsequent marriage is not, directly or indirectly, to be considered. However, if you are the paying spouse and your household income from any source significantly increases, your ex-spouse's expenses may suddenly go up or he or she may argue that the amount was never sufficient.

If you are the one being paid, look at the most likely future. If you, for example, are a woman with good job skills who has been staying home to raise the kids and will now work outside the home and earn more than your spouse, a settlement and waiver of alimony may be to your advantage.

Be careful how the settlement is structured. If you simply take a promissory note for periodic payments, it could become uncollectible or even discharged in bankruptcy. You will not get help from the district attorney to collect as you would with alimony.

Child Support

The Department of Child Support Services handles child support. If you are paying support directly to your former spouse, he or she could turn collection over to this department. They may send you a letter saying that you are behind on support. They will take your former spouse's word for claims against you and you will have to prove that you are not behind on your payments.

If you are the payer and are employed, a *wage assignment* will have your employer deduct the support payment from your paycheck. If you are self-employed, you can have the money withdrawn electronically each month from your bank account.

Failure to pay can result in collection methods such as loss of a state license (like your driver's license, license to practice law, or license to sell real estate), seizure of property by the Franchise Tax Board, withholding of your tax refund by the IRS, and even jail time for contempt of court in extreme cases.

Two things you must do if you are the payer. First, keep good records. Do not count on your former spouse to know what you have paid and honestly admit it. Second, never fail to answer a complaint or question from the department. Ignoring letters and notices will almost always get you in trouble.

Record keeping is also important to determine the amount of support. Part of your record keeping should record time as well as money. If, for example, your spouse gets a new job requiring travel and the children are spending much more time with you, you may be entitled to an adjustment in the amount of support you pay or receive, depending on which side you are on.

The old system of collection by local District Attorney's offices did not work. Many people who regularly made payments were mistakenly hounded for not making them. The new system may be better, but there have been cases of the wrong people (same name) being dunned even though their age and Social Security numbers did not match. Try to straighten out any mistakes that arise by yourself until it looks hopeless. Then get a lawyer.

For further information contact your county office. Phone numbers for county offices can be found on the following chart. For more information about each county, visit the California Department of Child Support Services website at **www.childsup.ca.gov** and look under "Contact Local Office."

County	Number	County	Number
Alameda	510-639-7299	Orange	888-594-7600
Alpine	530-694-2235	Placer	530-889-5700
Amador	209-223-6318	Plumas	530-283-6264
Butte	530-538-7221	Riverside	909-955-4100
Calaveras	209-754-6780	Sacramento	916-875-7400
Colusa	530-458-0555	San Benito	831-636-4130
Contra Costa	925-957-7300	San Bernardino	909-799-1790
Del Norte	707-464-7232	San Diego	619-236-7600
El Dorado	530-621-5600	San Francisco	415-356-2700
Fresno	559-494-1090	San Joaquin	209-468-2601
Glenn	530-934-6527	San Luis Obispo	805-781-5734
Humboldt	707-441-3200	San Mateo	650-366-8221
Imperial	760-482-2300	Santa Barbara	805-568-2387
Inyo	760-873-3659	Santa Clara	888-687-7500
Kern	661-868-6500	Santa Cruz	831-454-3700
Kings	559-584-1425	Shasta	530-225-5300
Lake	707-262-4300	Sierra	888-823-2845
Lassen	530-251-2630	Siskiyou	530-841-2950
Los Angeles	800-615-8858	Solano	888-823-2735
Madera	559-675-7885	Sonoma	888-271-4214
Marin	415-507-4068	Stanislaus	209-558-3000
Mariposa	209-966-3400	Sutter	530-822-7338
Mendocino	707-463-4216	Tehama	530-527-3110
Merced	209-381-1300	Trinity	530-623-1306
Modoc	530-233-6216	Tulare	599-713-5700
Mono	760-924-1720	Tuolumne	209-533-6400
Monterey	831-755-3200	Ventura	805-654-5200
Napa	707-253-4251	Yolo	530-661-2880
Nevada	530-271-5437	Yuba	530-749-6000

The website will also give you toll-free numbers and fax numbers. Since phone numbers can change, it is recommended that you visit the website for current listings.

WHICH DIVORCE PROCEDURE TO USE

Technically, there are two divorce procedures (*summary* and *regular*); however, this book refers to three procedures because of differences in how you will handle certain situations. The three procedures are:

1. summary divorce procedure;

2. uncontested regular divorce procedure; and,

3. contested divorce procedure.

Residency Requirement. Before you can use any procedure either you or your spouse must have lived in California for at least six months. You or your spouse must have lived in the county where your divorce case is being filed for at least three months, immediately before filing your **PETITION** with the court. If you do not meet these residency requirements and need to file immediately, an attorney may be able to guide you around this obstacle.

NOTE: *Read the entire book once before you begin filling out any court forms.*

Summary Divorce Procedure

The *summary procedure* uses a different set of forms from the usual uncontested and contested divorce. To be eligible for the summary procedure, you must satisfy many requirements. Chapter 6 provides more specific details about this divorce procedure.

Uncontested Divorce Procedure

If you cannot qualify for the summary procedure, you will have to use the uncontested procedure or the contested procedure. The *uncontested procedure* is mainly designed for those who are in agreement, but cannot use the summary procedure because there are children or substantial property involved. The uncontested procedure may also be used if your spouse does not respond to your **PETITION** or cannot be located. (As stated earlier, Chapter 7 provides more details about the uncontested procedure.)

Contested Divorce Procedure

The *contested divorce procedure* is necessary if you and your spouse cannot agree. This may be the result of disagreement over custody of the children, the payment of child support or spousal support, the division of your property, or any combination of these items. If you determine that you will use the contested divorce procedure, you will first need to read Chapter 7 to get a basic understanding of the forms and procedures, and then read Chapter 9 for additional instructions on the contested situation. (Be sure to read both chapters before you start filling out forms.)

If your case becomes contested, it is time to seriously consider getting a lawyer. If you do not think you can afford a lawyer, you may be able to require your spouse to pay for your lawyer. Find a lawyer who will give you a free or reduced-cost initial consultation. He or she will explain your options regarding lawyer's fees. (See Chapter 3 for more information about lawyers.)

General Procedures

Both the California Legislature and California Judicial Council have taken steps to assist people in completing their divorce on their own. The California Legislature created the *Family Law Facilitator Act* (FLFA) to aid families that cannot afford a lawyer. (See Family Code Secs. 10000–10012.) It is designed to provide a speedy, conflict-reducing system for resolving issues of child support, spousal support, and health insurance that is cost-effective and accessible to families that cannot afford legal representation.

Under the FLFA, each county must maintain an Office of the Family Law Facilitator that will help in various areas, including:

- child and spousal support;

- health insurance;

- nullity of marriage (annulment);

- custody;

- domestic violence;

- ✪ educational materials;

- ✪ order enforcement;

- ✪ completing forms;

- ✪ preparing support schedules;

- ✪ meetings with the spouses;

- ✪ reviewing documents; and,

- ✪ preparing formal orders consistent with the court's announced orders.

Call the clerk of the superior court in your county to find out more about the program and whether you can take advantage of it.

The California Judicial Council, which is the policy-making body of the courts, has produced three videos and related brochures in the area of general divorce law (including legal separation and nullity), applications for restraining orders, and responses to applications for restraining orders. The videos and brochures are specifically designed to aid persons representing themselves in the divorce courts. You can find these materials at every Family Law Facilitator office in the county, as well as related offices such as legal aid clinics, domestic violence clinics, victim witness assistance offices, and libraries. These videos are a direct response by the California Judicial Council to the fact that the great majority of child support cases in the courts are managed not by attorneys, but by persons representing themselves.

AN INTRODUCTION TO LEGAL FORMS

Almost all forms you will use changed in some way as of 2005. Many were modified only by adding "or domestic partner" after "spouse." Others have undergone more extensive changes. A few are new. This book reflects the changes made through July 2007. Forms change each year and sometimes at midyear. Always check with the court clerk to be sure you are using a current form. Filing an outdated form could delay your case.

Most of the forms in this book are adopted by the Judicial Council of California and their use is mandatory. Although most are self-explanatory, some can be confusing. If you have difficulty understanding the forms, you should consult a lawyer. You can tear the forms out of this book to file with the court. However, it is best to make photocopies of the forms and keep the originals blank to use in case you make mistakes or need additional copies.

You should type the information on the forms. If typing is not possible, print the information required on the forms. Be sure your writing can be easily read or the clerk may not accept your papers for filing.

NOTE: *Some, if not all, of the counties require the use of black ink on the forms. Therefore, whenever you sign a form, or if you print the information instead of typing, be sure to use a pen with black ink. It is always advisable to type the forms or call the clerk beforehand to find out if you can print on the forms.*

Forms can be filled out on the Internet. Type "California Judicial Council" into a search engine and open the site for forms. Find the correct form by comparing the form number on the form in this book with the form on the site. Once you have filled in the form, print it, and then clear it as recommended on the site.

Courts have various rules that have absolutely nothing to do with the law, but if not observed, your documents will not be accepted. These rules vary from court to court, requiring you to check with the clerk as to what is and is not required. Listed below are some of the more common practices.

- Almost all courts require two-hole punching of documents at the top.

- Most courts require your original documents to be typed.

- The type size and style of the font you use to type your documents should be that on a standard typewriter. If you are using a computer for typing a document for which there is not a standardized form, use a type size and font that is at least as large as Courier 12-point type. A font equivalent to Courier is permitted.

✪   Use only one side of the paper.

✪   Have an extra copy of the *face sheet* (the first page) of all documents presented for filing.

✪   Although the state-wide Rules of Court do not always *mandate* use of the Judicial Council forms (like those supplied in the back of this book), use them in *all* cases anyway as the local courts will almost always require their use.

✪   Identify all originals by putting a self-sticking removable note stating *original* on the first page of all original documents.

✪   Many courts now require a brief identification of the document for all non-Judicial Council forms at the bottom of every page beneath the page number, such as, "Ex-Parte Petition" or "Declaration."

Each form found in Appendix B of this book is referred to by both the title of the form and a form number. Be sure to check the form number because some of the forms have similar titles. The form number is found in the top outside corner of the first page of each form. Also, a list of the forms, by both number and name, is found at the beginning of Appendix B.

You will notice that the forms in Appendix B have the same heading information in the top portion of the form. The first box contains your name, address, phone number, and fax number if you have one (unless you had an attorney, in which case your attorney's information would go here). After the words "Attorney for," type your name, then a comma followed by the phrase *"In Propria Persona,"* which means that you are representing yourself. The shortening of *In Propria Persona* to *In Pro Per* is acceptable. In the next box, type in the name of the county for the superior court where you reside, along with the court's address.

Next, you need to type your full name on the line marked "Petitioner," and your spouse's full name on the line marked "Respondent." Do not use nicknames or shortened versions of names. You should use the names as they appear on your marriage license, if possible. You will not be able to fill in the case number until after you file your **PETITION** with the clerk. The clerk will assign a case number and will stamp it on your **PETITION** and any other papers you file. You must fill in the case number on all papers you file later.

ATTORNEY OR PARTY WITHOUT ATTORNEY*(Name, state bar number, and address)*	FOR COURT USE ONLY
MARY D. NOUGH 3333 HALIFAX RD. GARDEN GROVE, CA 99999 TELEPHONE NO.: 714-000-0000 FAX NO.: 714-000-0000 ATTORNEY FOR *(Name)*: MARY D. NOUGH, In Propria Persona	
SUPERIOR COURT OF CALIFORNIA, COUNTY OF ORANGE STREET ADDRESS: 341 The City Drive MAILING ADDRESS: PO Box 14170 CITY AND ZIP CODE: Orange, CA 92868 BRANCH NAME: Lamoreaux Justice Center -- Family Law	
MARRIAGE OF PETITIONER: MARY D. NOUGH RESPONDENT: BEAU E. NOUGH	
PETITION FOR [X] **Dissolution of Marriage** [ ] **Legal Separation** [ ] **Nullity of Marriage** [ ] AMENDED	CASE NUMBER: 0000000

When completed, the top portion of your forms will resemble the above example.

At the bottom of the forms are places for you to fill in the date, sign your name, and type or print your name. The clerk's office follows the rules to the letter and will reject your papers even if a seemingly insignificant box that should be checked is not. This can be irritating, but it does eliminate problems that could occur later.

At some time during the divorce proceeding, you may need to make a declaration (a statement under penalty of perjury) to the court, either to further explain something or in connection with a court form that does not have sufficient space for the information required. This book provides for that eventuality with a general **DECLARATION** (see form 26, p.267) and with an **ADDITIONAL PAGE**. (see form 27, p.269.) Both of these forms have the required information and perjury statement to pass through court.

FILING WITH THE COURT CLERK

Once you have decided which forms you need and have them prepared, it is time to file your case with the court clerk. Make at least
three copies of each form (the original for the clerk, one copy for yourself, one for your spouse, and one extra just in case the clerk asks for
two copies or you decide to hire an attorney later).

Filing is actually fairly simple. Call the court clerk's office. Locate the
phone number under the county government section in your phone
directory. Ask the clerk the following questions (along with any other
questions that come to mind, such as where the clerk's office is
located and what its hours are).

- ✪   How much is the filing fee for a dissolution of marriage?

- ✪   Does the court have any special forms (other than the official
       forms) that need to be filed with the **PETITION**? (If there are spe-
       cial forms that are not in this book, obtain them from the
       clerk's office. There may be a fee, so ask.)

- ✪   How many copies of the **PETITION** and other forms do you need
       to file with the clerk?

Take your **PETITION** and any other forms you determine you need to
the clerk's office. The clerk handles many different types of cases, so
be sure to look for signs telling you which office or window is appropriate for your case. Look for signs that say such things as "Family
Court," "Family Division," "Filing," and the like.

The clerk will examine the papers and then do one of two things—
either accept them for filing (and either collect the filing fee or direct
you to where to pay it), or tell you that something is not correct. If you
are told something is wrong, ask the clerk to explain to you what is
wrong and how to correct the problem. Although clerks are not permitted to give legal advice, the types of problems they spot often are
minor and they can tell you how to make the necessary corrections.

NOTIFYING YOUR SPOUSE

A basic sense of fairness requires that a person be notified of a legal proceeding that involves him or her. Use the **SUMMONS (FAMILY LAW)** to do this. (see form 1, p.197.) If you are using the summary dissolution procedure, you do not need to worry about the information in this section (your spouse will have to sign the petition, so it will be obvious that he or she knows about the divorce). However, in all other cases, you are required to notify your spouse that you have filed for divorce. This gives your spouse a chance to respond to your **PETITION**. If you are unable to find your spouse (and therefore cannot have him or her personally served), review Chapter 10. The notice requirements as they relate to particular situations are discussed in later chapters.

Notice of Filing the Petition

The usual way to notify your spouse that you filed for a divorce is called *personal service*. This is when the sheriff, marshal, or someone else personally delivers the papers to your spouse. You, being a party to the case, are not permitted to serve your spouse. However, a friend or relative over 18 may serve your spouse.

Call the sheriff's or marshal's office in the county where your spouse lives and ask how much it will cost to have him or her served with divorce papers and what forms of payment they accept (they may not accept personal checks). If you obtain the form from the clerk, make sure you get the form designated **SUMMONS (FAMILY LAW)**.

NOTE: *This section does not apply to the summary dissolution. If you use the summary dissolution procedure, you do not use the* **SUMMONS (FAMILY LAW)**.

Complete the **SUMMONS (FAMILY LAW)** as follows.

◈ Complete the "Notice to Respondent" by typing in your spouse's name.

◈ Type your name after "Petitioner's name is."

◈ In item 1, type the name and address of the court.

◈ In item 2, type your name, address, and phone number.

⬦ In the bottom box under item 2, check "a." Your spouse is being served as an individual.

⬦ Take form 1 to the clerk's office, along with your other documents, (see Chapter 7) and the clerk will issue the **SUMMONS** by affixing the clerk's signature to it.

NOTE: *You must put in the case number on all other forms once the clerk assigns the number.*

⬦ After your spouse is served with a copy of this **SUMMONS (FAMILY LAW)** (and any other documents discussed in Chapter 7), file the **PROOF OF SERVICE OF SUMMONS** with the clerk. (see form 2, p.199.)

Warning:

On the back of the **SUMMONS (FAMILY LAW)** you will see a notice in English and Spanish. It states that you have read the notice and that you must abide by the automatic restraining orders printed there. This applies to you and your spouse. If you violate them by taking the children out of the state without consent, by transferring any funds without consent, or in any other way, you are in contempt of court and exposed to both civil and criminal court sanction.

Serve only copies of forms. Never serve the originals of the documents; keep those for filing with the court. If a friend or relative will serve your spouse, provide one copy of the documents to be served. If the sheriff's or marshal's office will serve the papers, it is best to go to that office with at least two sets of all papers. You will have to write instructions as to the location of your spouse and times that you expect your spouse to be present at the location. It is a good idea to give a picture of your spouse to the person doing the serving. After your spouse is served, you will receive back the **PROOF OF SERVICE OF SUMMONS** from the marshal or sheriff for filing with the court. If a friend or relative serves the papers, he or she will need to complete the **PROOF OF SERVICE OF SUMMONS**.

The **Proof of Service of Summons** form shows four ways to serve your spouse.

1. Method "3.a," *personal service*, as previously discussed, is by far the best method.

2. Method "3.b," refers to *substituted service*. You use this when several attempts have been made to personally serve your spouse, but he or she is obviously trying to avoid the service. If that is the situation, hire a registered process server who will do the service legally and complete the **Proof of Service of Summons** correctly.

3. Method "3.c," *mail and acknowledge service*, is used when you know your spouse's address and believe he or she will sign a form acknowledging service and send it back.

4. Method "3.d," *other service*, can be used if your spouse is out of state. For this method to work, your spouse will obviously have to be cooperative. If your spouse is out of state and not cooperative, you will need an attorney's assistance.

If you use method "3.c" you will need a form called a **Notice and Acknowledgment of Receipt**. (see form 5, p.207.) Although this is an easy way to serve the initial papers, provided your spouse cooperates and sends the signed form back, personal service is still the better way to go.

Complete the top portion of the **Notice and Acknowledgment of Receipt** (form 5, p.207) the same as all the others. Insert your spouse's name after "To:" (under the caption), then sign and date it in the middle of the page where indicated. Place an "x" in each applicable box under "I agree I received the following:". You would normally only place an "x" in the box for a copy of the **Summons** and of the **Petition**. Send your spouse two copies of the form by first class mail (not certified or registered mail), one for your spouse's file and one to return to you with his or her original signature, together with a self-addressed stamped envelope. And do not forget to include copies of the documents you checked.

Your spouse enters two dates—when the form was received and when it was signed. Your spouse then signs and prints his or her name.

Service by this method is complete on the date it is signed at the bottom by your spouse. The thirty-day response period begins to run from that date. Remember that you must also complete and file a **Proof of Service of Summons** (form 2), attach it to the **Notice and Acknowledgment of Receipt** (form 5) bearing your spouse's original signature, and then file both forms with the clerk. Do not forget to check box "3c" on the **Proof of Service of Summons**. (see form 2, p.199.) It is recommended that you use personal service whenever you can.

Other Notices

Once your spouse has been served with the *initiating documents*, namely the **Summons (Family Law)** (form 1, p.197), **Petition** (form 3, p.201), and a blank **Response** (form 21, discussed in Chapter 7), you may serve copies of other documents on your spouse by mail. You cannot mail the copies yourself nor can you hand the copies to your spouse because you are a party in the action. Have a friend, relative, or process serving company mail or personally serve them.

NOTE: *As of January 1, 2005, domestic partners have their own* **Petition** *and* **Response** *forms. (see form 3A and 21A.) The forms are basically the same as the marriage forms and the same instructions for filling them in can be used.*

You will need to file a **Proof of Service By Mail** (see form 28, p.271) or a **Proof of Personal Service** (see form 34, p.285), which are different from the **Proof of Service of Summons** (form 2, p.199). The person who signs either **Proof of Service** must be the person who placed the documents in the mail or who personally handed the documents to your spouse.

Fill out either **Proof of Service** completely, but do not have the person who will serve it (either by mail or personally) sign or date it. Staple a completed, but unsigned and undated, copy of the **Proof of Service** to the back of the copy of the document being served and have that copy served. The person who served the copy signs and dates the original proof of service after he or she has served the document(s). Then staple the original **Proof of Service** to the original document and file it, keeping a copy of the document to which is attached the signed and dated proof of service for your records. (This may sound unduly complicated but one cannot sign that he or she did something until after doing it.)

Court Hearing Date

You can get a date for the final hearing to get the divorce when you have completed all of the required documents. (Additional required documents are discussed later.) After all of your required forms are filed, ask the clerk for the procedure for setting a hearing. They will instruct you on what to do next. Clerks are not allowed to give legal advice, but they will tell you what form or procedure their court uses to set a hearing date. Once you get a hearing date, make sure you notify your spouse of such date, time, place, and courtroom number in writing. Then, you need to complete a **Proof of Service By Mail** (see form 28, p.271) for filing with the court, along with the form you served by mail. If you want a hearing date for some immediate or temporary relief, you will have to prepare an order-to-show cause or motion papers. This subject is briefly discussed in Chapter 11 under the section "Temporary Support and Custody."

Be aware that the clerk will not accept any papers for filing unless they are accompanied by a **Proof of Service** (form 28 or 34), which shows you have served your spouse with copies of the papers you want to file. The legal system requires all parties to notify the other parties of documents being filed.

COURTROOM MANNERS

There are certain rules of procedure that are used in a court. These are really rules of good conduct, or good manners, and are designed to keep things orderly. Many of the rules are written down, although some are unwritten customs that have developed over many years. They are not difficult, and most of them do make sense. Following these suggestions will make the judge respect you for your maturity and professional manner. It will also increase the likelihood that you will get the things you request.

Show Respect for the Judge

Showing respect basically means, do not make the judge angry at you. Be polite and call the judge *Your Honor* when you speak to him or her. Say things such as "Yes, Your Honor," or "Your Honor, I brought proof of my income," when addressing the court.

Many of the following rules also relate to showing respect for the court. This also means wearing appropriate, business-like clothing, such as a coat and tie for men and a suit or a dress for women. This especially means no T-shirts, blue jeans, shorts, or revealing clothing.

Listen   Whenever the judge talks, you listen. Even if the judge interrupts you, stop talking immediately and listen. Judges can become rather upset if you do not allow them to interrupt.

One at a Time   Only one person can talk at a time. Each person is allotted his or her own time to talk in court. The judge can only listen to one person at a time, so do not interrupt your spouse when it is his or her turn. And as difficult as it may be, stop talking if your spouse interrupts you. Ask and let the judge tell your spouse to keep quiet and let you have your say.

Talk to the Judge, not Your Spouse   Many people get in front of a judge and begin arguing with the other party. They turn away from the judge, face their spouse, and argue as if they were in the room alone. Whenever you speak in a courtroom, look only at the judge. Try to pretend that your spouse is not there. Remember, you are there to convince the judge that you should have certain things; you do not need to convince your spouse.

Wait Your Turn   Talk only when it is your turn. The usual procedure is for you, as the Petitioner, to present your case first. When you are done saying all you came to say, your spouse will have a chance to say whatever he or she came to say. Let your spouse have his or her say. When your spouse is finished, you will get another chance to respond to what has been said.

Stick to the Subject   Many people cannot resist the temptation to get off the track and start telling the judge all the problems with their marriage over the past twenty years. This wastes time and aggravates the judge. Stick to the subject and answer the judge's questions simply and accurately.

Keep Calm   Judges like things to go smoothly in their courtrooms. They do not like shouting, name calling, crying, or other displays of emotion.

do not respect your spouse, act like you do. All you have
to your spouse as "Mr. Smith" or "Ms. Smith" (using your
correct name, of course).

ATING

requires compromise. If you start with the minimum for
are willing to settle, you cannot compromise. How far from
settlement you start depends on how much you think
re to give up. Is your spouse usually a reasonable person
she only be satisfied if you have given up most of what
ly proposed?

thing else you do, preparation is extremely important.
ow all your assets and liabilities, as well as the ramifica-
. You must know exactly what you really want and what
ng to let go. It is seldom that either spouse ends up with
e or she wants. Be realistic.

t your spouse go first. You will get a better idea of where
tart and how much compromise may be necessary. You
d out what is really important to your spouse. If those
ot very important to you, you have a good bargaining

egin negotiating, you should try to set a point that you
eyond. For example, if you have decided that there are
property that you absolutely must have, and your spouse
is only willing to agree to let you have three, it is time to end the bargaining session and go home.

Keep in mind that the court will try to divide property equally and will use child support guidelines. If your spouse is unreasonable, be prepared to submit a more reasonable plan to the judge.

Additional Considerations Some additional considerations to keep in mind when negotiating a settlement are taxes and debt. The tax consequences of the divided property can significantly affect its ultimate value. Consult an accountant if large sums are involved.

Example:

You and your spouse own 100 shares of stocks A and B. All shares are worth $10 per share, but stock A was purchased for $5 per share, while stock B was purchased for $15 per share. If you take stock A and sell the shares, you will pay tax on the profit. If your take stock B and sell the shares, you will keep all the proceeds and have a tax write-off from its loss in value. Even though you each receive $1000 worth of stock, if sold under these circumstances, the net proceeds from stock A are much less. Keep the tax ramification in mind and use it in negotiating.

Be very careful with debts. You may think that you are getting a great settlement because your spouse is agreeing to take on most of your joint debt. If your spouse is not a responsible person or has a job that is not secure, you may end up paying the debts you thought you avoided. Creditors do not let you off the hook because of your divorce settlement. If your spouse quits making payments, the creditors will come after you. If your spouse suffers a job loss, it is not going to do you any good to go back to court and complain that your spouse is not living up to your agreement. If your spouse does not pay on time, your credit may be damaged. You may not even be aware of this until you apply for credit.

NOTE: *After a divorce, you should obtain your credit report at least once a year. Obtaining your credit report more often is recommended if your spouse has agreed to pay joint debts.*

chapter 6

Summary Dissolution Procedure

In certain circumstances, you may be able to take advantage of California's *summary dissolution procedure*. In order to use this procedure, you must meet certain requirements which are listed below. If you qualify, this is an inexpensive and easy way to get your divorce, with one caution—make sure that both you and your spouse are sure you agree on this procedure. If either of you change your mind within the six-month waiting period, you have just wasted a lot of time.

REQUIREMENTS

The summary dissolution procedure requires only a few forms, and although there are many requirements as you will see from the following, they are clear and easy to understand. To qualify for a summary dissolution you must meet *all* the following requirements. You and your spouse:

✪   have been married less than five years on the date you file your **Joint Petition for Summary Dissolution of Marriage**;

✪   have no children together that were adopted or born before or during the marriage (and the wife is not pregnant now);

✪   do not own or have an interest in any real estate (house, con-
    dominium, rental property, land, or a one-year lease or option
    to buy);

✪   do not owe more than $5,000 for debts acquired since the date
    of your marriage (do not count auto loans);

✪   have less than $33,000 worth of property acquired during the
    marriage (do not count money you owe on the property or auto
    loans);

✪   do not have separate property worth more than $33,000 (do
    not count money you owe on the property or auto loans);

✪   agree that neither spouse will ever get spousal support;

✪   must both sign the **JOINT PETITION FOR SUMMARY DISSOLUTION OF
    MARRIAGE** and pay the court filing fees or get a fee waiver;

✪   have signed an agreement that divides your property and
    debts before filing the **JOINT PETITION FOR SUMMARY DISSOLUTION
    OF MARRIAGE**;

✪   at least one spouse has lived in California for the last six
    months and in the county where you plan to file for the last
    three months; and,

✪   have read the *Summary Dissolution Information Booklet*.

If you qualify under all of the above, you should go to the courthouse
and pick up the necessary forms. Call first because sometimes the
forms are located at another branch of the court. Ask for the
Summary Dissolution Booklet and for the forms that you will need.

If you do not meet all of the above conditions, you may not use the
summary dissolution procedure. However, you may still want to read
this section, as it may help you understand the standard procedure
better. If the only requirement you do not meet is that you cannot
agree on the division of your property, you may want to reconsider
your position on the property. Read this chapter and have your

spouse read it. Then compare the summary dissolution procedure to the standard procedures in Chapter 7 and Chapter 8 of this book. Once you see how much easier the summary procedure is, you may want to try harder to resolve your differences over the property.

The Procedure   Basically, the procedure is as follows.

- ✪ You and your spouse complete the **JOINT PETITION FOR SUMMARY DISSOLUTION OF MARRIAGE** and attach the worksheets from the *Summary Dissolution Booklet.* (see form 22, p.259.)

- ✪ You file form 22 with the court clerk.

- ✪ You and your spouse wait six months.

- ✪ You or your spouse file the **REQUEST FOR JUDGMENT, JUDGMENT OF DISSOLUTION OF MARRIAGE, AND NOTICE OF ENTRY OF JUDGMENT** (form 23, p.261).

- ✪ The court grants your divorce without the need of a court hearing.

– Caution –
With the summary dissolution procedure, neither of you may receive spousal support and there is no appeal.

JOINT PETITION FOR SUMMARY DISSOLUTION OF MARRIAGE

The **JOINT PETITION FOR SUMMARY DISSOLUTION OF MARRIAGE** is the form used to open your case and ask for a divorce. (see form 22, p.259.) Complete form 22 as follows.

- ◈ Complete the top portion of the form according to the instructions in Chapter 5.

- ◈ Fill in the marriage date for item 2.

◈ Items 3 to 8 are reminders to you of the qualifications required to use this procedure.

◈ Item 10 directs you to complete and attach copies of the worksheets on pages 8, 10, and 12 of the *Summary Dissolution Booklet* that you have picked up from the clerk's office.

◈ In item 11, check box "a" if you have no community assets or liabilities. If you have community assets or liabilities, check box "b," and type up a *Property Settlement Agreement* according to the sample in the *Summary Dissolution Booklet*. Then attach that agreement to the **JOINT PETITION FOR SUMMARY DISSOLUTION OF MARRIAGE**.

◈ Item 12 verifies that you do not believe that your marriage can be saved.

◈ Check the box for item 13 if the wife or husband wishes to have his or her former name restored. Type in his or her complete former name.

◈ In the box at the top of the second page, fill in your name and your spouse's name where indicated. The case number will be filled in when you file your papers and the clerk assigns a case number.

◈ Items 17 and 18 ask for your mailing addresses.

◈ Sign and date the form where indicated, signing exactly as your names appear on the front of the form.

There is a filing fee you will have to pay, so if you did not ask when you picked up the forms, call ahead to find out the amount and the acceptable forms of payment (cash, money order, or check). If the clerk will take a check, find out how the clerk wants it to read. After the clerk files and stamps your copies, give one copy to your spouse. You should sign the form in California, but if for some reason you need to sign it while out of the state, have your signature notarized.

REQUEST FOR JUDGMENT, JUDGMENT OF DISSOLUTION OF MARRIAGE, AND NOTICE OF ENTRY OF JUDGMENT

After six months and one day from the date of filing the **JOINT PETITION FOR SUMMARY DISSOLUTION OF MARRIAGE** (form 22, p.259), you can file the **REQUEST FOR JUDGMENT, JUDGMENT OF DISSOLUTION OF MARRIAGE, AND NOTICE OF ENTRY OF JUDGMENT**. (see form 23, p.261.) This is really three forms combined into one. Complete form 23 as follows.

❖ Complete the top portion of the form according to the instructions in Chapter 5.

❖ In item 1, type in the date you filed the **JOINT PETITION FOR SUMMARY DISSOLUTION OF MARRIAGE** (form 22, p.259).

❖ In item 3, check box "a" if you want your dissolution to be effective immediately. If you want your dissolution to be effective at a date later than the time you file it, you must check box "b," and type in the date you want it to become effective and the reason for wanting this date.

❖ Sign your name, fill in the date, and type or print your name where indicated.

   NOTE: *This form need only be signed and dated by one spouse.*

❖ If the wife wants her former name restored and she did not request it on the **JOINT PETITION FOR SUMMARY DISSOLUTION OF MARRIAGE**, she can do so now by checking the box for item 4, typing in her full former name, and signing where indicated.

❖ Item 5 at the bottom of the form is for the judge to complete.

❖ On the back of form, type in your names and case number in the boxes at the top, and both your and your spouse's address in the boxes shown.

   NOTE: *Be sure to make several copies of the original after you complete it. The clerk will want at least three copies and maybe more depending on the county. Always have an extra copy for your files and for your spouse.*

NOTICE OF REVOCATION OF PETITION FOR SUMMARY DISSOLUTION

The **NOTICE OF REVOCATION OF PETITION FOR SUMMARY DISSOLUTION** is self-explanatory. (see form 24, p.263.) If, during the six-month waiting period, you and your spouse decide to get back together, or if either of you decide to use the standard divorce procedure, this is the form to use. This is the easiest of all of the forms. Simply type it as you did the other forms. Sign it, date it, and fill in your and your spouse's addresses at the bottom. Take it to the clerk's office and file it. Take at least four copies with you. You do not need your spouse's signature to do this. Either spouse can revoke the summary dissolution procedure during the six months.

If you do not revoke the divorce during the six months, one of you must file the **REQUEST FOR JUDGMENT, JUDGMENT OF DISSOLUTION OF MARRIAGE, AND NOTICE OF ENTRY OF JUDGMENT** (form 23, p.261). If you do not, the court may dismiss your case for lack of action on your part.

Uncontested Divorce Procedure

There are two ways that a case can be considered *uncontested*. One is when you and your spouse reach an agreement on every issue in the divorce, but do not qualify for the summary procedure. To be in this situation you must be in agreement on:

- ✪ how your property is to be divided;

- ✪ how your debts are to be divided;

- ✪ which of you will have custody of the children, and in what percentage of time;

- ✪ how much child support is to be paid; and,

- ✪ whether any alimony is to be paid, and if so, how much and for how long a period of time.

The other type of uncontested divorce is where your spouse does not respond to your **PETITION**. If your spouse is served (see Chapter 5 for more information about service) and does not respond, you will need to file certain forms. If you cannot find your spouse, you will need to file additional forms (see Chapter 11).

To begin your uncontested divorce procedure, the following forms should be taken to the court clerk in all cases (see Chapter 5 for filing instructions):

- ✪ any required *local forms*;

- ✪ **SUMMONS (FAMILY LAW)** (form 1, p.197); and,

- ✪ **PETITION** (form 3, p.201 for marriage) or (form 3A, p.203 for domestic partnership).

Other official forms, some mandatory and some depending upon your situation, will also need to be filed. These include the following.

- ✪ **REQUEST TO ENTER DEFAULT** (form 12, p.225).

- ✪ **DECLARATION FOR DEFAULT OR UNCONTESTED DISSOLUTION OR LEGAL SEPARATION** (form 13, p.227).

- ✪ **DECLARATION REGARDING SERVICE OF DECLARATION OF DISCLOSURE AND INCOME AND EXPENSE DECLARATION** (form 9, p.219).

- ✪ **APPEARANCE, STIPULATIONS, AND WAIVERS** (form 11, p.223).

- ✪ **SCHEDULE OF ASSETS AND DEBTS** (form 7, p.211).

- ✪ **INCOME AND EXPENSE DECLARATION** (form 8, p.215).

- ✪ **PROOF OF SERVICE OF SUMMONS** (form 2, p.199).

- ✪ **EARNINGS ASSIGNMENT ORDER FOR SPOUSAL SUPPORT** (form 20, p.253).

- ✪ **ORDER/NOTICE TO WITHHOLD INCOME FOR CHILD SUPPORT** (form 46, p.323).

- ✪ **JUDGMENT** (form 17, p.247).

- ✪ **NOTICE OF ENTRY OF JUDGMENT** (form 19, p.251).

✪ **STIPULATION TO ESTABLISH OR MODIFY CHILD SUPPORT AND ORDER** (form 15, p.233).

✪ **MARITAL SETTLEMENT AGREEMENT (MSA)** (form 16, p.235).

These and other additional forms are found in Appendix B and are discussed as appropriate in this book.

Once you complete and file the necessary forms, you have the choice of either:

✪ delivering or mailing your papers to the court and getting your judgment back in the mail or

✪ appearing before the judge to get your judgment.

If you choose to go to court, you will first have to apply for a court date. Local practice may vary, so be sure to ask the clerk's office for the procedure to obtain your judgment. Your forms will have to be in order to get your judgment, regardless of method.

As mentioned earlier, some courts require a cover sheet to be filed with your **PETITION**. You will have to call the clerk in your particular county to find out if a cover sheet is required. If it is, you can obtain the form from the clerk.

SUMMONS (FAMILY LAW)
The **SUMMONS (FAMILY LAW)** (see form 1, p.197) needs to be completed with the original issued by the court clerk and a copy served on your spouse along with the **PETITION**. (See Chapter 5 for information on completing form 1 and serving your spouse.)

PETITION
The **PETITION** must be completed in all cases. (see form 3, p.201 for marriage or form 3A, p.203 for domestic partnership.) This is the

paper you file to begin your case. The **PETITION** may also be accompanied by other forms depending upon your situation.

Complete the **PETITION** as follows. (The following instructions for form 3 are based on the assumption that you and your spouse are in agreement on everything.)

◈   Complete the top portion of the form according to the instructions in Chapter 5.

◈   In the "Petition For" box, check the box for "Dissolution of Marriage." Do not check the box for "Amended" unless you've made a substantial error and are refiling the **PETITION**.

◈   In item 1, check the box that applies. Check both boxes if both of you satisfy the residency requirements.

◈   In item 2, provide the requested information as to the date of separation. This is the date you decided to divorce; it is not the date you and your spouse temporarily separated to test the marriage. An attorney's advice is recommended if there are separation date issues as the date affects community property, etc.

◈   In item 3, check either "a" or "b," and provide the requested statistical information if you check "b."

◈   If there are minor children of the marriage, note that item "3c" requires you to complete the **DECLARATION UNDER UNIFORM CHILD CUSTODY JURISDICTION AND ENFORCEMENT ACT (UCCJEA)**. (see form 4, p.205.)

◈   Item "3d" refers to a "voluntary declaration of paternity" form. This form is used primarily by social workers at the hospitals to establish paternity for children born out of wedlock. If the spouse in the divorce case is the father who signed the form at the hospital and did not rescind it within a short time thereafter, he cannot deny being the father.

◈   Check the box that applies for item 4, and type under "Item" those pieces of property that you claim are your separate (not community) property. If there is not enough space, check the box marked "in Attachment 4," and attach a page containing this information, labeling it "Attachment 4 to Petition." If your spouse claims certain property as separate, list that property and type either "Petitioner" or "Respondent" under the "Confirm to" section. ("Confirm to" means that you agree that the property listed belongs to you or your spouse as his or her separate property.)

◈ Fill out the top portion on the back of the form just like you did with the other forms.

◈ In item 5, check box "a" if there are no assets or obligations for the court to divide. In other words, you have no community property. If you do have community property, you should check box "b" or "c." Check box "b" if you and your spouse have written, or will write, a **Marital Settlement Agreement (MSA)** (form 16) in which you divide the community property. Check box "c" if you do not have, and do not intend to have, a written **MSA**.

If there is enough room below item 5 for you to list the assets and obligations that need dividing, list them in that space. If you need more space check the box marked "in Attachment 5b." Then list the assets and obligations on an **Additional Page** (form 27, p.269), label it "Attachment 5 to Petition," and staple it to the **Petition**.

◈ In item 6, check boxes "a" and "(1)," indicating you are requesting dissolution of your marriage based on the ground of irreconcilable differences.

◈ Item 7, boxes "a" through "i": References to "children" are to the minor children of your marriage and to those still unborn if the wife is pregnant. (It does not include stepchildren or children 18 years of age and older.) The duty of support continues for an unmarried child who (1) has reached 18; (2) is a full-time high school student; and (3) is not self-supporting. If all three apply, support will continue until the time the child completes the twelfth grade or attains the age of 19 years, whichever occurs first.

Check these boxes as follows:

○ Item "a": Check the box under "Joint." *Legal custody* refers to the decision-making aspects of child rearing, such as religious training, medical decisions, special needs, and the like. Routinely, both spouses jointly participate in these decisions unless there are extraordinary problems. If a special problem exists, check the box for the spouse that will retain sole legal custody.

○ Item "b": If you check physical custody for one spouse, then the other spouse is necessarily reduced to having only visitation rights with the children.

○ Item "c": If you decide that one spouse will have physical custody, then the other necessarily has visitation rights. Check the box so indicating that.

○ Item "d": Check this box if the two of you had children together before your marriage and parentage was established by a voluntary declaration of paternity.

○ Item "e": Ignore this item. You do not have an attorney so there are no attorney's fees.

○ Item "f": If you have decided that one spouse will pay spousal support, check the box showing which spouse will pay.

 NOTE: *The form states payment will be by wage assignment. This is mandatory unless you and your spouse agree otherwise.*

○ Item "g": Check this box if you and your spouse agree that you will not pay spousal support to your spouse.

○ Item "h": Check this box if you checked item 4 or item "5b" above.

✪ Item "i": If the petitioner wants her or his former name restored, check this box and type in the full former name.

◈ Item 8 is a notice about child support and item 9 is a verification that you have read the restraining orders on the **Summons (Family Law)** (form 1, p.197).

◈ Date and sign the form where indicated at the bottom. Above the second dotted line marked "(Type or Print Name)," type or print your name with the phrase "In Pro Per" (short for "In Propria Persona") after it. That phrase simply means you are acting as your own attorney. Your **Petition** is now ready for filing.

DECLARATION UNDER UNIFORM CHILD CUSTODY JURISDICTION AND ENFORCEMENT ACT (UCCJEA)

The **Declaration Under Uniform Child Custody Jurisdiction and Enforcement Act (UCCJEA)** (see form 4, p.205) must be completed and attached to the **Petition** (form 3, p.201 or 3A, p.203) if there are minor children of the marriage. Form 4 is straightforward and needs no explanation. If you must use form 4, file it along with the **Petition**.

STARTING YOUR DIVORCE PROCEEDING

The documents discussed are required to get the divorce going. Before you have your spouse served, be sure you have done the following.

❑ Completed the **Summons (Family Law)** (form 1, p.197).

❑ Completed and filed the **Petition** (form 3, p.201 for marriage or form 3A, p.203 for domestic partnership).

❑ Completed and filed the **Declaration Under Uniform Child Custody Jurisdiction and Enforcement Act (UCCJEA)** (form 4, p.205).

❏   Completed and filed any other documents required by the court.

❏   Had the clerk issue the **SUMMONS (FAMILY LAW)** (form 1, p.197).

You now need to serve these documents on your spouse. See the section in Chapter 5 on "Notifying Your Spouse" for details on how to go about having your spouse served.

PRELIMINARY DECLARATION OF DISCLOSURE

Sometimes one spouse may feel inclined to hide certain property, despite the restraining orders referred to on the back of the **SUMMONS (FAMILY LAW)** (form 1, p.197). To avoid this, the law requires both spouses to voluntarily reveal to the other all the property (both separate or community) that he or she has on the **DECLARATION OF DISCLOSURE**. (see form 6, p.209.)

NOTE: *There are both a Preliminary and a Final DECLARATION OF DISCLOSURE. They are the same form but are served at different times, with the final version being used for updating purposes.*

Although you and your spouse may waive the Final **DECLARATION OF DISCLOSURE**, you may not waive the Preliminary **DECLARATION OF DISCLOSURE**. Each spouse must serve the other with the Preliminary **DECLARATION OF DISCLOSURE** within sixty days from the date you serve your spouse with the initial documents (the **SUMMONS (FAMILY LAW)** (form 1, p.197), **PETITION** (form 3, p.201 for marriage or form 3A, p.203 for domestic partnership), and any local forms). You can also serve the **SCHEDULE OF ASSETS AND DEBTS** (form 7, p.211) with the initial papers.

Both spouses owe a duty of fair dealing and full disclosure to the other. If a spouse is found to have deliberately hidden property or to have disclosed it without sufficient particularity, the court can prevent the noncomplying spouse from presenting evidence on issues that should have been covered in the **DECLARATION OF DISCLOSURE** and sanction such noncomplying spouse with a money penalty. Because the Code requires this be done by a legal motion, you may want to contact an attorney if you find yourself in this situation.

Neither the Preliminary nor Final **DECLARATION OF DISCLOSURE** is filed with the court, but the **DECLARATION REGARDING SERVICE OF DECLARATION OF DISCLOSURE AND INCOME AND EXPENSE DECLARATION** is filed. (see form 9, p.219.) Form 9 is brief and contains only two items—first, whether you are the respondent or petitioner and second, when and how you served the final **DECLARATION OF DISCLOSURE** on your spouse. The Preliminary **DECLARATION OF DISCLOSURE** forms must be exchanged between you and your spouse. (see form 6, p.209.)

Complete the **DECLARATION OF DISCLOSURE** as follows.

- ◈ Complete the top portion of the form according to the instructions in Chapter 5.

- ◈ Check box 1 and complete and attach the **SCHEDULE OF ASSETS AND DEBTS** (form 7, p.211).

- ◈ Check box 2 and complete and attach the **INCOME AND EXPENSE DECLARATION** (form 8, p.215).

- ◈ Check box 3 and write and attach a statement as the form requires.

- ◈ Check box 4 and write and attach a statement as to any information you have that would affect a community obligation.

- ◈ Check box 5 and write and attach a statement if you know of any investment opportunity that arose since your separation.

If you have no information that applies under boxes 3, 4, and 5, indicate that fact on the form itself beneath the item. For example, if you have no information of any investment opportunity in item 5, write "I have no knowledge of any investment opportunity since separation." Then sign, print your name, and serve it on your spouse.

SCHEDULE OF ASSETS AND DEBTS

The **SCHEDULE OF ASSETS AND DEBTS** is a four-page form with the first three pages relating to assets and the last page for debts. (see form 7, p.211.) You must:

✪   list all your property—separate and community;

✪   indicate under the column "Sep. Prop." whether any separate property is husband's "H" or wife's "W" (leave this column blank if the item is community property);

✪   show the approximate date you obtained the property;

✪   show the gross fair market value; and,

✪   show the amount of the debt against it.

Complete the **SCHEDULE OF ASSETS AND DEBTS** as follows.

◈   Complete the top portion of the form according to the instructions in Chapter 5.

◈   Under item 1, list all real property, and attach a copy of the deed, with its legal description and latest lender's statement.

◈   Under item 2, list all *special* furniture separately. (If you or your spouse want to list everything to avoid an argument later, that is fine.)

◈   Under item 3, identify valuable items and use the fair market value.

◈   Under item 4, describe your cars and boats and attach a copy of the pink slip, if you have it, or the registration, and show the value and loans.

◈   Under items 5, 6, and 7, identify the financial institution, the account number, and attach the latest statement.

◈ Under item 8, list any cash. Do not include amounts listed in items 5, 6, or 7.

◈ Under item 9, list any expected tax refund not yet received.

◈ For item 10, call your insurance agent to find out the cash value of any life insurance you have. If the policy has a value, attach a copy of the declaration page of the policy and the information you obtained from the agent.

◈ Item 11 is self-explanatory, but make sure to be complete.

◈ Under items 12 and 13, you may need to contact your company's pension department or the administrator of the plan you have at work. Retirement accounts are community property for that portion of the time worked from marriage to time of separation. You may be surprised at the large value. These include profit sharing plans, 401(k) plans, defined benefit plans, and the like.

   NOTE: *If either of you have a substantial retirement account, you should seek professional advice as to how to handle these items.*

◈ Item 14 is asking for the value of any money owed you from someone else.

◈ For item 15, you must attach the IRS K-1 partnership form and/or the IRS Schedule C form included in your income tax return. All business interests should be described here including corporations, limited liability companies, or any other interest.

◈ Under item 16, list any other assets not mentioned.

◈ If you need more space to list everything, use attachment pages and label each attachment page with the name and number of your case. For any such pages, total the two right-hand columns and write the totals in item 17.

◈ In item 18, write in the totals for the two right-hand columns.

◈   On page 4 of the form, list your debts under the appropriate headings in items 19 through 24. The only item requiring explanation is item 21, "Support Arrearages." If you are behind in spousal or child support payments from a previous marriage, list the amounts here. You need to attach a copy of the court order showing the support to be paid and a statement showing the arrearage dates and amounts. If you need more space to list everything, use attachment pages and label each attachment page with the name and number of your case. For any such pages, total the "Total Owing" column and write the total in item 25. In item 26, write in the total for this column.

◈   Check the box for item 27 if you have attached any additional pages, and write in the number of additional pages.

◈   Fill in the date, print your name, and sign your name where indicated at the bottom of page four.

If you do not have all of the information for this Preliminary **DECLARATION OF DISCLOSURE**, put "Unknown." If your spouse has all the paperwork and it is not accessible to you, try to get it. The law requires diligence to complete this form.

INCOME AND EXPENSE DECLARATION

The **INCOME AND EXPENSE DECLARATION** (see form 8, p.215) is the second form that must be attached to the Preliminary **DECLARATION OF DISCLOSURE**.

There is a simplified **FINANCIAL STATEMENT** (form 10, p.221) that may be substituted for the **INCOME AND EXPENSE DECLARATION** (form 8, p.215). Read the instructions on the back of the form to see if you qualify. If you think any of the disqualifications may arise during the case, use form 8. You are not required to use the simplified form just because you qualify.

Complete the **INCOME AND EXPENSE DECLARATION** as follows.

◈ Complete the top portion of the first page according to the instructions in Chapter 5.

◈ Item 1 asks for information about your employer, the number of hours that you work, and your pay. Be sure to attach your pay stubs for the last two months and black out the Social Security number. If you are self-employed, skip this section.

◈ Item 2 asks for your age and formal education. No proof need be filed with the form.

◈ Item 3 requires information as to how and when you filed tax returns. You do not have to attach tax returns but be sure that the tax returns are available for your court hearing.

◈ Item 4 asks for your spouse's or domestic partner's income. If you do not know, estimate and give a short explanation of the reason for the amount estimated. You might say "saw one of spouse's paychecks" or "was told by partner."

◈ Item 5. Fill in all information required for your income. Be sure there are no discrepancies between this item and item 1.

◈ Item 6. If you have rental property, you will need to furnish income and expenses for each. Use your tax return schedule and always black out your Social Security number.

◈ Item 7. If you are self-employed, you answer the questions and attach the required documentation either in the form of a profit and loss statement or schedule C from your tax return. If you have more than one business, submit separate records for each.

◈ Item 8. Disclose any other income. If you received a gift or inheritance, it may be separate property that you keep. It still has to be disclosed.

◈ Item 9. If you have changed jobs and now have less income, you may need to explain to the court that you are doing the best you can. If the court believes that you are voluntarily making less than you should be (underemployed), you may have to pay a higher amount of support than your income would normally require.

✦ Item 10. The questions are self-explanatory except for "g." These are not expenses that have to be tax deductible. They are the actual expenses necessary to doing the job that you have, whether allowed as deductions by IRS or not.

✦ Item 11. Listing your assets does not mean that your spouse or partner is entitled to half. This is not the time to show which are separate property. Just list them.

✦ Item 12. If this applies, fill in as best you can. It is a way for the court to get an idea if others are helping, or could help, with your expenses. Estimate earnings or ask the party involved.

✦ Item 13 asks for expenses (actual), how much you think your expenses are (estimated), or how much you think your expenses will be (proposed need). Check the appropriate box and fill in the amounts. You can now see the reason for item 12. If you are spending $300 per week for groceries because you have deadbeat friends or relatives living with you who do not chip in, this may not be a legitimate expense when it comes to figuring out support. Fill out item 14 before totaling as you will need the figure from item 14 for line "p."

✦ Item 14. List your installment payments like your car payment, furniture payment, and credit card payments. Put the total on line "p" of item 13.

✦ Item 15. If you are requesting attorney's fees, fill in this item.

✦ Items 16–18 apply to child support. If this applies, fill in the time you spend with your child or children and your costs. Be sure these are your expenses and not covered by your employer or insurance.

✦ Item 19 covers special situations not yet listed. If it applies, fill it in and attach any documentation to support your claims.

✦ Item 20. The form is complete enough that most people do not need to add anything. If you have a special situation not covered so far, add it now.

You are signing this form under penalty of perjury. The court will understand if you make an honest mistake, but deliberate lies usually end with your spouse or partner getting more than he or she would normally get.

SERVING YOUR SPOUSE

You must serve your spouse with a copy of your Preliminary **DECLARATION OF DISCLOSURE** (form 6), the attached **SCHEDULE OF ASSETS AND DEBTS** (form 7), and **INCOME AND EXPENSE DECLARATION** (form 8). Service can be by mail. Complete and file the **DECLARATION REGARDING SERVICE OF DECLARATION OF DISCLOSURE AND INCOME AND EXPENSE DECLARATION** (form 9) to show that you complied with the law by serving your spouse with the Preliminary **DECLARATION OF DISCLOSURE** (form 6). For your own records in case you are challenged, complete and keep in your file the original **PROOF OF SERVICE BY MAIL** (form 28) that you used in mailing the **DECLARATION OF DISCLOSURE** to your spouse.

WHEN YOUR SPOUSE WILL NOT COOPERATE

So what happens if your spouse won't exchange the **DECLARATION OF DISCLOSURE** (form 6, p.209) with you? You then need to make a record of your attempt to get him or her to exchange the form. You do that by mailing a copy of your **DECLARATION OF DISCLOSURE** to your spouse's last known address, and at least one certified and one regular letter informing your spouse of his or her legal duty to serve you with his or her Preliminary **DECLARATION OF DISCLOSURE**. Then, using the **DECLARATION**, write a statement as to what you have done to try to get your spouse to comply and file it with the court. (see form 26, p.267.) The purpose for doing this is to anticipate a judge's question as to why both **DECLARATION OF DISCLOSURE** forms were not exchanged.

The last paragraph of the statement must state: "I declare under penalty of perjury under the laws of the State of California that the foregoing is true and correct." Insert the date, type or print your name, and sign the document. Form 26 already has this required information. If you need more space, use an **ADDITIONAL PAGE** and label it "Attachment to Declaration." Type the case name and number at the top of the **ADDITIONAL PAGE**. (see form 27, p.269.)

FINAL DECLARATION OF DISCLOSURE

The Final **DECLARATION OF DISCLOSURE** may be waived by you and your spouse if you have a **MARITAL SETTLEMENT AGREEMENT (MSA)** (see form 16, p.235), or if the divorce is a *default* divorce (i.e., when your spouse either does not respond to the **PETITION**, or responds, but does not show up at court on the trial date). (see form 6, p.209.) Remember, however, that you must have served the Preliminary **DECLARATION OF DISCLOSURE** on your spouse because that requirement is not waived.

The Final **DECLARATION OF DISCLOSURE** is the same as the Preliminary **DECLARATION OF DISCLOSURE**, except that the Final updates the Preliminary. If your case becomes contested, both you and your spouse need to serve the final **DECLARATION OF DISCLOSURE** on each other not later than forty-five days before the first assigned trial date. If your case is uncontested, but you and your spouse do not waive the Final **DECLARATION OF DISCLOSURE** in the **MARITAL SETTLEMENT AGREEMENT (MSA)** (form 16, p.235) or in the **DECLARATION FOR DEFAULT OR UNCONTESTED DISSOLUTION** (form 13, p.227), you both need to exchange your Final **DECLARATION OF DISCLOSURE** forms at the time you prepare your MSA. Neither the preliminary nor the Final **DECLARATION OF DISCLOSURE** is filed with the court, but each of you must file a **DECLARATION REGARDING SERVICE OF DECLARATION** (form 9, p.219) for the Preliminary **DECLARATION OF DISCLOSURE** in any event.

STIPULATION FOR CHILD SUPPORT

Some courts require a **STIPULATION TO ESTABLISH OR MODIFY CHILD SUPPORT AND ORDER** and some do not. (see form 15, p.233.) Generally, the **MARITAL SETTLEMENT AGREEMENT (MSA)** (form 16, p.235) replaces form 15. The word stipulation means agreement, and there is no need for two agreements where one will suffice. Nevertheless, some courts require both of these forms. Complete the **STIPULATION TO ESTABLISH OR MODIFY CHILD SUPPORT AND ORDER** as follows.

❖ Complete the top portion of the forms according to the instructions in Chapter 5.

❖ In item 1, check box "a" and enter the net incomes of both spouses (you already determined this on the **INCOME AND EXPENSE DECLARATION** (form 8, p.215). If you have an attorney friend who has one of the computer programs certified by the courts, you may check box "b" instead and attach the printout.

❖ Check the appropriate boxes and enter the information for items 2 and 3 in detail, making sure it corresponds to the information you entered for hardship on the **INCOME AND EXPENSE DECLARATION** (form 8, p.215).

❖ If you know the amount from the support guidelines, fill in this amount in item 4, along with the name of the person who will be paying support (you or your spouse).

❖ Check item 5 if you and your spouse agree to the amount determined by the guideline.

❖ Check item 6, and not item 5, if you and your spouse do not agree to the guideline amount and wish a different amount. Enter the amount to which you do agree.

❖ Complete the item 7 boxes as applicable and remember to total all amounts contributing to the child support in the box "7c."

❖ Fill in the names and case number called for in the box at the top of the second page of the form.

❖ Item 8 is self-explanatory as to health insurance.

❖ For item 9, it is recommended that the **ORDER/NOTICE TO WITHHOLD INCOME FOR CHILD SUPPORT** (form 46, p.323) not be stayed. A wage assignment eliminates potential disagreement and potential attorneys fees later by having the support paid directly by the payor's employer to the payee spouse.

> ◈ The balance of the form is self-explanatory, but do not forget to date the form, print your name and sign it, and type "In Pro Per" after your name so the court knows you are representing yourself.

> **NOTE:** *Form 15 has not yet been modified to include domestic partners. If you are a domestic partner and need to use it, insert "partner" to replace "mother" and "father."*

MARITAL SETTLEMENT AGREEMENT (MSA)

The **MARITAL SETTLEMENT AGREEMENT** (**MSA**) is the document in which you and your spouse state your agreement regarding matters such as property division, spousal support, child support, custody, and visitation. (see form 16, p.235.) You will note that form 16 contains optional provisions for you to choose from by checking a box. It is more common for the **MSA** to be prepared individually, rather than using a form. This check-the-box format may, or may not, be acceptable to the court in your county. It would be advisable for you to re-type form 16, using only those provisions that apply to your agreement.

The following information will help you to either fill out form 16 or develop an original **MSA** using form 16 as a guideline.

> ◈ In the first, unnumbered paragraph, type in the date, the wife's name, and the husband's name on the three blank lines.

> ◈ In paragraph 1, type in the date of your marriage.

> ◈ In paragraph 2, type in the date you and your spouse agree is the separation date.

> ◈ In paragraph 3, fill in the county and case number.

◆ In paragraph 4, check the first box if no children were born or adopted during your marriage. If you have children, check the second box and type in their names and birthdates.

◆ In paragraph 5, type in your and your spouse's Social Security numbers on the appropriate lines.

◆ In paragraph 6, check the box beside the statement that reflects your situation. If you check the second box, type in a brief description of the health problem or problems.

◆ In paragraph 7, type in the names of employers and monthly income for you and your spouse on the appropriate lines.

◆ Paragraphs 8 through 12 are general statements that you are making relating to the agreement.

◆ In paragraphs 13 through 16, list your and your spouse's community and separate property in the appropriate paragraphs. If real property is included, type the complete address and full legal description. If the legal description is lengthy, make a clear copy of it and attach it to the **MSA**, stating in the appropriate paragraph of the **MSA** that "the legal description to this property is attached as Exhibit A and incorporated herein by this reference."

The real property is often the only substantial asset. If there are children, you may want to arrange that one spouse remain in the home with the children until a later time if it makes economic sense. If you do so agree, include a clause in the **MSA** that the house will be sold at some date in the future and the proceeds divided evenly. During the time one spouse remains in the home with the children, that spouse would normally pay the upkeep of the home, including mortgage, taxes, and insurance. However, the cost of a capital improvement, such as a new roof or other major repair, would normally be divided equally between the parties.

NOTE: *If there is substantial equity in the home, seek the help of an attorney for the drafting of this particular issue.*

◈   Paragraphs 18 through 22 concern the division of debt among the parties and claims against the other's property.

◈   List the wife's debts in paragraph 19, dividing them into the three categories listed, and list the husband's debts similarly in paragraph 20.

◈   Regarding paragraph 23, if either you or your spouse has substantial retirement or other employee benefits, remember that such benefits are community property to the extent they were earned during the marriage to the time of separation.

   NOTE: *If the value is substantial, talk to an attorney and see an actuary so you know the community property value.*

   Half of the community value is yours. Any such item must be included in the **MSA** and must be the subject of an additional court order, called a *QDRO* (which stands for *Qualified Domestic Relations Order*). This QDRO is then sent to the administrator of the plan or account, who in turn takes the appropriate community property interest out of the employee spouse's account and creates an account for the other spouse.

◈   In paragraph 24, check the box for the sub-paragraph that reflects your agreement regarding spousal support, and fill in any other items that need completing in the sub-paragraph you select. A reasonable period of time for spousal support is one-half the length of the marriage, but the judge can order a greater or lesser period of time. This does not apply to marriages of long duration (more than ten years). When the parties intelligently agree between themselves as to spousal support, such agreement will normally stand.

   NOTE: *Life insurance may be used as a support tool.*

◈   In paragraph 25, check the box for the sub-paragraph that reflects your agreement regarding child custody and fill in any other items that need completing in the sub-paragraph you select. Note that form 16 has a standard visitation schedule in the event you and your spouse do not agree as to what is reasonable. (If you wish to have a different schedule, you will need to re-type the form and insert the schedule you desire.)

❖ In paragraph 26, check the appropriate boxes and fill in the information required to reflect your agreement on child support.

> **NOTE:** *The remaining paragraphs contain general contract language to make your agreement binding. The* **MSA** *is a contract between you and your spouse creating legal rights and responsibilities you both must follow.*

❖ You and your spouse will need to date and sign the **MSA** before a notary public.

> **NOTE:** *If you and your spouse develop complicated ways for support to be paid, or certain property to be divided—have a lawyer look over your agreement. You do not want to return to court because you did not foresee the legal consequences.*

Remember that in an **MSA**, you and your spouse can divide your property any way you want. If you do not agree, and leave it to the court to divide, the court must divide the property equally and will perhaps divide it in a way you do not want. The judge would much prefer to have you settle everything yourself and just present the completed **JUDGMENT** for his or her signature.

If you have an **MSA**, it must be attached with the **JUDGMENT** (form 17, p.247). Check box 4i of the **JUDGEMENT** and attach the **MSA** to it.

To resolve your issues, unless you have no community property, no children, no community debts, and no support issues, you will need an **MSA**. That is the only way your case can be settled, unless, of course, you go to trial and get a judgment.

RESPONDING TO THE DIVORCE FILING

Your spouse is required to file a **RESPONSE** (form 21, p.255) within thirty days after being served with a copy of the **SUMMONS (FAMILY LAW)** (form 1, p.197) and **PETITION** (form 3, p.201). If your spouse does not file a **RESPONSE** within this time period, you may seek a default by filing a **REQUEST TO ENTER DEFAULT**. (see form 12, p.225.)

The **REQUEST TO ENTER DEFAULT** is used in either of the following situations:

❂   your spouse is personally served and fails to file a **RESPONSE** within thirty days (and you do not give an extension of time) or

❂   you cannot locate your spouse.

Once a default is entered, it prevents your spouse from participating further in your divorce case.

In many cases, provided the two of you have agreed on everything, the default of your spouse will be by agreement to save the **RESPONSE** filing fee. If you and your spouse are not in agreement, but for whatever reason he or she does not bother to respond to the **SUMMONS (FAMILY LAW)** (form 1, p.197) and **PETITION** (form 3, p.201 or form 3A, p.203) within the thirty days, you can file the **REQUEST TO ENTER DEFAULT** (form 12, p.225).

Default

Once the clerk enters your spouse's default, your spouse cannot contest the proceeding, and you can go ahead with the forms you need to complete your case and get your divorce. (Note that because your defaulted spouse could obtain an attorney to try to set aside the default, it makes more sense to let your spouse file a response even if it is late.)

There are some subtle traps that could throw you off track if you proceed by default. For example, if you are the husband/petitioner and your wife wants her maiden name back, you would check the box on the **JUDGMENT** form that accomplishes this. But if you and your wife agree to proceed by way of default to save the response filing fee, your papers might be bounced by the clerk because your wife would be asking the court to change her name when she has not appeared in the case. However, if she appears in the case, a response filing fee is due. Some courts will accept your wife's signature on the **JUDGMENT** without requiring a response fee.

You and your spouse may also wish to stipulate (agree) to something after the default has been entered. In that case, the court may not accept the agreement unless the response filing fee is paid.

Exactly what makes the clerk ask for a response filing fee varies from county to county. Certainly, the response filing fee is due if your spouse files a **RESPONSE**. (see form 21, p.255.) But sometimes your spouse agrees that the divorce can proceed by default because you have agreed on everything and he or she wants to save the response filing fee, which is approximately $280.

Even if your spouse does not file a **RESPONSE**, he or she may still have to pay the response fee. As an example, if your spouse signs a **MARITAL SETTLEMENT AGREEMENT (MSA)** in San Diego or San Francisco county, your spouse would not have to pay the fee, but in Orange County your spouse would have to pay the fee. Be sure to call the clerk to find out the particular county's policy.

Often it is more efficient, even when you and your spouse have no disagreement, to have the other spouse file a **RESPONSE** and pay the response filing fee. This eliminates traps and encourages exchange of required documents such as the Preliminary **DECLARATION OF DISCLOSURE** forms. But, because the **RESPONSE** makes the matter contested, you would both have to sign and file the **APPEARANCE, STIPULATIONS, AND WAIVERS** (form 11, p.223) when you request your **JUDGMENT** to tell the court that your matter is really *uncontested*.

When the **JUDGMENT**, with the **MSA**, is ready to be submitted to the court for signature granting the divorce, you would file an **APPEARANCE, STIPULATIONS, AND WAIVERS** (form 11, p.223) with the **JUDGMENT**. This tells the court that both of you agree the action may now proceed as an uncontested, as opposed to a default, divorce. This eliminates a trial and also permits you to obtain your divorce without a court appearance, if you so choose.

Opinions differ on this, and how best to proceed may depend on local practice. If there is little property and no substantial issues, you may want to proceed by default just to avoid having one spouse pay the response filing fee. But if you decide to proceed by default, or must proceed by default because your spouse has not filed a **Response**, complete the **Request to Enter Default** (form 12, p.225) as follows.

◈ Complete the top portion of the form according to the instructions in Chapter 5.

◈ For items 2 and 3, check the applicable boxes. If you do not attach the **Income and Expense Declaration** (form 8, p.215) and the **Property Declaration** (form 14, p.229), you must explain why in items (a) through (e). If there are no issues of support, property, custody, or attorney's fees, you do not need to attach these forms. If there are such issues, but all issues are addressed in a **Marital Settlement Agreement (MSA)**, you would only need to attach the **Income and Expense Declaration** forms. (However, you may want to check with the clerk to confirm local policy.) Item (f) refers to a paternity proceeding so leave it blank.

If the form requires you to attach the documents, remember that the Preliminary **Declaration of Disclosure** already includes this information, so all you need to do is attach an updated **Income and Expense Declaration**. The **Property Declaration** is very similar to the **Schedule of Assets and Debts**. Simply transfer the information from one form to the other and state in the last two columns of the **Property Declaration** your proposal as to who gets what. Then sign and print your name and date it.

◈ Item 3, "Declaration," requires you to give the clerk a copy of the form (with any attachments) and an envelope with sufficient postage on it addressed to respondent's last known address or to respondent's attorney if he or she has one. Use the court clerk's address for the return address on the envelope because the clerk will do the mailing.

NOTE: *To avoid rejections by the clerk's office, be sure that you complete the places where you need to date, print your name, and sign.*

Your spouse has thirty days to file a **RESPONSE**, so you cannot file a **REQUEST TO ENTER DEFAULT** until the thirty-first day. If the thirtieth day falls on a weekend or court holiday, the time is extended to the next court day. Your spouse may have filed the **RESPONSE,** but neglected to serve you with a copy. Check the court file before you file the **REQUEST TO ENTER DEFAULT** to make sure.

◈   In item 4, check the box at the top waiving costs and disbursements, enter the date, your printed name, your signature, and the place you signed.

◈   In item 5, sign, print, date, and fill in the place you sign just as above, provided your spouse in not in the military.

File the form and any attachments with the clerk and provide the clerk with two copies for mailing back to respondent and to you. Do not forget the stamped envelopes, one addressed as item 3 states and the other addressed to you. Type the clerk's return address on the envelopes, as stated under item 3.

DECLARATION FOR DEFAULT OR UNCONTESTED DISSOLUTION

The **DECLARATION FOR DEFAULT OR UNCONTESTED DISSOLUTION** (see form 13, p.227) is used when your spouse either defaults (does not file a **RESPONSE** to the **SUMMONS (FAMILY LAW)** and **PETITION**), or you and your spouse agree on all issues. In either of these two cases, you can seek a **JUDGMENT** without having to go to court. If your spouse has defaulted, you can file this form with the **REQUEST TO ENTER DEFAULT** (form 12, p.225), the proposed **JUDGMENT** (form 17, p.247), and the **NOTICE OF ENTRY OF JUDGMENT** (form 19, p.251). In the second case where your spouse has not defaulted (has filed a **RESPONSE**), but the two of you agree on all issues, you file the **DECLARATION FOR DEFAULT OR UNCONTESTED DISSOLUTION** (form 13, p.227) with the **APPEARANCE, STIPULATION, AND WAIVERS** (form 11, p.223), which states that your spouse agrees to no longer contest any issues.

If you already filed the **Request to Enter Default** (form 12, p.225) and received a copy back showing the default was entered, attach a copy to the **Declaration for Default or Uncontested Dissolution** (form 13, p.227) so the clerk makes no mistake that the default was in fact entered.

However, if support is an issue, you might want to get a court date. The reason is that if the judge reviewing your papers has a question about the matter, especially child support, and you have chosen this declaration route rather than a hearing, the judge cannot get an answer. Also, the clerk may return your entire package because you have forgotten to check a box on one of the forms.

In either case, your papers will be sent back to you for correction and resubmission or with a note to set the matter for a court hearing. Either way, you will have to resubmit your papers. If you feel confident your documents are in order and the support agreed to is at or near guideline, try using the **Declaration for Default or Uncontested Dissolution**. Otherwise, get a court date and appear. Even though you appear, you may still get sent home with directions to resubmit. But you have got a chance the judge will permit you to make changes on the spot or give oral evidence to overcome some deficiency.

NOTE: *The* **Declaration for Default or Uncontested Dissolution** *(form 13, p.227) can also be used for legal separation. You may hear it referred to as* **Declaration for Default or Uncontested Dissolution or Legal Separation**.

Complete the **Declaration for Default or Uncontested Dissolution** as follows.

◈ Complete the top portion of the form according to the instructions in Chapter 5.

◈ Check the box in the caption area for "Dissolution."

◈ In item 3, check the box for "Petition."

◈ In item 4, check "a" if your spouse has not filed a **Response**, and you have already filed the **Request to Enter Default** (form 12, p.225). Check "b" if your spouse has filed a **RESPONSE** to the **PETITION** and you filed the **APPEARANCE, STIPULATIONS, AND WAIVERS** (form 11, p.223), which tells the court that your spouse has agreed not to contest any issues.

◈ In item 5, you must check either "a" or "b." If you do not have a **MARITAL SETTLEMENT AGREEMENT (MSA)** (form 16, p.235), you must check either box "b(1)" or "b(2)." The "stipulated judgment" box at "5a" is checked when you or your spouse show up in court on the day of the trial but settle the case before the trial begins.

◈ In item 6, complete the boxes as applicable. If you become confused, refer to Chapter 7 and review the sections on Preliminary **DECLARATION OF DISCLOSURE** and Final **DECLARATION OF DISCLOSURE**. You would normally leave box "a" blank and check box "c" if you have an **MSA**, and box "b" if you do not.

◈ If you have custody and visitation issues, make sure your proposed **JUDGMENT** addresses them and check the boxes for items 7 and 8.

◈ In item 9, ignore the "Family support" box unless you have talked with an attorney and are confident of your actions. If spousal support is an issue, attach a current **INCOME AND EXPENSE DECLARATION** (form 8, p.215), unless you have already filed it, and check at least one of the boxes. You would check box "a" if you do not want spousal support now or in the future; box "b" if you do not want spousal support now but may want it later; and "c" if you have covered the subject in the **MSA** (which is part of the **JUDGMENT**).

◈ Items 10 through 13 are self-explanatory. The only box needing some clarification is box "d" in item 13. If your spouse intentionally reduces his or her gross income in order to pay less child or spousal support, and you can prove it, the court may order support based not your spouse's actual earnings but rather on the amount he or she has the ability to earn.

◈ Item 14 would only be checked if you checked box "3d" on the **PETITION**.

◈ Leave the item 15 box blank because you do not have an attorney.

◈ Items 16 through 20 are self-explanatory.

◈ Do not check box 21. This box would only be checked if you need an immediate judgment (after the six-month mandatory wait) stating that you are no longer married and are keeping all other issues (such as property, custody, and support) open to be decided later.

◈ Ignore box 22, which is for legal separations.

◈ Date, sign, and print your name where indicated.

> **NOTE:** *If you are asking for a custody order in a default where your spouse has not been served by personal service and has not appeared in the case, you should file a certified copy of the birth certificates of all children with the clerk.*

APPEARANCE, STIPULATIONS, AND WAIVERS

The **APPEARANCE, STIPULATIONS, AND WAIVERS** requires a response fee to be paid with it if your spouse has not filed a **RESPONSE**. (see form 11, p.223.) Form 11 is used when local court policy requires a response fee if a **MARITAL SETTLEMENT AGREEMENT (MSA)** is filed with, or as part of, the **JUDGMENT**. As mentioned in the discussion on the **MSA**, some courts require a response fee and some do not when an **MSA** is filed with the **JUDGMENT**. If your county requires the fee, then your spouse files the **APPEARANCE, STIPULATIONS, AND WAIVERS** (form 11, p.223) instead of the **RESPONSE**, and pays the fee. The concept is that you must pay for the right to have a court consider your requests. Because your spouse is asking the court to consider requests made in the **MSA**, he or she must pay (in counties requiring it). Form 11 is also used when the case changes from contested to uncontested.

Example:

You and your spouse disagreed on several issues so your spouse filed a **RESPONSE**. But now you both agree on all issues. The two of you would then sign and file form 11, telling the court that the case can proceed as uncontested and that you are waiving your right to a trial.

Complete the **APPEARANCE, STIPULATIONS, AND WAIVERS** as follows.

❖ Complete the top portion of the form according to the instructions in Chapter 5.

Item 1

❖ Check box "a" if your spouse has not filed a **RESPONSE**.

❖ Check box "b" only if your spouse has already filed a **RESPONSE**. (If he or she has, no additional filing fee is paid.)

❖ Check box "c" only if your spouse is in the military and is waiving his or her rights as a member of the military.

Item 2

❖ Check box "a."

❖ Check box "b" because you have got no triable issues.

❖ Check box "c."

❖ Check box "d" if you and your spouse have signed a **MARITAL SETTLEMENT AGREEMENT** or will submit a **STIPULATION OF JUDGMENT**.

❖ Check box "e" if you and your spouse have signed a **MARITAL SETTLEMENT AGREEMENT** or will submit a **STIPULATION OF JUDGMENT**.

❖ Check box "f" if it applies to your case.

◈ Fill out item 3 if you and your spouse are agreeing to something not covered in items 1 and 2. Give specifics in your
agreement.

◈ Sign and date the form.

MILITARY SERVICE CONSIDERATIONS

If you know for sure your spouse is *not* in the military, date, sign, and
enter the place where you signed, in item 5 of the **REQUEST TO ENTER
DEFAULT** (form 12, p.225) as previously stated. But what if you do not
know for sure and cannot really sign item 5 of the **REQUEST TO ENTER
DEFAULT**? Then do not sign item 5. The clerk should still enter the
default under the law. The only problem is that if your spouse is
active in the military, he or she may be able to set aside (void) the
default judgment pursuant to the *2003 Servicemembers Civil Relief
Act*, and you would have to start over.

Do not get confused. For clarification, the default you obtain from the
clerk after filing the **REQUEST TO ENTER DEFAULT** is different from the
default judgment. The default here pertains to your spouse not
responding to the **PETITION** within the time allowed. Even though you
have the default, you must still obtain the judgment, referred to in
such case as a default judgment.

If you cannot state unequivocally that your spouse is not in the military, you can file a statement showing facts that will support a
reasonable presumption that your spouse is not in the military.

Maybe you do not have a clue whether your spouse is in the service,
but you want to protect against a possible setting aside of the judgment if it turns out he or she is in the military. In that case, use the
MEMORANDUM OF REQUEST FOR MILITARY SERVICE STATUS to find out if your
spouse is active in the military and where. (see form 25, p.265.) If your
spouse is not active in the military, you can sign item 5 on the **REQUEST
TO ENTER DEFAULT** or file the negative responses from the military service branches. (You may want to call the military branches beforehand
to determine if there is any fee for them sending the information.)

You will need to make seven copies of the **MEMORANDUM OF REQUEST FOR MILITARY SERVICE STATUS** (form 25, p.265) and mail one to each of the seven addresses listed on the form. Be sure to enclose a stamped envelope addressed to yourself with each one. Each branch will then check its records and send you a written statement as to whether or not your spouse is in that branch. If a response shows your spouse to be in the military, you can send him or her notice of the divorce and try to reach an agreement so you can use the uncontested procedure. If such attempts fail, you should contact an attorney.

JUDGMENT

The **JUDGMENT** officially tells the world you are divorced. (see form 17, p.247.) It contains all of the terms you and your spouse agreed to, or what the judge orders. If a provision is not in the **JUDGMENT**, you cannot enforce it in court. An oral agreement you have with your spouse carries no weight.

The **JUDGMENT** shows the effective date of your divorce, which cannot be earlier than six months and a day from the date you served your spouse with the **SUMMONS (FAMILY LAW)**. You can request a later effective date if the date is crucial for some reason, such as qualifying for your spouse's Social Security or for tax reasons.

Your judgment will consist of the **JUDGMENT** (form 17, p.247) with various attachments and the **MARITAL SETTLEMENT AGREEMENT (MSA)** (form 16, p.235) if you have one. The **JUDGMENT** form includes a box to check if you are attaching a **MARITAL SETTLEMENT AGREEMENT (MSA)**. This eliminates the practice of some courts requiring the **MSA** to be retyped into mandatory judge language and included within the **JUDGMENT** itself, and then also requiring it to be attached to the **JUDGMENT** as an exhibit. (The **MSA** is discussed on p.120.)

NOTE: *Judgment refers to what the court orders that finalizes your divorce, while* **JUDGMENT** *refers to the form you will complete reflecting those orders.*

Complete the **JUDGMENT** (form 17, p.247) as follows.

◈ Complete the top portion of the form according to the instructions in Chapter 5.

◈ In item 1, leave the boxes blank unless you have previously obtained personal conduct restraining orders.

> **NOTE:** *Item 1 is applicable only if you obtained personal conduct restraining orders against your spouse and they are still in effect. There are two types of restraining orders—personal conduct restraining orders and property restraining orders. A property restraining order would be an order granting you exclusive possession of your home during the dissolution proceeding.*
>
> *You can obtain both types of protective orders in the dissolution proceeding, but if you are seeking personal conduct orders you must use the forms under the Domestic Violence Protection Act, Sections 6200–6390 of the Family Code.*
>
> *This book does not instruct you on personal conduct restraining orders because an excellent informational booklet entitled* Domestic Violence Restraining Orders Instruction Booklet *with forms is available free from the court clerk. If you obtain personal conduct restraining orders, you would attach them to the* **JUDGMENT** *form as indicated in Item 1. (see form 17, p.247.)*

◈ In item 2, check the box for "default or uncontested" if you opted for the court hearing method, and check the other box if you are going to file everything with the clerk's office and avoid a court appearance. Leave all the other boxes blank, except check box "2c" if you want a court hearing.

◈ In item 3, after the colon, enter the date your spouse was served with the **SUMMONS (FAMILY LAW)** (form 1, p.197) or the date he or she filed a **RESPONSE**. Check the box marked "respondent was served with process" if you filled in the date your spouse was served with the **SUMMONS (FAMILY LAW)**. Check the box marked "respondent appeared" if you filled in the date your spouse filed a **Response**.

◈ Check item "4a" and box "1". If you do not need a particular date, leave the space after the colon blank. If you want a particular date, type the date after the colon. (Skip items "4b," "4c," "4d," and "4e.")

◈ In item "4f," check the box for a former name being restored and type it in full.

◈ In item "4g," check the box.

◈ Check item "4h" if the **Judgment** provides for child support, and attach (staple) the **Notice of Rights and Responsibilities— Health Care Cost and Reimbursement Procedures Information Sheet on Changing a Child Support Order** (form 18, p.249) to the **Judgment**. If you do not attach these forms, the clerk will probably reject the **Judgment**. The third form, **Child Support Case Registry Form** is NOT attached to the **Judgment**, but rather submitted to the clerk separately. (see form 38, p.295.)

NOTE: *The* **Child Support Case Registry Form** *does not have to be submitted at the time of filing the* **Judgment**, *but can be submitted within ten days from the date of the* **Judgment**.

If there is a change of information on the **Child Support Case Registry Form** (form 38, p.295), you must update with a new form and provide it to the clerk within ten days of the change. This is confidential information and the form is not *filed*, meaning it is not included in your public courthouse file but sent to a state agency for informational purposes. Use the instruction sheet included with the form to complete it. Both you and your spouse must each file a separate form.

◈ Items "4i" through "4m" refer to several forms as follows.

   ✪   **Marital Settlement Agreement** (form 16, p.235).

✪   **Child Custody and Visitation Order Attachment** (form 40, p.301).

✪   **Supervised Visitation Order** (form 40A, p.303).

✪   **Stipulation and Order for Custody and/or Visitation of Children** (form 41, p.313).

✪   **Child Support Information and Order Attachment** (form 42, p.315).

✪   **Non-Guideline Child Support Findings Attachment** (form 43, p.317).

✪   **Stipulation to Establish or Modify Child Support and Order** (form 15, p.233).

✪   **Spousal or Family Support Order Attachment** (form 44, p.319).

These attachment forms need only be completed if you do not have an **MSA** or a stipulated judgment. Without an **MSA**, the judge will make his or her decisions with the help of the above attachment forms.

◆   Check item "4i" at the top of page 2 if you and your spouse signed a **Marital Settlement Agreement** (form 16, p.235).

◆   It is unlikely you would check item "4j." A stipulation (agreement) for judgment is used when you and your spouse do not have a **Marital Settlement Agreement** and are contesting issues, but when the two of you show up at the courthouse on the trial date, you agree to everything without trial. You would then complete the *stipulation for judgment* form available inside the courtroom. However, you would still have to prepare the formal **Judgment** (form 17, p.247) and file it at the court later, along with the above attachment forms.

◆   Item "4k" asks for the names and birthdates of children.

❖ If Item "4l" applies, check the box that applies and attach the form as required.

❖ If Item "4m" applies, check the box that applies and submit the required form.

❖ Item "4n" requires any agreement or order for spousal support. Check the box that applies and submit the required form.

❖ Item "4o" refers to the division of property. Check the box that applies and submit the required form.

NOTE: *Items "4k" through "4o" show the importance of a* MARITAL SETTLEMENT AGREEMENT. *You will avoid many extra steps and uncertainty if you and your spouse or partner can agree and sign one.*

❖ At item "4p," describe any pertinent information not covered above. Be sure to document any information you submit.

– Caution –

Be sure to attach the form NOTICE OF RIGHTS AND RESPONSIBILITIES—HEALTH CARE COSTS AND REIMBURSEMENT PROCEDURES/INFORMATION SHEET ON CHANGING A CHILD SUPPORT ORDER (form 18, p.249). Without this attachment your JUDGMENT will be returned to you without the judge's signature.

Additionally, the JUDGMENT requires you to submit an additional form called the CHILD SUPPORT CASE REGISTRY FORM. (form 38, p.295.) This form does not have to be submitted at the time you submit the JUDGMENT, but you must do so within ten days of the JUDGMENT date. This form is simply handed to the clerk so DO NOT attach it to the JUDGMENT.

EARNINGS ASSIGNMENT ORDER FOR SPOUSAL SUPPORT

The **EARNINGS ASSIGNMENT ORDER FOR SPOUSAL SUPPORT** is mandatory for all spousal support orders. (see form 20, p.253.) This form is served on the paying spouse's (*obligor*) employer who must by law withhold the support amount up to 50% of the obligor's wages and send it to the receiving spouse (*obligee*). It is up to the obligee spouse to have the order served on the employer. You must also serve with the order a blank **REQUEST FOR HEARING REGARDING EARNINGS ASSIGNMENT FOR SPOUSAL SUPPORT** form and the information sheet that goes with it. (see form 48, p.333.) Once it is served, the employer has ten days in which to process the order. Even if you cannot locate the employer, you still must submit this form with the **JUDGMENT** so that you will have it when you do locate the present or future employer. Although you can agree with your spouse to ask the court to stay (hold) the order on certain grounds, the court will remove such stay upon your declaration that the payments have been late.

It is probably better for both of you not to ask for a stay. By law, the employer may not in any way impair the employee spouse's status with the company. The regular payment of the support by the employee's employer establishes a record for the support payments for both spouses and eliminates argument as to whether a payment was missed or late.

Complete the **EARNINGS ASSIGNMENT ORDER FOR SPOUSAL SUPPORT** (form 20, p.253) as follows.

- ❖ Complete the top portion of the form according to the instructions in Chapter 5.

- ❖ Check the box under the title of the form only if you are modifying a previous order.

- ❖ Complete "To the Payor" by typing in the paying spouse's full name and birth date.

- ❖ In item 1, check the appropriate box and enter the amount of support ordered by the court; then total the amounts at "1c."

◈ In item 2, type in your name and address.

◈ Skip item 3, unless back support is included.

◈ Skip item 5, unless you are modifying a previous order.

◈ Item 8 will normally be blank.

◈ Skip item 9, unless back support is included.

The **EARNINGS ASSIGNMENT ORDER FOR SPOUSAL SUPPORT** will not work if your spouse is an independent contractor and has no specific employer, is the type that changes jobs constantly, or is self-employed. In these cases, ask for the payments to be made by electronic funds transfer. The judge has discretion to order that the paying spouse set up an account at a financial institution designated for the payment of child support when a wage assignment order would be ineffective.

ORDER/NOTICE TO WITHHOLD INCOME FOR CHILD SUPPORT

The **ORDER/NOTICE TO WITHHOLD INCOME FOR CHILD SUPPORT** is a federal form that must be used for all child support orders and is enforceable across state lines. (see form 46, p.323.) The procedure is similar to that for wage assignments for spousal support in that it is served on the payor's employer by first class mail along with a blank **REQUEST FOR HEARING REGARDING EARNINGS ASSIGNMENT FOR SPOUSAL SUPPORT** (form 48, p.333).

NOTICE OF ENTRY OF JUDGMENT

The purpose of the **NOTICE OF ENTRY OF JUDGMENT** is to establish when the **JUDGMENT** was entered in the records of the court. (see form 19, p.251.) Complete the **NOTICE OF ENTRY OF JUDGMENT** as follows.

◈ Complete the top portion of the form according to the instructions in Chapter 5.

◈   Check the box in item 1.

◈   In the bold box showing the "Effective date of termination of marital or domestic partnership status," leave it blank and let the clerk fill in the date.

◈   Type in your name and address and that of your spouse in the two boxes at the bottom of the form.

Supply the clerk with two stamped envelopes with the clerk's address as the return address. One should be addressed to you and the other addressed to your spouse. If you do not know your spouse's address, type in the last known address.

Domestic Partnerships

The law governing domestic partnerships changed drastically as of January 1, 2005. Domestic partners in California are now treated like a married couple; yet, there are some notable exceptions explored later in this chapter.

DECLARATION OF DOMESTIC PARTNERSHIP

California defines domestic partners as those who have filed a valid **DECLARATION OF DOMESTIC PARTNERSHIP** with the California Secretary of State. (see form 49, p.337.) The declaration can also be obtained from the Secretary of State's office or downloaded from **www.ss.ca.gov/dpregistry**.

To be eligible to file, the couple must meet the following requirements:

- ✪ both share a common residence;

- ✪ neither person is married to someone else or is a member of another domestic partnership with someone else that has not been terminated, dissolved, or adjudged a nullity;

✪ the two persons are not related by blood in a way that would prevent them from being married to each other;

✪ both are at least 18 years of age;

✪ either:

  • both are members of the same sex or

  • if members of the opposite sex, one or both are over the age of 62; and,

✪ both are capable of consenting to the domestic partnership.

NOTE: *"Common residence" means that both domestic partners share the same residence. It is not necessary that the legal right to possess the common residence be in both of their names. Two people have a common residence even if one or both have additional residences. Domestic partners do not cease to have a common residence if one leaves the common residence but intends to return.*

Once a declaration has been filed the couple has the same rights and responsibilities as a married couple. This applies to inheritance, spousal and child support, property ownership, debts of a partner, and any other responsibility governed only by California law.

EXCEPTIONS FROM MARRIAGE

Federal law does not recognize domestic partnerships. This affects status for income tax filing, Social Security, military benefits, and any other federal benefits that are accorded to a husband and wife.

As of January 1, 2007, California allows domestic partners to file state tax returns with the same burdens and benefits as a married couple. The law takes effect in 2007 so most taxpayers will not file until 2008. If you need to file before then, check with your tax preparer.

Since many states do not recognize domestic partnerships, California may not have jurisdiction over property located in another state if one or both of the partners has left California. This is true even though both partners agree in the declaration to be governed by California law whether they reside in California or elsewhere.

By contrast, California accepts relationships sanctioned by other states if similar to California's. The Family Code section reads as follows:

> *299.2. A legal union of two persons of the same sex, other than a marriage, that was validly formed in another jurisdiction, and that is substantially equivalent to a domestic partnership as defined in this part, shall be recognized as a valid domestic partnership in this state regardless of whether it bears the name domestic partnership.*

TERMINATION OF A DOMESTIC PARTNERSHIP

There are two ways to terminate a domestic partnership. One is by court action similar to dissolution of marriage. If you are in this situation, follow the procedures for married couples except for the forms included in this chapter. Always check with the court clerk of your county for any forms or procedures that may be required. This is true for married couples as well.

If you meet the following requirements, you can end your partnership by filing a **NOTICE OF TERMINATION OF DOMESTIC PARTNERSHIP** with the Secretary of State. (see form 50, p.339.) The partnership is terminated six months after the filing unless one of the parties revokes the termination. The forms can also be downloaded from the Secretary of State's web address at **www.ss.ca.gov/dpregistry**.

The Secretary of State publishes a brochure entitled *Terminating a California Registered Domestic Partnership*. You should read through this brochure in its entirety. Some of the key requirements for terminating a domestic partnership it outlines include the following.

✪ You and your partner have no children together, and neither is pregnant.

✪ You and your partner have been registered domestic partners for five years or less.

✪ Neither party has any interest in real property, in California or elsewhere, except in the lease of the residence where either of you lives (as long as the lease does not include an option to purchase and ends within one year from the date that you file the **NOTICE OF TERMINATION OF DOMESTIC PARTNERSHIP**).

✪ You and your partner do not have any debts (excluding automobile debts) that either or both of you incurred after you registered as domestic partners totaling more than approximately $5,000.

✪ You and your partner do not have assets (excluding automobiles and encumbrances) totaling more than approximately $33,000 *and* you and your partner have executed an agreement that lists how the assets and/or debts will be divided.

✪ Both you and your partner have executed an agreement setting forth how you are going to divide your assets and the assumptions of liabilities of the community property, and have executed any documents, title certificates, bills of sale, or other evidence or transfer necessary to effectuate the agreement.

✪ Both you and your partner waive any rights to support from the other.

✪ Both you and your partner have read and understood the brochure prepared by the Secretary of State describing the requirements of terminating a domestic partnership.

✪ Both you and your partner wish to terminate your domestic partnership.

REVOKING THE TERMINATION

If within six months of filing the Termination, either party mails to the Secretary of State a Revocation of Termination of Domestic Partnership with a copy mailed to the other partner, the Termination is cancelled.

Even after the termination is completed, a party can go to court and ask to set the termination aside if one of the following is shown:

- ✪ that the partnership did not meet all the Secretary of State's requirements at the time the **NOTICE OF TERMINATION OF DOMESTIC PARTNERSHIP** was filed;

- ✪ that you were treated unfairly in the **PROPERTY SETTLEMENT AGREEMENT**. This is possible if you find out that the things you agreed to give your partner were much more valuable than you thought when you filed;

- ✪ that you signed the **NOTICE OF TERMINATION OF DOMESTIC PARTNERSHIP** against your will. This is possible if you can show that your partner used threats or other kinds of unfair pressure to get you to go along with the **PROPERTY SETTLEMENT AGREEMENT** or the termination; or,

- ✪ that there are serious mistakes in the original agreement. Various kinds of other mistakes may make the termination invalid, but you will have to go to court to prove the mistakes. You should consult with an attorney for more information about setting aside a termination.

If you have properly registered and want to end the relationship, but are not eligible to use the **NOTICE OF TERMINATION OF DOMESTIC PARTNERSHIP**, you must follow the same basic procedures as a married couple. You can use form 3A, **PETITION—DOMESTIC PARTNERSHIP**, instead of form 3, **PETITION—MARRIAGE**, and form 21A, **RESPONSE— DOMESTIC PARTNERSHIP**, instead of form 21, **RESPONSE—MARRIAGE**. The forms are virtually the same except for the references to domestic partners rather than a married couple.

The other forms required for a married couple have been revised to include domestic partners and should be used by domestic partners the same as used by married couples. Be sure to check with the county clerk to see if any local forms are required.

With the uncertainty in many areas of domestic partnerships, it is advisable to consult an attorney before registering as domestic partners or ending the relationship through court proceedings. Some attorneys are beginning to advertise as attorneys for gay and lesbian relationships. Check the Internet and Yellow Pages.

Contested Divorce Procedure

For our purposes, a contested divorce will be defined based on its complexity. Even though you may technically be going through a contested divorce, the definition is not that you and your spouse cannot agree on everything. Many of the things you want will be contested by your spouse. The important thing is that you are working together toward getting the divorce.

If you and your spouse are arguing over some specific piece of property and have exhausted possibilities for a negotiated settlement, you probably are not going to need to go to extreme measures. You each will tell the judge why you should get the property and the judge will make the decision. If the value of the property is disputed, you may need an independent appraisal.

However, if your spouse is fighting you at every turn, refusing to turn over information you need, or demanding unreasonable child custody arrangements, you are involved in a contested divorce for the purposes of this chapter. You probably want to see a lawyer. This is especially true if your spouse has hired a lawyer.

There are several good reasons to hire an attorney in a contested matter. If you believe your spouse is hiding assets, for example, you may have to produce witnesses who know of the assets, subpoena records, or even hire an investigator to locate them. If the assets are worth the cost of a private investigator, they are worth the price of a lawyer.

If your spouse is just unreasonable, you may be better off if he or she hires a lawyer. You should speak to the lawyer and ask if it would be of any value to negotiate. The lawyer may give you some idea of the firmness of your spouse's position. Sometimes lawyers like the other spouse better than their own client.

If your spouse has a lawyer, you must strictly comply with procedure. Pay special attention to required notices to your spouse and copies of filed documents that you must give your spouse. You and your spouse will be interested in the substantive issues. The lawyer will seize on any procedural mistakes that you make. Having to repeat procedures will cause you unreasonable delay and extra paperwork. This can lead to your finally throwing in the towel and giving up things that you could be awarded.

Be cautious about signing any papers until you are certain you understand what they mean. You should have an attorney review any papers prepared by your spouse's lawyer before you sign them.

If there is no chance to reach agreement except by your giving in to everything, at least you know where you stand. You can then decide whether you can live with your spouse's demands, fight the battle yourself, or hire a lawyer.

COLLECTING INFORMATION

The court rules require each party serve on the other the Preliminary **DECLARATION OF DISCLOSURE** (form 6, p.209). (See Chapter 7 for a detailed discussion of form 6.) If your spouse is not cooperating and will not provide the forms, you may have to try to get the information yourself. You will need to have the information available at the hearing. This will require you to get subpoenas issued. You can make a motion to compel your spouse to give you the documents, but now you are getting into a more complicated matter. It may be wiser to check with an attorney.

The Preliminary and Final **DECLARATION OF DISCLOSURE** (form 6, p.209) are designed to eliminate or reduce the need for spouses to serve interrogatories, document production requests, subpoenas, and other forms of discovery. *Discovery* is a legal term meaning legal process to obtain information about the other party's personal and business affairs.

Of course, you may still have to rely on formal discovery if your spouse refuses to cooperate. Also, if you do not trust your spouse and there are substantial assets, you will want to subpoena the information directly from the source, such as your spouse's bank or employer. You will probably need a lawyer's help for this.

PROPERTY AND DEBTS

The judge looks at your property and debts and must divide the community property equally. At the same time, the judge will confirm any separate property to the spouse owning it. If the property is part separate and part community, as, for example, retirement benefits from a job you had both before and during marriage, only that portion earned between the date of your marriage and the date of your separation is community property. In that case, depending upon the type of retirement plan, you may need an actuary to figure how much is community and how much is separate.

Property Declaration

You will need to complete another form called the **PROPERTY DECLARATION**. (see form 14, p.229.) You have already completed this for the most part. Look at the **SCHEDULE OF ASSETS AND DEBTS** (form 7, p.211) that you and your spouse had to serve on each other with a **DECLARATION OF DISCLOSURE**. (see Chapter 7.) The **PROPERTY DECLARATION** (form 14, p.229) will be the same, updated to the time of the hearing, along with a proposed property division. The judge will use that form to divide the property.

If you have very young children and the house payment is approximately equal to what the custody spouse would have to pay for rent anyway, you might want an order in which the custody spouse and the children live in the house for a period of time, say until the children reach a certain age, and then the house would be sold and the proceeds divided. In the meantime, the spouse living in the home would pay normal maintenance expenses and the mortgage payment. If you get to this level of complication, you might want an attorney's help.

NOTE: *You will not need form 15 if you and your spouse have completed a* **Marital Settlement Agreement (MSA)**. *(see form 16, p.235.)*

Notice that the **Property Declaration** (form 14, p.229) is much the same as the **Schedule of Assets and Debts** (form 7, p.211), except it includes the net value and your proposal for division. If you need continuation pages, use **Additional Pages** (form 27, p.269). You must use separate forms for the community property and the separate property. Complete the forms just as you did the **Schedule of Assets and Debts**, but this time distribute the amount in the third column (the net fair market value) in either the petitioner's or the respondent's column.

In dividing the property, consider:

- ✪ what you really want;

- ✪ what you would like to have;

- ✪ what you do not care about either way;

- ✪ what your spouse really wants;

- ✪ what your spouse would like to have; and,

- ✪ what your spouse does not care about either way.

Start a list of what each of you should end up with using the categories listed above. You will eventually end up with a list of things you can probably get with little difficulty (what you really want and your spouse does not care about), those which you will fight over (what you both really want), and those which need to be divided but can probably be easily divided equally (what you both do not really care about).

At the hearing, the judge will probably try to get you to work out your disagreements, but he or she will not put up with arguing for very long. In the end, he or she will divide the items you cannot agree upon, or order you to sell those items and divide the money you get.

For the few items that are really important to you, it may be necessary to prove why you should get them. It will help if you can convince the judge of one or more of the following.

- ✪ You paid for the item out of your own earnings or funds, not community funds.

- ✪ You are the one who primarily uses the item.

- ✪ You use the item in your employment, business, or hobby.

- ✪ You are willing to give up something else you really want in exchange for the item.

- ✪ The item is needed for your child (assuming you will have custody).

The best thing you can do is make the division reasonably fair and equal, regardless of how angry you are at your spouse. Even if the judge changes some of it to appear fair to your spouse, you will most likely get more of what you want if you do offer a few suggestions. (No, this is not an exception to the negotiating rule of letting your spouse make the first offer because at this point you are no longer just negotiating with your spouse. You are now negotiating with the judge. You are trying to impress the judge with your fairness—not trying to convince your spouse.)

Special problems arise if a claim of separate property becomes an issue. This may be in terms of your spouse trying to get your separate property, or in terms of you trying to get property you feel your spouse is wrongly claiming to be separate.

It is also a good idea to have documents that prove the property you claim to be separate property is actually separate property. These would be papers showing that:

✪   you bought the item before you were married (such as dated sales receipts);

✪   you inherited the item as your own property (such as certified copies of wills and probate court papers); or,

✪   you got the property by exchanging it for property you had before you got married, or exchanging it for property you received as a gift or through an inheritance (such as a statement from the person you made the exchange with, or some kind of receipt showing what was exchanged).

In order to make a claim on what would otherwise appear to be your spouse's separate property, you need to ask for it in your **PETITION** (form 3, p.201). To get at assets your spouse is claiming are separate assets, you will need to collect the following types of evidence.

✪   Papers showing that the community helped pay for the asset (such as a check from a community property bank account, or from your separate account if you and your spouse had previously agreed in writing that you would maintain a separate property bank account). For example, suppose your spouse owned a house before marriage. During the marriage, some of the mortgage payments or repairs were made with community property money (or with your separate account money if you had a separate account). The community is entitled to reimbursement of such contribution to your spouse's separate property. (In such case, you would be entitled to one-half of the reimbursement because community property is owned fifty-fifty by you and your spouse.) You are also entitled to reimbursement for funds from your separate account provided it was not a gift. You would need to bring to court copies of the cancelled checks showing such payments.

A separate account means a separate property account as discussed above and not an account where community funds are kept as a convenience for bill paying or some other reason.

✪   Papers showing that the asset was improved or increased in value during your marriage.

Example 1:

Your spouse owned the house before you were married. During your marriage, you and your spouse added a family room to the house. This will enable you to make a claim for some of the value of the house.

Example 2:

Your spouse owned the house before you were married. The day before you got married, the house was worth $85,000. Now the house is appraised at $115,000. You can claim part of the $30,000 of increased value if the community (you or your spouse using community property funds) made some of the mortgage payments.

NOTE: *This area becomes very complex and often requires the help of an accountant as well as that of an attorney.*

The judge will probably announce who gets what at the end of the hearing. Take notes of the order if you can keep up. Also ask the court clerk for a copy of the *minute order*. The minute order will contain the judge's ruling unless it is complicated. In that case, ask the court clerk or the court reporter for a copy of the transcript of that part of the hearing in which the judge issued the order. It will take a few days and you will have to pay for the transcript, but at least you will have the exact order.

When you are sure you have the order right, prepare the **JUDGMENT** and have your spouse sign it. Then you will have to take it to the judge's clerk for the judge's signature. Complete the **JUDGMENT** as described in Chapter 7.

CHILD CUSTODY AND VISITATION

Generally, if you are the wife, the odds are in favor of you getting custody. But do not depend on it. Start out by reviewing the guidelines the judge will use to decide the custody question. These can be found in Chapter 4. For each item listed in that section, write down an explanation of how that item applies to you. This will be your argument when you have your hearing with the judge.

Many custody battles revolve around the moral fitness of one or both of the parents. If you become involved in this type of custody fight, you should consult a lawyer. Charges of moral unfitness (such as illegal drug use, child abuse, and immoral sexual conduct) can require long court hearings involving the testimony of many witnesses, as well as the hiring of private investigators. For such a hearing, you will require the help of an attorney who knows the law, what questions to ask witnesses, and the rules of evidence.

The current issue getting all the attention is domestic violence. As with any important issue in the spotlight, some people take advantage. If you are falsely accused of domestic violence, consult a lawyer immediately. Because of the attention to the subject, you may have to prove you are not guilty rather than the other way around. If there is any record of domestic violence, such as hospital visits with suspicious injuries, temporary restraining orders, or arrests for domestic violence, you have a serious problem. Even if there is no record, your spouse may produce witnesses, usually friends, who may testify to abuse by you. Since these allegations could affect the custody of your children, do not take any chances. Get a lawyer.

If you are the victim of domestic violence, supply as much evidence as possible. Hospital records, 911 calls, and restraining orders are all very credible. If you have never reported the domestic violence, witnesses who can testify to seeing you with bruises after hearing arguments may be your best evidence.

Be realistic. If you and your spouse argued frequently—not uncommon for people being divorced—was there really domestic violence? Telling the judge that there was emotional abuse when neighbors will testify that you hollered just as loud as your spouse is not going to help your case. Further false and unproven allegation of domestic violence may hurt your credibility in court on other issues. Do not hide domestic violence—just do not make it up.

However, if the only question is whether you or your spouse has been the main caretaker of the child, you can always have friends, neighbors, and relatives come into the hearing to testify on your behalf. It may not be necessary to have an attorney. But if you need to subpoena unwilling witnesses to testify, you will probably need one. The judge's decision regarding custody will be placed into the **JUDGMENT**.

CHILD SUPPORT

In California, as in most states, the question of child support is a matter of a mathematical calculation. Getting the guideline child support amount depends upon the accuracy of the income information presented to the judge. If you feel fairly sure that the information your spouse presents is accurate, or that you have accurate information about his or her income, there is not much to argue. The judge will simply take the income information provided, determine the amount of custody time each spouse has, use a computer to calculate the amount to be paid, and order that amount to be paid.

In most cases, there is not much room to argue about the amount of child support, so there usually is not a need to get an attorney. If you claim your spouse has not provided accurate income information, it will be up to you to prove this to the judge by showing the income information you have obtained from your spouse's employer or other source of income.

The areas open for argument are whatever *special needs* are claimed by the party asking for child support and whether the party paying child support has other children he or she is obligated to support. Once again, it will be necessary for that party to provide proof of the cost of these special needs by producing billing statements, receipts, or other papers to show the amount of these needs.

Refer to Chapter 4 for a more complete discussion on child support. The judge's decision regarding child support will have to be put into the **JUDGMENT**. (Read Chapter 7 for instructions on preparing the **JUDGMENT**.)

SPOUSAL SUPPORT (ALIMONY)

A dispute over spousal support (alimony) may require a lawyer, especially if there is a request for permanent alimony because of a disability. Such a claim may require the testimony of *expert witnesses* (such as doctors, accountants, and actuaries).

In setting spousal support, the judge looks at criteria in Family Code Section 4320. Generally, the categories are:

- ✪ the standard of living during the marriage, taking into consideration the marketable skills of the supported party and the job market for such skills, expenses for training to further develop such skills, and the need for any retraining to acquire other more marketable skills;

- ✪ the supported party's impairment of his or her earning capacity by the period devoted to domestic duties;

- ✪ the extent to which the party seeking support contributed to the attainment of an education, training, a career, or a license of the supporting party;

- ✪ the supporting party's ability to pay;

- ✪ the needs of each party based on the standard of living during the marriage;

- ✪ the obligations, assets, and separate property of each party;

- ✪ the duration of the marriage, age, and health of the parties;

- ✪ the ability of the supported party to work without unduly interfering with the needs of the dependent children in the custody of supported party;

- ✪ the immediate tax consequences, if any;

- ✪ the balance of the hardships of each party;

✪   the goal that the supported party shall be self-supporting within a reasonable period, with "reasonable period" defined as one-half the length of the marriage; and,

> **NOTE:** *This implies that spousal support will generally be for a period determined by one-half the length of the marriage. Remember, however, that unless you and your spouse agree differently, the judge must retain the power to award spousal support indefinitely in marriages of long duration (ten years or more).*

✪   any other factors the judge considers fair.

You might want to talk to an attorney after considering the above criteria. If your spouse makes a great deal of money or if you sacrificed your career to help him or her, some substantial support may be at stake.

The Court Hearing

Since most people are unfamiliar with court proceedings, the court hearing can be somewhat traumatic. The best way to be confident in your ability to present your case is to know that you are properly prepared.

PREPARATION

To set a court hearing date, you will have to pick up a form from the clerk's office as these forms vary from court to court. All the forms are similar in that they inform the court that the case is ready for trial and ask for a time estimate. When you file that form, the clerk will normally send out a notice of the trial date to you and your spouse. To be on the safe side, it is recommended that you also notify your spouse in writing of the trial date, time, and place. You can do that with a letter, but make sure you complete a **PROOF OF SERVICE BY MAIL** after you mail it. (see form 28, p.271.) Take the letter and attached proof of service to the court hearing just in case your spouse does not show up. If the clerk's notice is missing from the court file, you will have your notice ready and the matter will not have to be continued due to lack of proof your spouse had notice of the hearing.

When you go to court, bring:

- ✪ your entire file, organized so you can locate papers quickly if asked to do so;

- ✪ your three most recent pay stubs and copies of your recent income tax returns;

- ✪ additional papers showing the financial condition of yourself and your spouse, including his or her pay stubs;

- ✪ the **JUDGMENT** (form 17, p.247) filled out to the extent the information is available and at least four copies;

- ✪ the **NOTICE OF ENTRY OF JUDGMENT** (form 19, p.251) filled out to the extent the information is available, along with four copies;

- ✪ the **MARITAL SETTLEMENT AGREEMENT (MSA)** (form 16, p.235) if you and your spouse have completed one; and,

- ✪ **DECLARATION REGARDING SERVICE OF DECLARATION OF DISCLOSURE AND INCOME AND EXPENSE DECLARATION** (form 9, p.219) for both the Preliminary and Final **DECLARATION OF DISCLOSURE** (form 6, p.209), with a copy of each if you have not already filed them with the clerk.

All of these forms were previously discussed. Sometimes the clerk's office makes a mistake and the judge does not have all of the papers you filed in the court file. That is why you need to bring copies of all the papers you have filed to prove they have been filed.

THE HEARING

Your hearing will probably take place in one of the smaller courtrooms, not like those you see on television or in the movies. The judge calls your case by name (*e.g.*, "Smith v. Smith"). A listing of the cases scheduled will be posted outside the courtroom door. Make sure you check in and tell the bailiff or clerk inside the courtroom that you are present and ask what number your case is on the docket. When the judge (or commissioner) calls your case, he or she will look over your papers and start asking you questions. He or she may ask you, as the petitioner, to present your case. Styles among judges vary, so be prepared.

Before the judge calls your case, the clerk will review your papers and tell you if there is something missing. Hopefully, you will be able to fix any problem. The judge may review your papers before you get to say anything and point out various legal deficiencies, if any exist. Whatever style you confront, answer courteously. Do not be afraid to speak up and ask the judge if he or she could call your case at the end of the *calendar* (later that morning or afternoon) to give you time to obtain a missing document. If it will take longer than that, or if you left the papers at home, ask the judge if you could bring the papers to him or her the next day. Your goal is to get the case finished without the judge continuing (postponing) it.

Assuming your papers are in order, the judge will eventually ask you four general questions.

1.   Have you been a resident of California for at least six months and of the county for at least three months?

2.   Have irreconcilable differences arisen in your marriage?

3.   Are those differences irremediable?

4.   Would any kind of counseling save the marriage?

You must answer "yes" to the first three and "no" to the last.

If you have updated the **INCOME AND EXPENSE STATEMENT**, be sure to file it with the courtroom clerk. All of your financial information should be current as of the time of the hearing.

If there are issues you and your spouse have not been able to agree upon, tell the judge about them and present your proposed solution. If you have prepared a proposed **JUDGMENT** (form 17, p.247) because you do not have any complicated issues for the judge to rule on, and the judge rules the way you would expect, you can give the judge the original and four copies at the end of the hearing. You will also need the

NOTICE OF ENTRY OF JUDGMENT (form 19, p.251) along with two stamped envelopes (one addressed to you and the other to your spouse). Make sure the return address on the envelopes is the clerk's address, not yours. If the judge rules differently from how you have prepared the **JUDGMENT** and the difference is slight, ask the judge if you can make the correction right on the form. If the difference is major, you will have to go home and re-type it, and then submit it through the clerk's office. Make certain you have the judge's order correct.

You will also need the completed **EARNINGS ASSIGNMENT ORDER FOR SPOUSAL SUPPORT** (form 20, p.253) with at least two copies to give to the judge's clerk along with the **JUDGMENT**. Remember, you have to serve the file-stamped **EARNINGS ASSIGNMENT ORDER FOR SPOUSAL SUPPORT** signed by the judge on your spouse's employer.

If the unexpected occurs, such as your spouse testifying to something you were not prepared for, ask the judge for a *continuance* so you can get an attorney. The judge may not go along with your request (believing it should have been made before the hearing got underway), but try it anyway.

This book is not designed to get you through a contested divorce with substantial issues. If your divorce involves significant property disputes or major opposing positions as to income and expenses in connection with spousal or child support, the money you will pay to an attorney could be well spent. This book can give you a quick overview for simple divorces, but do not be fooled into thinking that reading this book or spending a few weekends in the law library will keep you from harm's way inside a courtroom.

PUBLIC ASSISTANCE

If you expect child support and receive public assistance, you must contact the Family Support Division of the local district attorney's office in your county. Child support payments will be made to the enforcement office, which will in turn pay you. New forms to cover this area are frequently generated, and the court will not hear your case unless the district attorney's office, who will be a participant in the case, is contacted. That office will help you with public assistance requirements for the **EARNINGS ASSIGNMENT ORDER FOR SPOUSAL SUPPORT** (form 20, p.253) and the other court forms including the **JUDGMENT**.

chapter 11

When You Cannot Find Your Spouse or Partner

Your spouse has run off and you have no idea of where he or she might be. So how do you have the sheriff or marshal deliver a copy of your summons and other papers to your spouse? The answer is, you cannot. Instead of personal service you will use a method of giving notice called *service by publication*, which can be complicated.

THE DILIGENT SEARCH

The court will only permit service by publication when you cannot locate your spouse. This includes the situation when the sheriff or marshal has tried several times to personally serve your spouse, but it appears that your spouse is hiding to avoid being served.

First, you will have to show that you cannot locate your spouse by letting the court know what you have done to try to find him or her. In making this search, you should try the following.

- ✪ Check the phone book and directory assistance in the area where you live.

- ✪ Check directory assistance in the area where you last knew your spouse to be living.

- ✪ Ask friends and relatives who could know where your spouse might be.

- ✪ Check with the post office where he or she last lived to see if there is a forwarding address (you can ask by mail if it is too far away).

- ✪ Check records of the tax collector and property assessor to see if your spouse owns property.

- ✪ Write to the Department of Motor Vehicles to see if your spouse has any car registrations.

- ✪ Check with any other sources you know that may lead you to a current address (such as landlords, prior employers, etc.).

- ✪ Check the registrar of voters.

- ✪ Hire an investigator (although a fee is required).

If you do come up with a current address, go back to personal service by the sheriff or marshal, but if not, continue with this procedure.

PREPARING AND FILING COURT PAPERS

Once you have made a diligent search, you need to tell the court what you have done to try to find your spouse, and request the court's permission to publish. This is done by filing an *ex parte* (meaning "without notice to the other party") application for a court order permitting you to publish the **SUMMONS (FAMILY LAW)** (form 1, p.197) in the newspaper instead of serving it on your spouse personally. Along with the ex parte application, you need to file a declaration stating your efforts to find your spouse.

Before you do any of the above, call the newspaper in the city of your spouse's last known address and ask if it is certified for legal advertising in that area and how much it costs. Shop around if there are other newspapers of general circulation in that particular area. Rates vary greatly. The newspaper may even have some forms you can use, and sometimes the person in charge of the legal advertising may help you with the procedure.

First determine if your local court has forms. If so, use the court's forms. If not, use the **Ex Parte Application for Publication of Summons Order; Declaration of Petitioner in Support Thereof; Memorandum of Points and Authorities** (form 36, p.289) and **Order for Publication of Summons** (form 37, p.293) from Appendix B. You will need to call the clerk and ask about the local ex parte procedure for publication orders. Follow the clerk's instructions.

Form 36 is a combined application and declaration. Be careful with the declaration portion of form 36 (this is the third and fourth page). A declaration normally contains information from your own personal knowledge, not from what someone has told you. This is important because, although you must declare your efforts to locate your spouse, you may also need another declaration from the person you may have hired to try to find your spouse. Because declarations must be on personal knowledge, such a third person should also complete a declaration showing his or her attempts to serve your spouse. For such a third person, use the **Declaration**. (see form 26, p.267.)

Complete the **Ex Parte Application for Publication of Summons Order; Declaration of Petitioner in Support Thereof; Memorandum of Points and Authorities** as follows.

Page 1:

◈ Type in your name, address, phone number, and fax number (if you have one) where indicated at the top of the form.

◈ Type in your name after the words "Attorney for." The following phrase, "In Propria Persona," means that you are acting as your own attorney.

◈ On the lines indicated, type in the county and division of the court, the case number, your name after the word "Petitioner," and your spouse's or partner's name after the word "Respondent." The clerk will fill in the lines marked "Date," "Time," and "Dept."

◈ In the first paragraph, type in your name after the word "Petitioner," your spouse's name after the word "Respondent," and the name of the newspaper in which you intend to publish the **Summons (Family Law)** on the third line.

Page 2:

◈ In the first paragraph, type in the date your **PETITION** was filed.

◈ In the last paragraph, type in your name.

◈ Type in the date and your name on the appropriate lines and sign your name on the line marked "(Petitioner's signature)."

Page 3:

◈ Type in your name after the words "Declaration of" and in the blank in the first paragraph.

◈ In the second paragraph, type in your spouse's name in the first blank, and the date you first tried to have your spouse served in the second blank. In the third paragraph, type in the date your **PETITION** was filed.

◈ In the blank at the beginning of the third paragraph, type in the name of the newspaper in which you intend to publish. On the lines after that paragraph, type in a brief explanation of why that newspaper is most likely to give notice to your spouse.

◈ On the lines after the fourth paragraph on this page, type in a list of all of your efforts to serve your spouse under all of the normal service procedures under the Code of Civil Procedure, Sections 415.10 to 415.40.

◈ On the lines after the fifth paragraph on this page, type in a list of the things you have done to try to locate your spouse. Specifically state how, when, and where you attempted to locate your spouse. Such efforts should include the items listed on pages 147 and 148. Include all the details. Remember that service by publication is a last resort, and it is usually unlikely to actually give notice to the respondent. Courts expect to see very diligent efforts to locate your spouse because if the **SUMMONS (FAMILY LAW)** is served by publication it is unlikely that your spouse will ever know about the dissolution.

◈ You do not need to notarize these papers, as long as your declaration includes the last paragraph: "I declare under penalty of perjury under the laws of the state of California that the above is true and correct. Signed at _____, California, on _____, _____."

◈ On the lines in the last paragraph on this page, type in the city where you signed this form and the date you signed it. Then sign your name on the line marked "Petitioner."

You will also need to be prepared with an order for the judge to sign, which permits you to publish the **Summons (Family Law)**. The **Order for Publication of Summons** (form 37, p.293) is provided for this purpose in the event your court does not have its own form. Complete the **Order for Publication of Summons** as follows.

◈ Complete the top portion of the form with the same information you filled in on form 36.

◈ In the first paragraph, type in your name after the word "Petitioner," and your spouse's or partner's name on the two lines after the word "Respondent."

◈ In the second paragraph, type in your spouse's or partner's name in the blank after the word "Respondent," the name of the newspaper in the second blank, and the name of the county or city in which the newspaper is published in the third blank.

◈ In the last paragraph, type your spouse's name in the blank after the word "Respondent." The judge will fill in the date and sign the form.

PUBLISHING

After you obtain a copy of the **Order for Publication of Summons** (form 37, p.293) signed by the judge, you will need to send or deliver it and a copy of the **Summons (Family Law)** (form 1, p.196) to the newspaper for publishing. There are certain publication requirements. For example, the **Summons (Family Law)** must be published at least once a week for four successive weeks, and there should be five days between the successive publications. The thirty days that your spouse has to file a **RESPONSE** to your **SUMMONS (FAMILY LAW)** begins to run on the twenty-eighth day after the first day of publication.

Special Circumstances

Each divorce is as individual as the people involved and it is not possible to anticipate all the *what if* possibilities. However, there are several situations that occur frequently enough to require a chapter to cover them.

WHEN YOU CANNOT AFFORD COURT COSTS

If you cannot afford to pay the filing fee and other costs associated with the divorce, you can file an **APPLICATION FOR WAIVER OF COURT FEES AND COSTS**. (see form 29, p.273.) In order to qualify for a waiver or partial waiver of the filing fee and costs, you must be *indigent*. If you are indigent, your income is probably low enough for you to qualify for public assistance (welfare).

The **APPLICATION FOR WAIVER OF COURT FEES AND COSTS** is self-explanatory and requires detailed financial information. To help you determine if you qualify, read the **INFORMATION SHEET ON WAIVER OF COURT FEES AND COSTS**. (see page 274.)

If the judge approves your application, he or she will issue an order declaring you indigent and waiving filing fees and other court costs. You will need to show a copy of this order to the court clerk so that you will be allowed to file your **PETITION** (form 3, p.201 or form 3A, p.203) without paying the filing fee. You will also need to provide a copy of this order to the sheriff's or marshal's office so that you can have your spouse served without paying the service fee. If you need to publish a service of summons in a newspaper, you will still need to pay the newspaper's fee. The waiver of fees applies only to fees charged by government agencies such as the court and sheriff's office. It does not require any private person or company to provide you with free services.

PROTECTING YOURSELF, YOUR CHILDREN, AND YOUR PROPERTY

Some people have three special concerns when getting prepared to file for a divorce:

- ✪ fear of physical attack by their spouse;

- ✪ fear that their spouse will take the children and go into hiding; and,

- ✪ fear that their spouse will try to take community property and hide it.

There are additional legal papers you can file if you feel you are in any of these situations.

Protecting Yourself   The California legislature, being especially sensitive to domestic violence, has tried to streamline procedures to protect the abused spouse. The legislature relegated all forms dealing with domestic violence to the Domestic Violence Protection Act, Sections 6200–6390 of the Family Code. An excellent informational booklet entitled *Domestic Violence Restraining Orders Instruction Booklet* with forms is available free from the court clerk.

Some courts have domestic violence clinics, and the clerks will always steer you to help if you have a domestic violence problem. Lawyers are helpful in this area, but may not be needed because of the many free resources available. Because the booklet may be a little overwhelming (ninety-eight pages), some courts have designated clerks to help persons complete the forms.

Protecting Your Children

If you fear physical violence directed at your children, you can use the same procedures you would use for protecting yourself from violence. If you are worried that your spouse may try to kidnap your children, you should make sure that the day care center, baby-sitter, relative, or whomever you leave the children with at any time, is aware that you are in the process of a divorce and that the children are only to be released to you personally (not to your spouse or to any other relative, friend, etc.). A public school may not be willing to prevent your spouse or someone else from picking up your child unless you obtain a temporary custody order stating your child is only to be released to you or someone you designate.

To prevent your spouse from taking the children out of the United States, you can apply for a passport for each child. Once a passport is issued, the government will not issue another. So get their passport and lock it up in a safe-deposit box. (This will not prevent them from being taken to Canada or Mexico, until stricter passport laws are finalized, but will prevent them from being taken overseas.) You can also file a motion to prevent the removal of the children from the state and to deny passport services, but this involves a level of complexity that an attorney is better equipped to handle.

Protecting Your Property

If you genuinely fear that your spouse will try to remove money from bank accounts, try to hide important papers showing what property you own, or try to hide items of property, you may want to take this same action before your spouse can. However, you can make a great deal of trouble for yourself with the judge if you do this to try to get these assets for yourself. So, make a complete list of any property you do take and be sure to include these items in your **Schedule of Assets and Debts** (form 7, p.211).

You may need to convince the judge that you only took these items temporarily, in order to preserve them. Do not spend any cash you take from a bank account or sell or give away any items of property you take. Any cash should be placed in a separate bank account, without your spouse's name on it, and kept separate from any other cash you have. Any papers, such as deeds, car titles, stock or bond certificates, etc., should be placed in a safe-deposit box without your spouse's name on it. The idea is not to take these things for yourself, but to get them in a safe place so that your spouse cannot hide them and deny they ever existed.

If your spouse is determined and resourceful, there is no guaranteed way to prevent the things discussed in this section from happening. All you can do is put as many obstacles in his or her way as possible and rely on legal remedies for the improper actions.

TEMPORARY SUPPORT AND CUSTODY

If your spouse has left you with the children, the mortgage, and monthly bills and is not helping you financially, then you may want to consider asking the court to order the payment of support for you and the children immediately while the divorce is pending. Of course, if you were the only person bringing in income and have been paying all the bills, do not expect to get any temporary support.

To get temporary support, you will need to prepare an **ORDER TO SHOW CAUSE** for temporary support and custody, as well as other papers, including your **DECLARATION**, which sets forth all your reasons for the request.

Order to Show Cause   An **ORDER TO SHOW CAUSE** (**OSC**) is a court ruling requiring your spouse to demonstrate why your request for temporary support should not be granted. (see form 30, p.277.) It is urged that you get an attorney if you need an **ORDER TO SHOW CAUSE**. **OSC** litigation requires a working knowledge of both law and procedure. The purpose of an **OSC** is to obtain quick legal relief when you and your spouse cannot come to an interim agreement on an immediate need such as support, custody, or living arrangements.

Complete the **ORDER TO SHOW CAUSE** as follows.

◈ Complete the top portion of the form according to the instruction in Chapter 5.

◈ Check the box relating to the type of relief you are requesting. If none of the boxes apply, check the "Other" box and type in the subject matter.

◈ In item 1, provide the name of your spouse.

◈ Complete item "2a" after you obtain the date, time, and department or room number from the clerk. The hearing date must be at least twenty-one calendar days from the time you serve your spouse. If service is by mail, notice time is increased to twenty-six days. Complete "2b" as applicable. Check box "2c" if applicable; you and your spouse will be required to attend mediation if you have issues of custody or visitation.

◈ In item 3, "a(1)" to "a(5)," check the boxes showing the documents you are serving on your spouse with the **OSC**. You will recognize "(1)" and "(3)" from previous sections in this book. Item "a(4)" refers to written legal arguments citing particular law where the relief requested is not standard and requires legal support. You would check item "3b" if the judge reduces the time required for notice of the hearing, and you would check items "3c" and "3d" if you are serving any ex parte or temporary restraining orders with the **OSC**.

Form 31 titled **APPLICATION FOR ORDER AND SUPPORTING DECLARATION** must be attached to the first page of the **ORDER TO SHOW CAUSE**. Complete it as follows.

◈ Items 1 through 4 refer to custody and support. Complete them as applicable. The "To be ordered pending the hearing" line in bold refers to ex parte requests.

◈ Complete and attach any of the following forms that are appropriate for your case: **CHILD CUSTODY AND VISITATION ORDER ATTACHMENT** (form 40, p.301), **CHILD ABDUCTION PREVENTION ORDER ATTACHMENT** (form 40B, p.305), **CHILDREN'S HOLIDAY SCHEDULE ATTACHMENT** (form 40C, p.307), **ADDITIONAL PROVISIONS—**

Physical Custody Attachment (form 40D, p.309), **Joint Legal Custody Attachment** (form 40E, p.311).

➔ Complete items 5 through 7 as applicable. Bear in mind that accompanying this form must be your **Declaration** which sets forth in clear and vivid language, facts and circumstances supporting why you need such relief. The facts and circumstances must be based on your personal knowledge, not on what someone has told you or what you think.

➔ Item 8 refers to requesting a shortened period of time for notice of the **OSC**.

➔ Item 9 refers to any other relief you need right away and not indicated on the form.

➔ Check both boxes at item 10 and type the reasons why you need the requested relief on an attached **Declaration** (form 26, p.267) unless you type what you want to say in the space provided.

Some courts do not permit you to testify at the hearing and consider your **OSC** request solely on the written documents. For that reason, your **Declaration** must be graphic, persuasive, and convincing.

If you are trying to get an order before the hearing on the **OSC**, you also need to attach the **Temporary Orders** to the **OSC** form. (see form 33, p.283.) You complete this form as applicable, bearing in mind that whatever relief you ask for must be supported with specific details based on first-hand knowledge. The same declaration you typed for the **Application for Order and Supporting Declaration** (form 31, p.279) is used for this form because all these forms are filed together. The purpose of your declaration is to provide the court with hard-hitting facts as to why the orders are urgent and necessary. Do not hold back, but be truthful.

If you are seeking any financial relief, you need to complete and file with these papers the **Income and Expense Declaration** (form 8, p.215) and if appropriate, the **Property Declaration** (form 14, p.229). Bring to the hearing other financial information you may have, such as IRS

W-2 forms, the last three wage statements for you and your spouse if you have them, the most recent federal and state income tax returns, loan applications during the past two years, and if a sole proprietor, copies of IRS 1099 forms, profit and loss statements, and balance sheets.

After you file the forms with the clerk and obtain the hearing date, you must serve the papers on your spouse so that he or she has twenty-one days notice if personally served, or twenty-six days notice if served by mail. If you are seeking *ex parte* relief (see below) and have given the telephonic notice required, the clerk will direct you to a particular courtroom.

Ex Parte orders. An even faster procedure is available called *ex parte orders*. This procedure is available when you need to get relief now and you cannot wait for the formal notice time required for an **OSC** hearing to elapse. Ex parte procedure differs from court to court, and you will have to call the court clerk. Ex parte refers to having a court hearing without notice to your spouse. In practice, courts require some kind of notice, usually by telephone, a certain number of hours before the hearing, unless notice would pose a danger.

NOTE: *If you do seek ex parte relief, you must bring to the courtroom your written declaration stating that you attempted to contact, or did contact, your spouse. Provide the details such as the telephone numbers you called, who you spoke with, when you called, that you fully informed such person of the nature of the hearing, and of the time and place of the hearing. Also, do not forget to file the* **Proof of Service** *of all of the documents at least five calendar days before the hearing after you have served your spouse.*

Notice of motion. Another procedure called *notice of motion* can sometimes be used in lieu of an **OSC**. The **OSC** procedure is most often used and is therefore recommended.

After the hearing, you will need to prepare the court's order. Since your need is immediate, you must ask the judge, if he or she grants your request, to make the order effective now and not wait until you can prepare a written order and return it to the judge.

The form used for the order is the **Findings and Order after Hearing** (see form 35, p.287) with the same attachment forms (forms 40 through 44) used for the **Judgment**. (see form 17, p.247.) These attachment forms are described in the discussion on **Judgment** in Chapter 7, so refer to those pages for instructions on completing them. There is one additional attachment used exclusively for the *Order to Show Cause* hearing, namely the **Property Order Attachment**. (see form 45, p.321.) This form is an order for property restraining orders and mirrors the requests you made in items 6 and 7 of the **Application for Order and Supporting Declaration**.

TAXES

As you are no doubt aware, the United States income tax code is complicated and ever changing. Therefore, it is impossible to give detailed legal advice with respect to taxes in a book such as this. Any such information could easily be out of date by the time of publication. Therefore, it is strongly recommended that you consult a tax expert about the tax consequences of a divorce. A few general concerns are discussed in this chapter to give you an idea of some of the tax questions that can arise.

Filing Tax Returns

Generally, married persons will pay less income tax by filing a joint return than by filing separate returns. Your filing status as being married or single is determined as of the end of the year. Thus, if your divorce is pending and you are separated from your spouse as of the end of the year, you can both agree to file a joint return.

Taxes and Family Support

Because of tax laws, spousal support and child support are combined into one payment called *family support*. To understand the significance of the term *family support*, you must understand that spousal support is deductible by the payor and taxable to the payee. That is, if you receive spousal support, you have to declare it as income on your tax return, but your spouse can deduct it from income on his or her return. Child support, on the other hand, is not deductible or taxable.

The Internal Revenue Service (IRS) labeled family support as disguised child support, and said that if a reduction in family support is associated with a contingency relating to a child, it is presumed to all be child support. The IRS applies two tests.

- ✪ If the support is reduced within six months before or after the child's eighteenth birthday, it will be considered child support.

- ✪ Where there is more than one child and more than one reduction in child support, and the two reductions are within one year before or after the two children reach an age which is the same between 18 and 24, it will be considered child support.

Taxes and Property Division

You and your spouse may be exchanging title to property as a result of your divorce. Generally, there will not be any tax to pay as the result of such a transfer. However, whoever gets the property will be responsible for any capital gain tax when the property is sold.

The IRS has issued numerous rulings about how property is to be treated in divorce situations. You need to be especially careful if you are transferring tax shelters or other complicated financial arrangements.

Taxes and Dependents

There are simple tax rules regarding child dependents. Whoever has custody gets to claim the children on his or her tax return (unless both parents file a special IRS form agreeing to a different arrangement each year). If you are sharing physical custody, the parent with whom the child lives for the most time during the year is entitled to claim the child as a dependent.

The IRS form to reverse this must be filed each year. Therefore, if you and your spouse have agreed that you will get to claim the children (even though you do not have custody), you should get your spouse to sign an open-ended form that you can file each year, so that you do not have to worry about it each year.

IRS Form 8332 is a simple form that the releasing parent signs. (see form 51, p.341.) The names of the child or children and years of released rights are all that are required. Instructions are provided on the form.

IF YOUR SPOUSE ALSO FILES FOR DIVORCE

It really makes no difference which spouse files first. However, once the papers are filed, you cannot then also file your papers as a Petitioner. Only one court will be able to hear your case and only one divorce can be granted. If your spouse has residence in a different county, it would be more convenient for you if you filed first in your own county. But other than that, the only effect is psychological. You must answer the **SUMMONS (FAMILY LAW)** and **PETITION** within thirty days, just as your spouse would. The other forms discussed in the book apply to both parties.

You answer the **SUMMONS (FAMILY LAW)** with the **RESPONSE**. (see form 21, p.255 or form 21A, p.257.) Look at the **PETITION** (form 3, p.201 or form 3A, p.203). You will see it is the same form as the **RESPONSE** other than for the caption, which is "Response" rather than "Petition." Complete the **RESPONSE** according to the same instructions in this book for the **PETITION**. The fee for filing the **RESPONSE** varies from county to county. Fees change often, even during the year, so you must call the clerk to find out what the fee is at the time you are ready to file your documents. Please refer to the discussion on the **PETITION** in Chapter 7—the same instructions are applicable to the **RESPONSE**.

NOTE: *In situations in which your spouse has the children and you find yourself served with divorce papers from another state, get an attorney—fast.*

THE FUTURE

Once your divorce is final you are legally free to get married again. If you ever find yourself thinking about marriage, be careful before getting married again. Now that you know and appreciate how difficult it can be to get out of a marriage, you have no excuse for rushing into another one. If you decide to get married, you would be wise to consider a premarital agreement. This is an agreement made before marriage. Both parties disclose all of their property and debts and agree how things will be handled in the event they separate. A premarital agreement can avoid a long and costly divorce.

Again, be sure that you are using current forms. Most forms in this book can be found on the website of the California Judicial Council. Type that name into any search engine. Follow the instructions to find the forms by either name or number. At the top or, more often, at the bottom of the form will be a date of the last revision. Check that date against the form(s) in this book. Use forms on the website with a later revision date. The instructions for filling out these forms will usually be easy to follow. On many the only change will be to include a box to be checked for Domestic Partnerships. Revisions are usually dated January 1 and, less commonly, July 1.

Glossary

A

action. A lawsuit, including a divorce.

adultery. The legal term describing a sexual relationship outside of marriage. Traditionally was a ground for divorce, but California is now a no-fault state.

affidavit. A written statement, signed before a notary public under oath.

alimony. Money paid by one party to the other, to assist in the other party's financial support.

annulment. *See* nullity.

antenuptial agreement. *See* premarital agreement.

B

best interest of the child. Standard by which the judge will make his or her decision regarding custody of the child.

blue book. Common reference name for publication containing prices for used cars.

C

case law. (1) The body of law developed through the courts. (2) The decisions courts have made.

case reporters. The books containing the published decisions of the courts.

cash out distribution. A distribution in which the property has been sold and the proceeds divided between the spouses, or when money is given by one spouse in exchange for keeping property (*e.g.*, husband gives up rights to money in bank account to keep his retirement account).

child support. The legal responsibility to provide financial and other beneficial care to the minor children of the marriage.

common stock. Class of stock of a corporation that entitles the owner to vote and to receive dividends after other creditors are paid.

community property. A legal concept of property ownership between a husband and wife, which separates what is jointly owned as part of the marital estate, and what is owned separately by each party.

contested divorce. A hearing in which parties are disputing major issues.

D

disposition (of an action). The final result taken in an action. This will usually either be a final judgment or a dismissal.

distribution in kind. A distribution of the actual property, not somehow transformed (*i.e.*, distribution of the marital furniture, not proceeds from the sale of the furniture).

Domestic Violence Restraining Orders Instruction Booklet. Instruction booklet available from the court to explain your rights and what protections are available should you be the victim of domestic violence.

domicile. The state of a person's main and permanent residence. This is more than mere residency. A person can have several residences, but only one domicile. Good proof of domicile in a particular state would be that you are registered to vote there, have a driver's license and car registration issued there, are employed or have your principal place of business there, and list that address on your income tax returns.

E

equitable distribution. A legal concept for how marital property is to be divided in a divorce. The concept seeks to divide property in a fair manner, after considering whatever factors are legally required to be considered in a particular state.

ex parte hearing. A court hearing without notice to your spouse.

ex parte orders. Orders of the court made with only one spouse's information known and no notice given to the other spouse to present evidence. (Often used with orders of protection in domestic violence situations.)

expert witness. A person that because of their skill, knowledge, or profession renders an opinion to the court about a matter in dispute.

F

family court. Court that hears divorce cases and other family related matters.

family support. (1) Term used to describe the combined amounts of alimony and child support. (2) Term used to claim a deduction for income tax purposes for money paid to the former spouse. (IRS has a definition to determine what part of family support is child support and not tax deductible, and what part is alimony and is tax deductible by the payor.)

G

gross income. The total of all income received before any deductions or other subtractions are made; includes money received from working, interest, dividend, and any other source.

I

In Propria Persona. Latin phrase meaning "in one's own person." In other words, a phrase used to describe a situation when one represents one's self in court without an attorney.

indigent. A person of extremely low income who, based on this income, qualifies for waivers of costs and fees.

irreconcilable differences. A nonspecific ground on which spouses divorce in California.

irremediable differences. Grounds for no-fault divorce based on the incompatibility of the spouses.

J

joint legal custody. Where both parents share custody and each has a right in the decision-making over the child's life.

L

legal custody. The term used to describe the parent who has decision-making power over the child for such things as schooling, religion, and medical care.

legal separation. A legal procedure in which courts make some orders concerning property, custody, and support, but parties remain married. Used primarily when religious beliefs do not allow for divorce.

M

marital property. Property that is considered by state law to be owned by both parties and is therefore subject to being divided between the parties.

marriage settlement agreement (MSA). Written agreement signed by both parties that divides their property, determines support (spousal and/or child), specifies custody, and addresses visitation.

mental cruelty. Grounds for divorce in which one spouse claims that the actions of the other resulted in mental or emotional abuse. Traditionally was a ground for divorce, but California is now a no-fault state.

minute order. An order of the court generally made while the parties are still present in front of the judge and made a part of the record. An oral order of the court that is subsequently written in the minutes of the court.

motion. A formal written request for the judge to take certain action.

N

net income. Income after certain allowable deductions and other subtractions have been made.

no-fault divorce. Proceeding in which spouses do not have to specify grounds/reasons why they are seeking a divorce. This is a practice in California for dissolutions of marriage.

nonmarital property. Property designated by state law as being the separate property of one of the parties. Nonmarital property is generally not subject to any claims by the spouse.

notice of motion. The notice that must be given to the other spouse when a court hearing has been set to hear a matter relating to the divorce.

nullity. Title of legal proceeding to declare a marriage invalid in the state of California.

O

obligee. The person receiving support.

obligor. The person paying support.

P

party. A person who files a divorce action, or the person a divorce action is filed against. The husband and wife are the parties in a divorce action.

payee. The person who is entitled to receive a payment of alimony or child support.

payor. The person who is obligated to pay alimony or child support.

personal service. When legal papers are personally delivered to a person by a sheriff or other authorized process server.

petition. *See* verified complaint.

petitioner. The person who files for divorce and initiates the paperwork.

physical custody. The term used to describe where the child actually spends the majority of his or her time.

pleading. A written paper filed in a lawsuit that gives a party's position, such as a complaint or an answer.

preferred stock. A class of stock giving the owner a preferential claim to dividends, but no voting rights.

premarital agreement. A written, legal contract signed by the parties before their marriage, which spells out what property is owned by each, and how property will be divided in the event of divorce.

prenuptial agreement. *See* premarital agreement.

process. In the law, this means the manner in which a person is compelled to appear in court or respond to a lawsuit. Generally, this is done by a summons or by a subpoena.

public assistance. Governmental support generally based on financial need.

Q

qualified domestic relations order (QDRO). A court ruling dividing a pension as part of the assets.

quasi-community property. The property acquired by one spouse in another state that would have been community property if acquired in California.

R

respondent. The person responding to the divorce papers.

S

separate debt. The debt that belongs to one spouse only and, therefore, is not part of the community property.

separate property. Property designated by state law as being the separate property of one of the parties. Nonmarital property is generally not subject to any claims by the spouse.

served. To be given official, legal notice of lawsuit papers.

service. To give official, legal notice of legal papers to a person.

service by publication. The process by which a spouse whose whereabouts cannot be determined is served with court papers regarding the divorce. It is a legal process in which certain information is published in a newspaper distributed in the community the spouse is believed to be or was last present.

service of process. To be served with a summons or a subpoena.

sole legal custody. When only one parent has custody and has the decision-making power over the child's life.

spousal support. *See* alimony.

summary dissolution. An expedited and uncontested divorce proceeding in which the spouses have limited property and debts.

Summary Dissolution Booklet. A booklet available from the clerk of the court that must be read and followed in order to use the summary dissolution procedures.

subpoena. A legal document notifying a witness that he or she must appear at a particular place and time to give testimony. This can either require appearance at court for a trial or hearing, or at some office for a deposition.

subpoena duces tecum. A particular kind of subpoena that requires the person to bring documents or other items when they appear to testify.

U

uncontested divorce. A hearing in which the parties are in agreement on nearly all issues.

unsecured debts. Loans or other money owed that is not protected with collateral. (Credit card debt is unsecured; an auto loan and a mortgage are not.)

V

verified complaint. A complaint that has been signed by a party under oath (such as before a notary public or the court clerk).

visitation. The right of the parent who does not have physical custody of the minor children to spend time with the children. (Term is being phased out because it implies that one parent visits his or her child instead of taking an active role in the child's life.)

voidable marriage. A marriage that is valid, but may be annulled.

W

wage and earning assignment order. Court order requiring the employer of the person obligated to make support payment deduct the payments directly from the employee's paycheck.

Appendix A: California Statues

The following are excerpts from the California Family Code and the California Code of Civil Procedure relating to property distribution, spousal support (alimony), and child support. These are not the only provisions relating to these subjects, and it is strongly recommended that you review all sections of these codes.

California Statutes
Family Code

3020. (a) The Legislature finds and declares that it is the public policy of this state to assure that the health, safety, and welfare of children shall be the court's primary concern in determining the best interest of children when making any orders regarding the physical or legal custody or visitation of children. The Legislature further finds and declares that the perpetration of child abuse or domestic violence in a household where a child resides is detrimental to the child.

(b) The Legislature finds and declares that it is the public policy of this state to assure that children have frequent and continuing contact with both parents after the parents have separated or dissolved their marriage, or ended their relationship, and to encourage parents to share the rights and responsibilities of child rearing in order to effect this policy, except where the contact would not be in the best interest of the child, as provided in Section 3011.

(c) Where the policies set forth in subdivisions (a) and (b) of this section are in conflict, any court's order regarding physical or legal custody or visitation shall be made in a manner that ensures the health, safety, and welfare of the child and the safety of all family members.

4050. In adopting the statewide uniform guideline provided in this article, it is the intention of the Legislature to ensure that this state remains in compliance with federal regulations for child support guidelines.

4052. The court shall adhere to the statewide uniform guideline and may depart from the guideline only in the special circumstances set forth in this article.

4053. In implementing the statewide uniform guideline, the courts shall adhere to the following principles:

(a) A parent's first and principal obligation is to support his or her minor children according to the parent's circumstances and station in life.

(b) Both parents are mutually responsible for the support of their children.

(c) The guideline takes into account each parent's actual income and level of responsibility for the children.

(d) Each parent should pay for the support of the children according to his or her ability.

(e) The guideline seeks to place the interests of children as the state's top priority.

(f) Children should share in the standard of living of both parents. Child support may therefore appropriately improve the standard of living of the custodial household to improve the lives of the children.

(g) Child support orders in cases in which both parents have high levels of responsibility for the children should reflect the increased costs of raising the children in two homes and should minimize significant disparities in the children's living standards in the two homes.

(h) The financial needs of the children should be met through private financial resources as much as possible.

(i) It is presumed that a parent having primary physical responsibility for the children contributes a significant portion of available resources for the support of the children.

(j) The guideline seeks to encourage fair and efficient settlements of conflicts between parents and seeks to minimize the need for litigation.

(k) The guideline is intended to be presumptively correct in all cases, and only under special circumstances should child support orders fall below the child support mandated by the guideline formula.

(l) Child support orders must ensure that children actually receive fair, timely, and sufficient support reflecting the state's high standard of living and high costs of raising children compared to other states.

4055. (a) The statewide uniform guideline for determining child support orders is as follows: $CS = K (HN - (H\%) (TN))$.

(b) (1) The components of the formula are as follows:

(A) CS = child support amount.

(B) K = amount of both parents' income to be allocated for child support as set forth in paragraph (3).

(C) HN = high earner's net monthly disposable income.

(D) H% = approximate percentage of time that the high earner has or will have primary physical responsibility for the children compared to the other parent. In cases in which parents have different time-sharing arrangements for different children, H% equals the average of the approximate percentages of time the high earner parent spends with each child.

(E) TN = total net monthly disposable income of both parties.

(2) To compute net disposable income, see Section 4059.

(3) K (amount of both parents' income allocated for child support) equals one plus H% (if H% is less than or equal to 50 percent) or two minus H% (if H% is greater than 50 percent) times the following fraction:

Total Net Disposable

Income Per Month	K
$0-800	0.20 + TN/16,000
$801-6,666	0.25
$6,667-10,000	0.10 + 1,000/TN
Over $10,000	0.12 + 800/TN

For example, if H% equals 20 percent and the total monthly net disposable income of the parents is $1,000, K = (1 + 0.20) X 0.25, or 0.30. If H% equals 80 percent and the total monthly net disposable income of the parents is $1,000, K = (2 - 0.80) X 0.25, or 0.30.

(4) For more than one child, multiply CS by:

2 children	1.6
3 children	2
4 children	2.3
5 children	2.5
6 children	2.625
7 children	2.75
8 children	2.813
9 children	2.844
10 children	2.86

(5) If the amount calculated under the formula results in a positive number, the higher earner shall pay that amount to the lower earner. If the amount calculated under the formula results in a negative number, the lower earner shall pay the absolute value of that amount to the higher earner.

(6) In any default proceeding where proof is by affidavit pursuant to Section 2336, or in any proceeding for child support in which a party fails to appear after being duly noticed, H% shall be set at zero in the formula if the noncustodial parent is the higher earner or at 100 if the custodial parent is the higher earner, where there is no evidence presented demonstrating the percentage of time that the noncustodial parent has primary physical responsibility for the children. H% shall not be set as described above if the moving party in a default proceeding is the noncustodial parent or if the party who fails to appear after being duly noticed is the custodial parent.

A statement by the party who is not in default as to the percentage of time that the noncustodial parent has primary physical responsibility for the children shall be deemed sufficient evidence.

(7) In all cases in which the net disposable income per month of the obligor is less than one thousand dollars ($1,000), there shall be a rebuttable presumption that the obligor is entitled to a low-income adjustment. The presumption may be rebutted by evidence showing that the application of the low-income adjustment would be unjust and inappropriate in the particular case. In determining whether the presumption is rebutted, the court shall consider the principles provided in Section 4053, and the impact of the contemplated adjustment on the respective net incomes of the obligor and the obligee. The low-income adjustment shall reduce the child support amount otherwise determined under this section by an amount that is no greater than the amount calculated by multiplying the child support amount otherwise determined under this section by a fraction, the numerator of which is 1,000 minus the obligor's net disposable income per month, and the denominator of which is 1,000.

(8) Unless the court orders otherwise, the order for child support shall allocate the support amount so that the amount of support for the youngest child is the amount of support for one child, and the amount for the next youngest child is the difference between that amount and the amount for two children, with similar allocations for additional children. However, this paragraph does not apply to cases where there are different

time-sharing arrangements for different children or where the court determines that the allocation would be inappropriate in the particular case.

(c) If a court uses a computer to calculate the child support order, the computer program shall not automatically default affirmatively or negatively on whether a low-income adjustment is to be applied. If the low-income adjustment is applied, the computer program shall not provide the amount of the low-income adjustment. Instead, the computer program shall ask the user whether or not to apply the low-income adjustment, and if answered affirmatively, the computer program shall provide the range of the adjustment permitted by paragraph (7) of subdivision (b).

4056. (a) To comply with federal law, the court shall state, in writing or on the record, the following information whenever the court is ordering an amount for support that differs from the statewide uniform guideline formula amount under this article:

(1) The amount of support that would have been ordered under the guideline formula.

(2) The reasons the amount of support ordered differs from the guideline formula amount.

(3) The reasons the amount of support ordered is consistent with the best interests of the children.

(b) At the request of any party, the court shall state in writing or on the record the following information used in determining the guideline amount under this article:

(1) The net monthly disposable income of each parent.

(2) The actual federal income tax filing status of each parent (for example, single, married, married filing separately, or head of household and number of exemptions).

(3) Deductions from gross income for each parent.

(4) The approximate percentage of time pursuant to paragraph (1) of subdivision (b) of Section 4055 that each parent has primary physical responsibility for the children compared to the other parent.

4057. (a) The amount of child support established by the formula provided in subdivision (a) of Section 4055 is presumed to be the correct amount of child support to be ordered.

(b) The presumption of subdivision (a) is a rebuttable presumption affecting the burden of proof and may be rebutted by admissible evidence showing that application of the formula would be unjust or inappropriate in the particular case, consistent with the principles set forth in Section 4053, because one or more of the following factors is found to be applicable by a preponderance of the evidence, and the court states in writing or on the record the information required in subdivision (a) of Section 4056:

(1) The parties have stipulated to a different amount of child support under subdivision (a) of Section 4065.

(2) The sale of the family residence is deferred pursuant to Chapter 8 (commencing with Section 3800) of Part 1 and the rental value of the family residence in which the children reside exceeds the mortgage payments, homeowner's insurance, and property taxes. The amount of any adjustment pursuant to this paragraph shall not be greater than the excess amount.

(3) The parent being ordered to pay child support has an extraordinarily high income and the amount determined under the formula would exceed the needs of the children.

(4) A party is not contributing to the needs of the children at a level commensurate with that party's custodial time.

(5) Application of the formula would be unjust or inappropriate due to special circumstances in the particular case. These special circumstances include, but are not limited to, the following:

(A) Cases in which the parents have different time-sharing arrangements for different children.

(B) Cases in which both parents have substantially equal time-sharing of the children and one parent has a much lower or higher percentage of income used for housing than the other parent.

(C) Cases in which the children have special medical or other needs that could require child support that would be greater than the formula amount.

4057.5. (a) (1) The income of the obligor parent's subsequent spouse or nonmarital partner shall not be considered when determining or modifying child support, except in an extraordinary case where excluding that income would lead to extreme and severe hardship to any child subject to the child support award, in which case the court shall also consider whether including that income would lead to extreme and severe hardship to any child supported by the obligor or by the obligor's subsequent spouse or nonmarital partner.

(2) The income of the obligee parent's subsequent spouse or nonmarital partner shall not be considered when determining or modifying child support, except in an extraordinary case where excluding that income would lead to extreme and severe hardship to any child subject to the child support award, in which case the court shall also consider whether including that income would lead to extreme and severe hardship to any child supported by the obligee or by the obligee's subsequent spouse or nonmarital partner.

(b) For purposes of this section, an extraordinary case may include a parent who voluntarily or intentionally quits work or reduces income, or who intentionally remains unemployed or underemployed and relies on a subsequent spouse's income.

(c) If any portion of the income of either parent's subsequent spouse or nonmarital partner is allowed to be considered pursuant to this section, discovery for the purposes of determining income shall be based on W2 and 1099 income tax forms, except where the court determines that application would be unjust or inappropriate.

(d) If any portion of the income of either parent's subsequent spouse or nonmarital partner is allowed to be considered pursuant to this section, the court shall allow a hardship deduction based on the minimum living expenses for one or more stepchildren of the party subject to the order.

(e) The enactment of this section constitutes cause to bring an action for modification of a child support order entered prior to the operative date of this section.

4058. (a) The annual gross income of each parent means income from whatever source derived, except as specified in subdivision (c) and includes, but is not limited to, the following:

(1) Income such as commissions, salaries, royalties, wages, bonuses, rents, dividends, pensions, interest, trust income, annuities, workers' compensation benefits, unemployment insurance benefits, disability insurance benefits, social security benefits, and spousal support actually received from a person not a party to the proceeding to establish a child support order under this article.

(2) Income from the proprietorship of a business, such as gross receipts from the business reduced by expenditures required for the operation of the business.

(3) In the discretion of the court, employee benefits or self-employment benefits, taking into consideration the benefit to the employee, any corresponding reduction in living expenses, and other relevant facts.

(b) The court may, in its discretion, consider the earning capacity of a parent in lieu of the parent's income, consistent with the best interests of the children.

(c) Annual gross income does not include any income derived from child support payments actually received, and income derived from any public assistance program, eligibility for which is based on a determination of need. Child support received by a party for children from another relationship shall not be included as part of that party's gross or net income.

4059. The annual net disposable income of each parent shall be computed by deducting from his or her annual gross income the actual amounts attributable to the following items or other items permitted

under this article:

(a) The state and federal income tax liability resulting from the parties' taxable income. Federal and state income tax deductions shall bear an accurate relationship to the tax status of the parties (that is, single, married, married filing separately, or head of household) and number of dependents. State and federal income taxes shall be those actually payable (not necessarily current withholding) after considering appropriate filing status, all available exclusions, deductions, and credits. Unless the parties stipulate otherwise, the tax effects of spousal support shall not be considered in determining the net disposable income of the parties for determining child support, but shall be considered in determining spousal support consistent with Chapter 3 (commencing with Section 4330) of Part 3.

(b) Deductions attributed to the employee's contribution or the self-employed worker's contribution pursuant to the Federal Insurance Contributions Act (FICA), or an amount not to exceed that allowed under FICA for persons not subject to FICA, provided that the deducted amount is used to secure retirement or disability benefits for the parent.

(c) Deductions for mandatory union dues and retirement benefits, provided that they are required as a condition of employment.

(d) Deductions for health insurance or health plan premiums for the parent and for any children the parent has an obligation to support and deductions for state disability insurance premiums.

(e) Any child or spousal support actually being paid by the parent pursuant to a court order, to or for the benefit of any person who is not a subject of the order to be established by the court. In the absence of a court order, any child support actually being paid, not to exceed the amount established by the guideline, for natural or adopted children of the parent not residing in that parent's home, who are not the subject of the order to be established by the court, and of whom the parent has a duty of support. Unless the parent proves payment of the support, no deduction shall be allowed under this subdivision.

(f) Job-related expenses, if allowed by the court after consideration of whether the expenses are necessary, the benefit to the employee, and any other relevant facts.

(g) A deduction for hardship, as defined by Sections 4070 to 4073, inclusive, and applicable published appellate court decisions. The amount of the hardship shall not be deducted from the amount of child support, but shall be deducted from the income of the party to whom it applies. In applying any hardship under paragraph (2) of subdivision (a) of Section 4071, the court shall seek to provide equity between competing child support orders. The Judicial Council shall develop a formula for calculating the maximum hardship deduction and shall submit it to the Legislature for its consideration on or before July 1, 1995.

4060. The monthly net disposable income shall be computed by dividing the annual net disposable income by 12. If the monthly net disposable income figure does not accurately reflect the actual or prospective earnings of the parties at the time the determination of support is made, the court may adjust the amount appropriately.

4061. The amounts in Section 4062, if ordered to be paid, shall be considered additional support for the children and shall be computed in accordance with the following:

(a) If there needs to be an apportionment of expenses pursuant to Section 4062, the expenses shall be divided one-half to each parent, unless either parent requests a different apportionment pursuant to subdivision (b) and presents documentation which demonstrates that a different apportionment would be more appropriate.

(b) If requested by either parent, and the court determines it is appropriate to apportion expenses under Section 4062 other than one-half to each parent, the apportionment shall be as follows:

(1) The basic child support obligation shall first be computed using the formula set forth in subdivision (a) of Section 4055, as adjusted for any appropriate rebuttal factors in subdivision (b) of Section 4057.

(2) Any additional child support required for expenses pursuant to Section 4062 shall thereafter be ordered to be paid by the parents in proportion to their net disposable incomes as adjusted pursuant to subdivisions (c) and (d).

(c) In cases where spousal support is or has been ordered to be paid by one parent to the other, for purposes of allocating additional expenses pursuant to Section 4062, the gross income of the parent paying spousal support shall be decreased by the amount of the spousal support paid and the gross income of the parent receiving the spousal support shall be increased by the amount of the spousal support received for as long as the spousal support order is in effect and is paid.

(d) For purposes of computing the adjusted net disposable income of the parent paying child support for allocating any additional expenses pursuant to Section 4062, the net disposable income of the parent paying child support shall be reduced by the amount of any basic child support ordered to be paid under subdivision (a) of Section 4055. However, the net disposable income of the parent receiving child support shall not be increased by any amount of child support received.

4062. (a) The court shall order the following as additional child support:

(1) Child care costs related to employment or to reasonably necessary education or training for employment skills.

(2) The reasonable uninsured health care costs for the children as provided in Section 4063.

(b) The court may order the following as additional child support:

(1) Costs related to the educational or other special needs of the children.

(2) Travel expenses for visitation.

4065. (a) Unless prohibited by applicable federal law, the parties may stipulate to a child support amount subject to approval of the court. However, the court shall not approve a stipulated agreement for child support below the guideline formula amount unless the parties declare all of the following:

(1) They are fully informed of their rights concerning child support.

(2) The order is being agreed to without coercion or duress.

(3) The agreement is in the best interests of the children involved.

(4) The needs of the children will be adequately met by the stipulated amount.

(5) The right to support has not been assigned to the county pursuant to Section 11477 of the Welfare and Institutions Code and no public assistance application is pending.

(b) The parties may, by stipulation, require the child support obligor to designate an account for the purpose of paying the child support obligation by electronic funds transfer pursuant to section 4508.

(c) A stipulated agreement of child support is not valid unless the local child support agency has joined in the stipulation by signing it in any case in which the local child support agency is providing services pursuant to Section 17400. The local child support agency shall not stipulate to a child support order below the guideline amount if the children are receiving assistance under the CalWORKs program, if an application for public assistance is pending, or if the parent receiving support has not consented to the order.

(d) If the parties to a stipulated agreement stipulate to a child support order below the amount established by the statewide uniform guideline, no change of circumstances need be demonstrated to obtain a modification of the child support order to the applicable guideline level or above.

4071. (a) Circumstances evidencing hardship include the following:

(1) Extraordinary health expenses for which the parent is financially responsible, and uninsured catastrophic losses.

(2) The minimum basic living expenses of either parent's natural or adopted children for whom the parent has the obligation to support from other marriages or relationships who reside with the parent. The court, on its own motion or on the request of a party, may allow these income deductions as necessary to accommodate these expenses after making the deductions allowable under paragraph (1).

(b) The maximum hardship deduction under paragraph (2) of subdivision (a) for each child who resides with the parent may be equal to, but shall not exceed, the support allocated each child subject to the order. For purposes of calculating this deduction,

the amount of support per child established by the statewide uniform guideline shall be the total amount ordered divided by the number of children and not the amount established under paragraph (8) of subdivision (b) of Section 4055.

(c) The Judicial Council may develop tables in accordance with this section to reflect the maximum hardship deduction, taking into consideration the parent's net disposable income before the hardship deduction, the number of children for whom the deduction is being given, and the number of children for whom the support award is being made.

4320. In ordering spousal support under this part, the court shall consider all of the following circumstances:

(a) The extent to which the earning capacity of each party is sufficient to maintain the standard of living established during the marriage, taking into account all of the following:

(1) The marketable skills of the supported party; the job market for those skills; the time and expenses required for the supported party to acquire the appropriate education or training to develop those skills; and the possible need for retraining or education to acquire other, more marketable skills or employment.

(2) The extent to which the supported party's present or future earning capacity is impaired by periods of unemployment that were incurred during the marriage to permit the supported party to devote time to domestic duties.

(b) The extent to which the supported party contributed to the attainment of an education, training, a career position, or a license by the supporting party.

(c) The ability of the supporting party to pay spousal support, taking into account the supporting party's earning capacity, earned and unearned income, assets, and standard of living.

(d) The needs of each party based on the standard of living established during the marriage.

(e) The obligations and assets, including the separate property, of each party.

(f) The duration of the marriage.

(g) The ability of the supported party to engage in gainful employment without unduly interfering with the interests of dependent children in the custody of the party.

(h) The age and health of the parties.

(i) Documented evidence of any history of domestic violence, as defined in Section 6211, between the parties, including, but not limited to, consideration of emotional distress resulting from domestic violence perpetrated against the supported party by the supporting party, and consideration of any history of violence against the supporting party by the supported party.

(j) The immediate and specific tax consequences to each party.

(k) The balance of the hardships to each party.

(l) The goal that the supported party shall be self-supporting within a reasonable period of time. Except in the case of a marriage of long duration as described in Section 4336, a "reasonable period of time" for purposes of this section generally shall be one-half the length of the marriage. However, nothing in this section is intended to limit the court's discretion to order support for a greater or lesser length of time, based on any of the other factors listed in this section, Section 4336, and the circumstances of the parties.

(m) The criminal conviction of an abusive spouse shall be considered in making a reduction or elimination of a spousal support award in accordance with Section 4325.

(n) Any other factors the court determines are just and equitable.

4323. (a) (1) Except as otherwise agreed to by the parties in writing, there is a rebuttable presumption, affecting the burden of proof, of decreased need for spousal support if the supported party is cohabiting with a person of the opposite sex. Upon a determination that circumstances have changed, the court may modify or terminate the spousal support as provided for in Chapter 6 (commencing with Section 3650) of Part 1.

(2) Holding oneself out to be the husband or wife of the person with whom one is cohabiting is not necessary to constitute cohabitation as the term is used in this subdivision.

(b) The income of a supporting spouse's subsequent spouse or nonmarital partner shall not be considered when determining or modifying spousal support.

(c) Nothing in this section precludes later modification or termination of spousal support on proof of change of circumstances.

10000. This division shall be known and may be cited as the Family Law Facilitator Act.

10001. (a) The Legislature finds and declares the following:

(1) Child and spousal support are serious legal obligations. The entry of a child support order is frequently delayed while parents engage in protracted litigation concerning custody and visitation. The current system for obtaining child and spousal support orders is suffering because the family courts are unduly burdened with heavy case loads and do not have sufficient personnel to meet increased demands on the courts.

10002. Each superior court shall maintain an office of the family law facilitator. The office of the family law facilitator shall be staffed by an attorney licensed to practice law in this state who has mediation or litigation experience, or both, in the field of family law. The family law facilitator shall be appointed by the superior court.

10005. (a) By local rule, the superior court may designate additional duties of the family law facilitator, which may include, but are not limited to, the following:

(1) Meeting with litigants to mediate issues of child support, spousal support, and maintenance of health insurance, subject to Section 10012. Actions in which one or both of the parties are unrepresented by counsel shall have priority.

(2) Drafting stipulations to include all issues agreed to by the parties, which may include issues other than those specified in Section 10003.

(3) If the parties are unable to resolve issues with the assistance of the family law facilitator, prior to or at the hearing, and at the request of the court, the family law facilitator shall review the paperwork, examine documents, prepare support schedules, and advise the judge whether or not the matter is ready to proceed.

(4) Assisting the clerk in maintaining records.

(5) Preparing formal orders consistent with the court's announced order in cases where both parties are unrepresented.

(6) Serving as a special master in proceedings and making findings to the court unless he or she has served as a mediator in that case.

(7) Providing the services specified in Division 15 (commencing with Section 10100). Except for the funding specifically designated for visitation programs pursuant to Section 669B of Title 42 of the United States Code, Title IV-D child support funds shall not be used to fund the services specified in Division 15 (commencing with Section 10100).

(8) Providing the services specified in Section 10004 concerning the issues of child custody and visitation as they relate to calculating child support, if funding is provided for that purpose.

(b) If staff and other resources are available and the duties listed in subdivision (a) have been accomplished, the duties of the family law facilitator may also include the following:

(1) Assisting the court with research and any other responsibilities which will enable the court to be responsive to the litigants' needs.

(2) Developing programs for bar and community outreach through day and evening programs, videotapes, and other innovative means that will assist unrepresented and financially disadvantaged litigants in gaining meaningful access to family court. These programs shall specifically include information concerning underutilized legislation, such as expedited child support orders (Chapter 5 (commencing with Section 3620) of Part 1 of Division 9), and preexisting, court-sponsored programs, such as supervised visitation and appointment of attorneys for children.

10007. The court shall provide the family law facilitator at no cost to the parties.

10008. (a) Except as provided in subdivision (b), nothing in this chapter shall be construed to apply to a child for whom services are provided or required to be provided by a local child support agency pursuant to Section 17400.

(b) In cases in which the services of the local child support agency are provided pursuant to Section 17400, either parent may utilize the services of the family law facilitator that are specified in Section 10004. In order for a custodial parent who is receiving the services of the local child support agency pursuant to Section 17400 to utilize the services specified in Section 10005 relating to support, the custodial parent must obtain written authorization from the local child support agency. It is not the intent of the Legislature in enacting this section to limit the duties of local child support agencies with respect to seeking child support payments or to in any way limit or supersede other provisions of this code respecting temporary child support.

Family Code Section 297. (a) Domestic partners are two adults who have chosen to share one another's lives in an intimate and committed relationship of mutual caring.

(b) A domestic partnership shall be established in California when both persons file a Declaration of Domestic Partnership with the Secretary of State pursuant to this division, and, at the time of filing, all of the following requirements are met:

(1) Both persons have a common residence.

(2) Neither person is married to someone else or is a member of another domestic partnership with someone else that has not been terminated, dissolved, or adjudged a nullity.

(3) The two persons are not related by blood in a way that would prevent them from being married to each other in this state.

(4) Both persons are at least 18 years of age.

(5) Either of the following:

(A) Both persons are members of the same sex.

(B) One or both of the persons meet the eligibility criteria under Title II of the Social Security Act as defined in 42 U.S.C. Section 402(a) for old-age insurance benefits or Title XVI of the Social Security Act as defined in 42 U.S.C. Section 1381 for aged individuals. Notwithstanding any other provision of this section, persons of opposite sexes may not constitute a domestic partnership unless one or both of the persons are over the age of 62.

(6) Both persons are capable of consenting to the domestic partnership.

(c) "Have a common residence" means that both domestic partners share the same residence. It is not necessary that the legal right to possess the common residence be in both of their names. Two people have a common residence even if one or both have additional residences. Domestic partners do not cease to have a common residence if one leaves the common residence but intends to return.

297.5. (a) Registered domestic partners shall have the same rights, protections, and benefits, and shall be subject to the same responsibilities, obligations, and duties under law, whether they derive from statutes, administrative regulations, court rules, government policies, common law, or any other provisions or sources of law, as are granted to and imposed upon spouses.

(b) Former registered domestic partners shall have the same rights, protections, and benefits, and shall be subject to the same responsibilities, obligations, and duties under law, whether they derive from statutes, administrative regulations, court rules, government policies, common law, or any other provisions or sources of law, as are granted to and imposed upon former spouses.

(c) A surviving registered domestic partner, following the death of the other partner, shall have the same rights, protections, and benefits, and shall be subject to the same responsibilities, obligations, and duties under law, whether they derive from statutes, administrative regulations, court rules, government policies, common law, or any other provisions or sources of law, as are granted to and imposed upon a widow or a widower.

(d) The rights and obligations of registered domestic partners with respect to a child of either of them shall be the same as those of spouses. The rights and obligations of former or surviving registered domestic partners with respect to a child of either of them shall be the same as those of former or surviving spouses.

(e) To the extent that provisions of California law adopt, refer to, or rely upon, provisions of federal law in a way that otherwise would cause registered domestic partners to be treated differently than spouses, registered domestic partners shall be treated by

California law as if federal law recognized a domestic partnership in the same manner as California law.

(f) Registered domestic partners shall have the same rights
regarding nondiscrimination as those provided to spouses.

(g) No public agency in this state may discriminate against any person or couple on the ground that the person is a registered domestic partner rather than a spouse or that the couple are registered domestic partners rather than spouses, except that nothing in this section applies to modify eligibility for long-term care plans pursuant to Chapter 15 (commencing with Section 21660) of Part 3 of Division 5 of Title 2 of the Government Code.

(h) This act does not preclude any state or local agency from exercising its regulatory authority to implement statutes providing rights to, or imposing responsibilities upon, domestic partners.

(i) This section does not amend or modify any provision of the California Constitution or any provision of any statute that was adopted by initiative.

(j) Where necessary to implement the rights of registered domestic partners under this act, gender-specific terms referring to spouses shall be construed to include domestic partners.

(k) (1) For purposes of the statutes, administrative regulations, court rules, government policies, common law, and any other provision or source of law governing the rights, protections, and benefits, and the responsibilities, obligations, and duties of registered domestic partners in this state, as effectuated by this section, with respect to community property, mutual responsibility for debts to third parties, the right in particular circumstances of either partner to seek financial support from the other following the dissolution of the partnership, and other rights and duties as between the partners concerning ownership of property, any ref-

erence to the date of a marriage shall be deemed to refer to the date of registration of a domestic partnership with the state.

(2) Notwithstanding paragraph (1), for domestic partnerships registered with the state before January 1, 2005, an agreement between the domestic partners that the partners intend to be governed by the requirements set forth in Sections 1600 to 1620, inclusive, and which complies with those sections, except for the agreement's effective date, shall be enforceable as provided by Sections 1600 to 1620, inclusive, if that agreement was fully executed and in force as of June 30, 2005.

299. (a) A registered domestic partnership may be terminated without filing a proceeding for dissolution of domestic partnership by the filing of a Notice of Termination of Domestic Partnership with the Secretary of State pursuant to this section, provided that all of the following conditions exist at the time of the filing:

(1) The Notice of Termination of Domestic Partnership is signed by both registered domestic partners.

(2) There are no children of the relationship of the parties born before or after registration of the domestic partnership or adopted by the parties after registration of the domestic partnership, and neither of the registered domestic partners, to their knowledge, is pregnant.

(3) The registered domestic partnership is not more than five years in duration.

(4) Neither party has any interest in real property wherever
situated, with the exception of the lease of a residence occupied by
either party which satisfies the following requirements:

(A) The lease does not include an option to purchase.

(B) The lease terminates within one year from the

date of filing of the Notice of Termination of Domestic Partnership.

(5) There are no unpaid obligations in excess of the amount described in paragraph (6) of subdivision (a) of Section 2400, as adjusted by subdivision (b) of Section 2400, incurred by either or both of the parties after registration of the domestic partnership, excluding the amount of any unpaid obligation with respect to an automobile.

(6) The total fair market value of community property assets, excluding all encumbrances and automobiles, including any deferred compensation or retirement plan, is less than the amount described in paragraph (7) of subdivision (a) of Section 2400, as adjusted by subdivision (b) of Section 2400, and neither party has separate property assets, excluding all encumbrances and automobiles, in excess of that amount.

(7) The parties have executed an agreement setting forth the division of assets and the assumption of liabilities of the community property, and have executed any documents, title certificates, bills of sale, or other evidence of transfer necessary to effectuate the agreement.

(8) The parties waive any rights to support by the other domestic partner.

(9) The parties have read and understand a brochure prepared by the Secretary of State describing the requirements, nature, and effect of terminating a domestic partnership.

(10) Both parties desire that the domestic partnership be
terminated.

(b) The registered domestic partnership shall be terminated
effective six months after the date of filing of the Notice of
Termination of Domestic Partnership with the Secretary of State pursuant to this section, provided that neither

party has, before that date, filed with the Secretary of State a notice of revocation of the termination of domestic partnership, in the form and content as shall be prescribed by the Secretary of State, and sent to the other party a copy of the notice of revocation by first-class mail, postage prepaid, at the other party's last known address. The effect of termination of a domestic partnership pursuant to this section shall be the same as, and shall be treated for all purposes as, the entry of a judgment of dissolution of a domestic partnership.

(c) The termination of a domestic partnership pursuant to
subdivision (b) does not prejudice nor bar the rights of either of the parties to institute an action in the superior court to set aside the termination for fraud, duress, mistake, or any other ground recognized at law or in equity. A court may set aside the termination of domestic partnership and declare the termination of the domestic partnership null and void upon proof that the parties did not meet the requirements of subdivision (a) at the time of the filing of the Notice of Termination of Domestic Partnership with the Secretary of State.

(d) The superior courts shall have jurisdiction over all
proceedings relating to the dissolution of domestic partnerships, nullity of domestic partnerships, and legal separation of partners in a domestic partnership. The dissolution of a domestic partnership, nullity of a domestic partnership, and legal separation of partners in a domestic partnership shall follow the same procedures, and the partners shall possess the same rights, protections, and benefits, and be subject to the same responsibilities, obligations, and duties, as apply to the dissolution of marriage, nullity of marriage, and legal separation of spouses in a marriage, respectively, except as provided in subdivision (a), and except that, in accordance with the consent acknowledged by domestic partners in the Declaration of Domestic

Partnership form, proceedings for dissolution, nullity, or legal separation of a domestic partnership registered in this state may be filed in the superior courts of this state even if neither domestic partner is a resident of, or maintains a domicile in, the state at the time the proceedings are filed.

299.2. A legal union of two persons of the same sex, other than a marriage, that was validly formed in another jurisdiction, and that is substantially equivalent to a domestic partnership as defined in this part, shall be recognized as a valid domestic partnership in this state regardless of whether it bears the name domestic partnership.

Code of Civil Procedure

415.40. A summons may be served on a person outside this state in any manner provided by this article or by sending a copy of the summons and of the complaint to the person to be served by first-class mail, postage prepaid, requiring a return receipt. Service of a summons by this form of mail is deemed complete on the 10th day after such mailing.

415.50. (a) A summons may be served by publication if upon affidavit it appears to the satisfaction of the court in which the action is pending that the party to be served cannot with reasonable diligence be served in another manner specified in this article and that either:

(1) A cause of action exists against the party upon whom service is to be made or he or she is a necessary or proper party to the action.

(2) The party to be served has or claims an interest in real or personal property in this state that is subject to the jurisdiction of the court or the relief demanded in the action consists wholly or in part in excluding the party from any interest in the property.

(b) The court shall order the summons to be published in a named newspaper, published in this state, that is most likely to give actual notice to the party to be served. If the party to be served resides or is located out of this state, the court may also order the summons to be published in a named newspaper outside this state that is most likely to give actual notice to that party. The order shall direct that a copy of the summons, the complaint, and the order for publication be forthwith mailed to the party if his or her address is ascertained before expiration of the time prescribed for publication of the summons. Except as otherwise provided by statute, the publication shall be made as provided by Section 6064

of the Government Code unless the court, in its discretion, orders publication for a longer period.

(c) Service of a summons in this manner is deemed complete as provided in Section 6064 of the Government Code.

(d) Notwithstanding an order for publication of the summons, a summons may be served in another manner authorized by this chapter, in which event the service shall supersede any published summons.

(e) As a condition of establishing that the party to be served cannot with reasonable diligence be served in another manner specified in this article, the court may not require that a search be conducted of public databases where access by a registered process server to residential addresses is prohibited by law or by published policy of the agency providing the database, including, but not limited to, voter registration rolls and records of the Department of Motor Vehicles.

Appendix B: Forms

Be sure to read the section "An Introduction to Legal Forms" in Chapter 5 before you begin using the forms in this appendix. The instructions for a particular form may be found by looking up the form number in the index. Make photocopies to use for both practice worksheets and the forms you will file with the court.

Publisher's Note: Previously, many second and subsequent pages to forms were shown upside down. California procedures have recently changed. All pages of all forms listed in this edition are current as of this publication.

Table of Forms

The following forms are included in this appendix.

SUMMONS (Family Law)

CITACIÓN (Derecho familiar)

NOTICE TO RESPONDENT *(Name):*

AVISO AL DEMANDADO (Nombre):

> **You are being sued.** *Lo están demandando.*

Petitioner's name is:

Nombre del demandante:

CASE NUMBER *(NÚMERO DE CASO):*

You have **30 calendar days** after this *Summons* and *Petition* are served on you to file a *Response* (form FL-120 or FL-123) at the court and have a copy served on the petitioner. A letter or phone call will not protect you.

If you do not file your *Response* on time, the court may make orders affecting your marriage or domestic partnership, your property, and custody of your children. You may be ordered to pay support and attorney fees and costs. If you cannot pay the filing fee, ask the clerk for a fee waiver form.

If you want legal advice, contact a lawyer immediately. You can get information about finding lawyers at the California Courts Online Self-Help Center *(www.courtinfo.ca.gov/selfhelp)*, at the California Legal Services Web site *(www.lawhelpcalifornia.org)*, or by contacting your local county bar association.

*Tiene **30 días corridos** después de haber recibido la entrega legal de esta Citación y Petición para presentar una Respuesta (formulario FL-120 ó FL-123) ante la corte y efectuar la entrega legal de una copia al demandante. Una carta o llamada telefónica no basta para protegerlo.*

Si no presenta su Respuesta a tiempo, la corte puede dar órdenes que afecten su matrimonio o pareja de hecho, sus bienes y la custodia de sus hijos. La corte también le puede ordenar que pague manutención, y honorarios y costos legales. Si no puede pagar la cuota de presentación, pida al secretario un formulario de exención de cuotas.

Si desea obtener asesoramiento legal, póngase en contacto de inmediato con un abogado. Puede obtener información para encontrar a un abogado en el Centro de Ayuda de las Cortes de California (www.sucorte.ca.gov), en el sitio Web de los Servicios Legales de California (www.lawhelpcalifornia.org) o poniéndose en contacto con el colegio de abogados de su condado.

NOTICE: The restraining orders on page 2 are effective against both spouses or domestic partners until the petition is dismissed, a judgment is entered, or the court makes further orders. These orders are enforceable anywhere in California by any law enforcement officer who has received or seen a copy of them.

AVISO: Las órdenes de restricción que figuran en la página 2 valen para ambos cónyuges o pareja de hecho hasta que se despida la petición, se emita un fallo o la corte dé otras órdenes. Cualquier autoridad de la ley que haya recibido o visto una copia de estas órdenes puede hacerlas acatar en cualquier lugar de California.

1. The name and address of the court are *(El nombre y dirección de la corte son):*

2. The name, address, and telephone number of the petitioner's attorney, or the petitioner without an attorney, are:
   (El nombre, dirección y número de teléfono del abogado del demandante, o del demandante si no tiene abogado, son):

Date *(Fecha):*   Clerk, by *(Secretario, por)* _____, Deputy *(Asistente)*

[SEAL]

NOTICE TO THE PERSON SERVED: You are served

AVISO A LA PERSONA QUE RECIBIÓ LA ENTREGA: *Esta entrega se realiza*

a. ☐   as an individual. *(a usted como individuo.)*

b. ☐   on behalf of respondent who is a *(en nombre de un demandado que es)*:

     (1) ☐   minor *(menor de edad)*

     (2) ☐   ward or conservatee *(dependiente de la corte o pupilo)*

     (3) ☐   other *(specify) (otro – especifique)*:

(Read the reverse for important information.)
(Lea importante información al dorso.)

Form Adopted for Mandatory Use
Judicial Council of California
FL-110 [Rev. January 1, 2006]

SUMMONS
(Family Law)

Family Code §§ 232, 233, 2040, 7700;
Code of Civil Procedure, §§ 412.20, 416.60–416.90
www.courtinfo.ca.gov

WARNING—IMPORTANT INFORMATION

WARNING: California law provides that, for purposes of division of property upon dissolution of a marriage or domestic partnership or upon legal separation, property acquired by the parties during marriage or domestic partnership in joint form is presumed to be community property. If either party to this action should die before the jointly held community property is divided, the language in the deed that characterizes how title is held (i.e., joint tenancy, tenants in common, or community property) will be controlling, and not the community property presumption. You should consult your attorney if you want the community property presumption to be written into the recorded title to the property.

STANDARD FAMILY LAW RESTRAINING ORDERS

Starting immediately, you and your spouse or domestic partner are restrained from

1. removing the minor child or children of the parties, if any, from the state without the prior written consent of the other party or an order of the court;

2. cashing, borrowing against, canceling, transferring, disposing of, or changing the beneficiaries of any insurance or other coverage, including life, health, automobile, and disability, held for the benefit of the parties and their minor child or children;

3. transferring, encumbering, hypothecating, concealing, or in any way disposing of any property, real or personal, whether community, quasi-community, or separate, without the written consent of the other party or an order of the court, except in the usual course of business or for the necessities of life; and

4. creating a nonprobate transfer or modifying a nonprobate transfer in a manner that affects the disposition of property subject to the transfer, without the written consent of the other party or an order of the court. Before revocation of a nonprobate transfer can take effect or a right of survivorship to property can be eliminated, notice of the change must be filed and served on the other party.

You must notify each other of any proposed extraordinary expenditures at least five business days prior to incurring these extraordinary expenditures and account to the court for all extraordinary expenditures made after these restraining orders are effective. However, you may use community property, quasi-community property, or your own separate property to pay an attorney to help you or to pay court costs.

ADVERTENCIA – INFORMACIÓN IMPORTANTE

ADVERTENCIA: De acuerdo a la ley de California, las propiedades adquiridas por las partes durante su matrimonio o pareja de hecho en forma conjunta se consideran propiedad comunitaria para los fines de la división de bienes que ocurre cuando se produce una disolución o separación legal del matrimonio o pareja de hecho. Si cualquiera de las partes de este caso llega a fallecer antes de que se divida la propiedad comunitaria de tenencia conjunta, el destino de la misma quedará determinado por las cláusulas de la escritura correspondiente que describen su tenencia (por ej., tenencia conjunta, tenencia en común o propiedad comunitaria) y no por la presunción de propiedad comunitaria. Si quiere que la presunción comunitaria quede registrada en la escritura de la propiedad, debería consultar con un abogado.

ÓRDENES DE RESTRICCIÓN NORMALES DE DERECHO FAMILIAR

En forma inmediata, usted y su cónyuge o pareja de hecho tienen prohibido:

1. *Llevarse del estado de California a los hijos menores de las partes, si los hubiera, sin el consentimiento previo por escrito de la otra parte o una orden de la corte;*

2. *Cobrar, pedir prestado, cancelar, transferir, deshacerse o cambiar el nombre de los beneficiarios de cualquier seguro u otro tipo de cobertura, tal como de vida, salud, vehículo y discapacidad, que tenga como beneficiario(s) a las partes y su(s) hijo(s) menor(es);*

3. *Transferir, gravar, hipotecar, ocultar o deshacerse de cualquier manera de cualquier propiedad, inmueble o personal, ya sea comunitaria, cuasicomunitaria o separada, sin el consentimiento escrito de la otra parte o una orden de la corte, con excepción las operaciones realizadas en el curso normal de actividades o para satisfacer las necesidades de la vida; y*

4. *Crear o modificar una transferencia no testamentaria de manera que afecte el destino de una propiedad sujeta a transferencia, sin el consentimiento por escrito de la otra parte o una orden de la corte. Antes de que se pueda eliminar la revocación de una transferencia no testamentaria, se debe presentar ante la corte un aviso del cambio y hacer una entrega legal de dicho aviso a la otra parte.*

Cada parte tiene que notificar a la otra sobre cualquier gasto extraordinario propuesto, por lo menos cinco días laborales antes de realizarlo, y rendir cuenta a la corte de todos los gastos extraordinarios realizados después de que estas órdenes de restricción hayan entrado en vigencia. No obstante, puede usar propiedad comunitaria, cuasicomunitaria o suya separada para pagar a un abogado o para ayudarle a pagar los costos de la corte.

SUMMONS
(Family Law)

FL-115

ATTORNEY OR PARTY WITHOUT ATTORNEY (Name, State Bar number, and address):	FOR COURT USE ONLY
TELEPHONE NO.: FAX NO. (Optional): E–MAIL ADDRESS (Optional): ATTORNEY FOR (Name):	

SUPERIOR COURT OF CALIFORNIA, COUNTY OF
STREET ADDRESS:
MAILING ADDRESS:
CITY AND ZIP CODE:
BRANCH NAME:

PETITIONER:

RESPONDENT:

PROOF OF SERVICE OF SUMMONS	CASE NUMBER:

1. At the time of service I was at least 18 years of age and not a party to this action. I served the respondent with copies   of:

   a. ☐ Family Law: Petition (form FL-100), Summons (form FL-110), and blank Response (form FL-120)

   —or—

   b. ☐ Family Law—Domestic Partnership: Petition—Domestic Partnership (form FL-103), Summons (form FL-110), and blank Response—Domestic Partnership (form FL-123)

   —or—

   c. ☐ Uniform Parentage: Petition to Establish Parental Relationship (form FL-200), Summons (form FL-210), and blank Response to Petition to Establish Parental Relationship (form FL-220)

   —or—

   d. ☐ Custody and Support: Petition for Custody and Support of Minor Children (form FL-260), Summons (form FL-210), and blank Response to Petition for Custody and Support of Minor Children (form FL-270)

   and

   e. ☐ (1) ☐ Completed and blank Declaration Under Uniform Child Custody Jurisdiction and Enforcement Act (form FL-105)

   (2) ☐ Completed and blank Declaration of Disclosure (form FL-140)

   (3) ☐ Completed and blank Schedule of Assets and Debts (form FL-142)

   (4) ☐ Completed and blank Income and Expense Declaration (form FL-150)

   (5) ☐ Completed and blank Financial Statement (Simplified) (form FL-155)

   (6) ☐ Completed and blank Property Declaration (form FL-160)

   (7) ☐ Order to Show Cause (form FL-300), Application for Order and Supporting Declaration (form FL-310), and blank Responsive Declaration to Order to Show Cause or Notice of Motion (form FL-320)

   (8) ☐ Other (specify):

2. Address where respondent was served:

3. I served the respondent by the following means (check proper box):

   a. ☐ Personal service. I personally delivered the copies to the respondent (Code Civ. Proc., § 415.10)
   on (date):   at (time):

   b. ☐ Substituted service. I left the copies with or in the presence of (name):
   who is (specify title or relationship to respondent):

   (1) ☐ (Business) a person at least 18 years of age who was apparently in charge at the office or usual place of business of the respondent. I informed him or her of the general nature of the papers

   (2) ☐ (Home) a competent member of the household (at least 18 years of age) at the home of the respondent. I informed him or her of the general nature of the papers

Page 1 of 2

Form Approved for Optional Use
Judicial Council of California
FL-115 [Rev. January 1, 2005]

PROOF OF SERVICE OF SUMMONS
(Family Law—Uniform Parentage—Custody and Support)

Code of Civil Procedure, § 417.10
www.courtinfo.ca.gov

	CASE NUMBER:
PETITIONER:	
RESPONDENT:	

3. b. (cont.) on (date):   at (time):

I thereafter mailed additional copies (by first class, postage prepaid) to the respondent at the place where the copies were left (Code Civ. Proc., § 415.20b) on (date):

A declaration of diligence   is attached, stating the actions taken to first attempt personal service.

c. ☐   Mail and acknowledgment service.   I mailed the copies to the respondent, addressed as shown in item 2, by first-class mail, postage prepaid, on (date):   from (city):

     (1) ☐   with two copies of the Notice and Acknowledgment of Receipt (Family Law) (form FL-117) and a postage-paid return envelope addressed to me. (Attach completed   Notice and Acknowledgment of Receipt (Family Law)   (form FL-117).) (Code Civ. Proc., § 415.30.)

     (2) ☐   to an address outside California (by registered or certified mail with return receipt requested). (Attach signed return receipt or other evidence of actual delivery to the respondent.)   (Code Civ. Proc., § 415.40.)

d. ☐   Other (specify code section):

     ☐   Continued on Attachment 3d.

4. The "NOTICE TO THE PERSON SERVED" on the Summons was completed as follows (Code Civ. Proc., §§ 412.30, 415.10, 474):

a. ☐   As an individual   or

b. ☐   On behalf of respondent who is a

     (1) ☐   minor. (Code Civ. Proc., § 416.60.)

     (2) ☐   ward or conservatee. (Code Civ. Proc., § 416.70.)

     (3) ☐   other (specify):

5. Person who served papers

Name:

Address:

Telephone number:

This person is

a. ☐   exempt from registration under Business and Professions Code section 22350(b).

b. ☐   not a registered California process server.

c. ☐   a registered California process server: ☐ an employee or   ☐ an independent contractor

     (1) Registration no.:

     (2) County:

d.   The fee for service was (specify): $

6. ☐   I declare under penalty of perjury under the laws of the State of California that the foregoing is true and correct.

–or–

7. ☐   I am a California sheriff, marshal, or constable,   and I certify that the foregoing is true and correct.

Date:

▶

_____   _____
(NAME OF PERSON WHO SERVED PAPERS)   (SIGNATURE OF PERSON WHO SERVED PAPERS)

    PROOF OF SERVICE OF SUMMONS
(Family Law—Uniform Parentage—Custody and Support)

FL-100

ATTORNEY OR PARTY WITHOUT ATTORNEY *(Name, State Bar number, and address):*	*FOR COURT USE ONLY*

TELEPHONE NO.:   FAX NO. *(Optional):*

E-MAIL ADDRESS *(Optional):*

ATTORNEY FOR *(Name):*

SUPERIOR COURT OF CALIFORNIA, COUNTY OF

STREET ADDRESS:

MAILING ADDRESS:

CITY AND ZIP CODE:

BRANCH NAME:

MARRIAGE OF

PETITIONER:

RESPONDENT:

PETITION FOR	CASE NUMBER:

  ☐ **Dissolution of Marriage**
  ☐ **Legal Separation**
  ☐ **Nullity of Marriage**   ☐ **AMENDED**

1. RESIDENCE (Dissolution only) ☐ Petitioner ☐ Respondent has been a resident of this state for at least six months and of this county for at least three months immediately preceding the filing of this *Petition for Dissolution of Marriage.*

2. STATISTICAL FACTS
   a. Date of marriage:
   b. Date of separation:
   c. Time from date of marriage to date of separation *(specify):*
      Years: Months:

3. DECLARATION REGARDING MINOR CHILDREN *(include children of this relationship born prior to or during the marriage or adopted during the marriage):*
   a. ☐ There are no minor children.
   b. ☐ The minor children are:

Child's name	Birthdate	Age	Sex

   ☐ Continued on Attachment 3b.
   c. If there are minor children of the Petitioner and Respondent, a completed *Declaration Under Uniform Child Custody Jurisdiction and Enforcement Act (UCCJEA)* (form FL-105) must be attached.
   d. ☐ A completed voluntary declaration of paternity regarding minor children born to the Petitioner and Respondent prior to the marriage is attached.

4. SEPARATE PROPERTY ☐
   Petitioner requests that the assets and debts listed ☐ in *Property Declaration* (form FL-160) ☐ in Attachment 4
   ☐ below   be confirmed as separate property.

Item	Confirm to

NOTICE: You may redact (black out) social security numbers from any written material filed with the court in this case other than a form used to collect child or spousal support.

Page 1 of 2

Form Adopted for Mandatory Use
Judicial Council of California
FL-100 [Rev. January 1, 2005]

PETITION—MARRIAGE
(Family Law)

Family Code, §§ 2330, 3409;
www.courtinfo.ca.gov

MARRIAGE OF (last name, first name of parties):	CASE NUMBER:

5. **DECLARATION REGARDING COMMUNITY AND QUASI-COMMUNITY ASSETS AND DEBTS AS CURRENTLY KNOWN**
    a. ☐ There are no such assets or debts subject to disposition by the court in this proceeding.
    b. ☐ All such assets and debts are listed ☐ in Property Declaration (form FL-160) ☐ in Attachment 5b.
        ☐ below (specify):

6. Petitioner requests
    a. ☐ dissolution of the marriage based on   d. ☐ nullity of voidable marriage based on
        (1) ☐ irreconcilable differences. (Fam. Code, § 2310(a).)   (1) ☐ petitioner's age at time of marriage.
        (2) ☐ incurable insanity. (Fam. Code, § 2310(b).)   (Fam. Code, § 2210(a).)
    b. ☐ legal separation of the parties based on   (2) ☐ prior existing marriage.
        (1) ☐ irreconcilable differences. (Fam. Code, § 2310(a).)   (Fam. Code, § 2210(b).)
        (2) ☐ incurable insanity. (Fam. Code, § 2310(b).)   (3) ☐ unsound mind. (Fam. Code, § 2210(c).)
    c. ☐ nullity of void marriage based on   (4) ☐ fraud. (Fam. Code, § 2210(d).)
        (1) ☐ incestuous marriage. (Fam. Code, § 2200.)   (5) ☐ force. (Fam. Code, § 2210(e).)
        (2) ☐ bigamous marriage. (Fam. Code, § 2201.)   (6) ☐ physical incapacity. (Fam. Code, § 2210(f).)

7. Petitioner requests that the court grant the above relief and make injunctive (including restraining) and other orders as follows:

	Petitioner	Respondent	Joint	Other
a. Legal custody of children to	☐	☐	☐	☐
b. Physical custody of children to	☐	☐	☐	☐
c. Child visitation be granted to	☐	☐		☐

      As requested in form: ☐ FL-311 ☐ FL-312 ☐ FL-341(C) ☐ FL-341(D) ☐ FL-341(E) ☐ Attachment 7c
    d. ☐ Determination of parentage of any children born to the Petitioner and Respondent prior to the marriage.
    e. Attorney fees and costs payable by .... ☐ ☐
    f. Spousal support payable to (earnings assignment will be issued) .... ☐ ☐
    g. ☐ Terminate the court's jurisdiction (ability) to award spousal support to Respondent.
    h. ☐ Property rights be determined.
    i. ☐ Petitioner's former name be restored to (specify):
    j. ☐ Other (specify):

       ☐ Continued on Attachment 7j.

8. Child support– If there are minor children born to or adopted by the Petitioner and Respondent before or during this marriage, the court will make orders for the support of the children upon request and submission of financial forms by the requesting party. An earnings assignment may be issued without further notice. Any party required to pay support must pay interest on overdue amounts at the "legal" rate, which is currently 10 percent.

9. I HAVE READ THE RESTRAINING ORDERS ON THE BACK OF THE SUMMONS, AND I UNDERSTAND THAT THEY APPLY TO ME WHEN THIS PETITION IS FILED.

I declare under penalty of perjury under the laws of the State of California that the foregoing is true and correct.

Date:

_____
(TYPE OR PRINT NAME)   ▶ _____
                                 (SIGNATURE OF PETITIONER)

Date:

_____
(TYPE OR PRINT NAME)   ▶ _____
                               (SIGNATURE OF ATTORNEY FOR PETITIONER)

FL-103

<table>
<tr><td>ATTORNEY OR PARTY WITHOUT ATTORNEY (Name, State Bar number, and address):</td><td rowspan="3">FOR COURT USE ONLY</td></tr>
</table>

TELEPHONE NO. :	FAX NO. (Optional):
E-MAIL ADDRESS (Optional):	
ATTORNEY FOR (Name):	

SUPERIOR COURT OF CALIFORNIA, COUNTY OF

STREET ADDRESS:

MAILING ADDRESS:

CITY AND ZIP CODE:

BRANCH NAME:

DOMESTIC PARTNERSHIP OF

PETITIONER:

RESPONDENT:

PETITION FOR	CASE NUMBER:
☐ **Dissolution of Domestic Partnership**	
☐ **Legal Separation of Domestic Partnership**	
☐ **Nullity of Domestic Partnership** ☐ **AMENDED**	

1. STATISTICAL FACTS
   a. Date of registration of domestic partnership or equivalent:
   b. Date of separation:
   c. Time from date of registration of domestic partnership to date of separation (specify):   Years   Months

2. RESIDENCE (Partnerships established out of state only)
   a. ☐ Our domestic partnership was established in another state (specify state):
   b. ☐ Petitioner ☐ Respondent has been a resident of this state of California for at least six months and of this county for at least three months immediately preceding the filing of this Petition for Dissolution of Domestic Partnership.

3. DECLARATION REGARDING MINOR CHILDREN (include children of this relationship born prior to or during this domestic partnership or adopted during this domestic partnership):
   a. ☐ There are no minor children.
   b. ☐ The minor children are:

Child's name	Birthdate	Age	Sex

   ☐ Continued on Attachment 3b.
   c. If there are minor children of the petitioner and respondent, a completed Declaration Under Uniform Child Custody Jurisdiction and Enforcement Act (UCCJEA) (form FL-105) must be attached.

4. SEPARATE PROPERTY
   Petitioner requests that the assets and debts listed ☐ in Property Declaration (form FL-160) ☐ in Attachment 4
   ☐ below   be confirmed as separate property.

Item	Confirm to

NOTICE: You may redact (black out) social security numbers from any written material filed with the court in this case other than a form used to collect child or partner support.

Page 1 of 2

Form Adopted for Mandatory Use
Judicial Council of California
FL-103 [New January 1, 2005]

PETITION—DOMESTIC PARTNERSHIP
(Family Law)

Family Code, §§ 299, 2330;
Cal. Rules of Court, rule 5.28
www.courtinfo.ca.gov

DOMESTIC PARTNERSHIP OF (Last name, first name of each party):	CASE NUMBER:

5. DECLARATION REGARDING COMMUNITY AND QUASI-COMMUNITY ASSETS AND DEBTS AS CURRENTLY KNOWN
   a. ☐ There are no such assets or debts subject to disposition by the court in this proceeding.
   b. ☐ All such assets and debts are listed ☐ in *Property Declaration* (form FL-160) ☐ in Attachment 5b.
      ☐ below *(specify):*

6. **Petitioner requests**
   a. ☐ dissolution of the domestic partnership based on
      (1) ☐ irreconcilable differences. (Fam. Code, § 2310(a).)
      (2) ☐ incurable insanity. (Fam. Code, § 2310(b).)
   b. ☐ legal separation of the domestic partnership based on
      (1) ☐ irreconcilable differences. (Fam. Code, § 2310(a).)
      (2) ☐ incurable insanity. (Fam. Code, § 2310(b).)
   c. ☐ nullity of void domestic partnership based on
      (1) ☐ incest. (Fam. Code, § 2200.)
      (2) ☐ bigamy. (Fam. Code, § 2201.)
   d. ☐ nullity of voidable domestic partnership based on
      (1) ☐ petitioner's age at time of registration of domestic partnership. (Fam. Code, § 2210(a)
      (2) ☐ prior existing marriage or domestic partnership. (Fam. Code, § 2210(b).)
      (3) ☐ unsound mind. (Fam. Code, § 2210(c).)
      (4) ☐ fraud. (Fam. Code, § 2210(d).)
      (5) ☐ force. (Fam. Code, § 2210(e).)
      (6) ☐ physical incapacity. (Fam. Code, § 2210(f).)

7. **Petitioner requests** that the court grant the above relief and make injunctive (including restraining) and other orders as follows:

	Petitioner	Respondent	Joint	Other
a. Legal custody of children to	☐	☐	☐	☐
b. Physical custody of children to	☐	☐	☐	☐
c. Child visitation granted to	☐	☐		☐

   As requested in form: ☐ FL-311 ☐ FL-312 ☐ FL-341(C) ☐ FL-341(D) ☐ FL-341(E) ☐ Attachment 7c.
   d. ☐ Determination of parentage of any children born to the Petitioner and Respondent prior to the domestic partnership.

| e. Attorney fees and costs payable by .... | ☐ | ☐ | | |
| f. Partner support payable to .... | ☐ | ☐ | | |

   g. ☐ Terminate court's jurisdiction (ability) to award partner support to respondent.
   h. ☐ Property rights be determined.
   i. ☐ Petitioner's former name be restored to *(specify):*
   j. ☐ Other *(specify):*

      ☐ Continued on Attachment 7j.

8. **Child support**–If there are minor children who were born to or adopted by the petitioner and respondent before or during this domestic partnership, the court will make orders for the support of the children upon request and submission of financial forms by the requesting party. An earnings assignment may be issued without further notice. Any party required to pay support must pay interest on overdue amounts at the "legal" rate, which is currently 10 percent.

9. **I HAVE READ THE RESTRAINING ORDERS ON THE BACK OF THE SUMMONS, AND I UNDERSTAND THAT THEY APPLY TO ME WHEN THIS PETITION IS FILED.**

I declare under penalty of perjury under the laws of the State of California that the foregoing is true and correct.

Date:

_____
(TYPE OR PRINT NAME)

▶

_____
(SIGNATURE OF PETITIONER)

Date:

_____
(TYPE OR PRINT NAME)

▶

_____
(SIGNATURE OF ATTORNEY FOR PETITIONER)

NOTICE: Dissolution or legal separation may automatically cancel the rights of a domestic partner under the other domestic partner's will, trust, retirement plan, power of attorney, pay-on-death bank account, survivorship rights to any property owned in joint tenancy, and any other similar thing. It does not automatically cancel the right of a domestic partner as beneficiary of the other partner's life insurance policy. You should review these matters, as well as any credit cards, other credit accounts, insurance polices, retirement plans, and credit reports, to determine whether they should be changed or whether you should take any other actions. However, some changes may require the agreement of your partner or a court order (see Fam. Code, §§ 231–235).

    PETITION—DOMESTIC PARTNERSHIP
(Family Law)

ATTORNEY OR PARTY WITHOUT ATTORNEY *(Name, State Bar number, and address)*:

FOR COURT USE ONLY

TELEPHONE NO.:   FAX NO. *(Optional)*:
E-MAIL ADDRESS *(Optional)*:
ATTORNEY FOR *(Name)*:

SUPERIOR COURT OF CALIFORNIA, COUNTY OF

STREET ADDRESS:
MAILING ADDRESS:
CITY AND ZIP CODE:
BRANCH NAME:

PETITIONER:

RESPONDENT:

**DECLARATION UNDER UNIFORM CHILD CUSTODY
JURISDICTION AND ENFORCEMENT ACT (UCCJEA)**

CASE NUMBER:

1. **I am a party** to this proceeding to determine custody of a child.

2. ☐ My present address is not disclosed. It is confidential under Family Code section 3429. I have listed the address of the children presently residing with me as confidential.

3. *(Number):* _____ minor children are subject to this proceeding as follows:
   (Insert the information requested below. The residence information must be given for the last FIVE years.)

a. Child's name		Place of birth	Date of birth		Sex
Period of residence	Address	Person child lived with *(name and present address)*		Relationship	
to present	☐ Confidential				
to					
to					
to					

b. Child's name		Place of birth	Date of birth		Sex
☐ Residence information is the same as given above for child a. *(If NOT the same, provide the information below.)*					
Period of residence	Address	Person child lived with *(name and present address)*		Relationship	
to present	☐ Confidential				
to					
to					

c. ☐ Additional children are listed on Attachment 3c. *(Provide all requested information for additional children.)*

Form Approved for Optional Use
Judicial Council of California
FL-105/GC-120 [Rev. January 1, 2007]

**DECLARATION UNDER UNIFORM CHILD CUSTODY
JURISDICTION AND ENFORCEMENT ACT (UCCJEA)**

Family Code, § 3400 et seq.
Probate Code, §§ 1510(f), 1512
www.courtinfo.ca.gov

SHORT TITLE:	CASE NUMBER:

4. Have you participated as a party or a witness or in some other capacity in another litigation or custody proceeding, in California or elsewhere, concerning custody of a child subject to this proceeding?

   ☐ No   ☐ Yes   *(If yes, provide the following information):*

   a. Name of each child:

   b. I was a: ☐ party ☐ witness ☐ other *(specify):*

   c. Court *(specify name, state, location):*

   d. Court order or judgment *(date):*

5. Do you have information about a custody proceeding pending in a California court or any other court concerning a child in this case, other than that stated in item 4?

   ☐ No   ☐ Yes   *(If yes, provide the following information):*

   a. Name of each child:

   b. Nature of proceeding: ☐ dissolution or divorce ☐ guardianship ☐ adoption ☐ other *(specify):*

   c. Court *(specify name, state, location):*

   d. Status of proceeding:

6. ☐ One or more domestic violence restraining /protective orders are now in effect. (Attach a copy of the orders if you have one.) The orders are from the following court or courts *(specify county and state):*

   a. ☐ Criminal: County/state: _____   c. ☐ Juvenile: County/state: _____
      Case No. *(if known):* _____   Case No. *(if known):* _____

   b. ☐ Family: County/state: _____   d. ☐ Other: County/state: _____
      Case No. *(if known):* _____   Case No. *(if known):* _____

7. Do you know of any person who is not a party to this proceeding who has physical custody or claims to have custody of or visitation rights with any child in this case?

   ☐ No   ☐ Yes   *(If yes, provide the following information):*

a. Name and address of person	b. Name and address of person	c. Name and address of person
☐ Has physical custody ☐ Claims custody rights ☐ Claims visitation rights	☐ Has physical custody ☐ Claims custody rights ☐ Claims visitation rights	☐ Has physical custody ☐ Claims custody rights ☐ Claims visitation rights
Name of each child	Name of each child	Name of each child

I declare under penalty of perjury under the laws of the State of California that the foregoing is true and correct.

Date:

▶

_____   _____
(TYPE OR PRINT NAME)   (SIGNATURE OF DECLARANT)

8. ☐ Number of pages attached after this page: _____

NOTICE TO DECLARANT: You have a continuing duty to inform this court if you obtain any information about a custody proceeding in a California court or any other court concerning a child subject to this proceeding.

FL-117

ATTORNEY OR PARTY WITHOUT ATTORNEY *(Name, State Bar number, and address)*:	FOR COURT USE ONLY
TELEPHONE NO.: FAX NO. *(Optional)*: E–MAIL ADDRESS *(Optional)*: ATTORNEY FOR *(Name)*:	

SUPERIOR COURT OF CALIFORNIA, COUNTY OF
STREET ADDRESS:
MAILING ADDRESS:
CITY AND ZIP CODE:
BRANCH NAME:

PETITIONER:

RESPONDENT:

OTHER:

NOTICE AND ACKNOWLEDGMENT OF RECEIPT	CASE NUMBER:

To *(name of individual being served)*: _____

NOTICE

The documents identified below are being served on you by mail with this acknowledgment form. You must personally sign, or a person authorized by you must sign, this form to acknowledge receipt of the documents.

If the documents described below include a summons and you fail to complete and return this acknowledgment form to the sender within 20 days of the date of mailing, you will be liable for the reasonable expenses incurred after that date in serving you or attempting to serve you with these documents by any other methods permitted by law. If you return this form to the sender, service of a summons is deemed complete on the date you sign the acknowledgment of receipt below. This is **not** an answer to the action. If you do not agree with what is being requested, you must submit a completed *Response* form to the court within 30 calendar days.

Date of mailing: _____

▶

_____   _____
(TYPE OR PRINT NAME)   (SIGNATURE OF SENDER—MUST NOT BE A PARTY IN THIS CASE
                                                                   AND MUST BE 18 OR OLDER)

ACKNOWLEDGMENT OF RECEIPT
(To be completed by sender before mailing)

I agree I received the following:

a. ☐ Family Law: *Petition* (form FL-100), *Summons* (form FL-110), and blank *Response* (form FL-120)

b. ☐ Family Law—Domestic Partnership: *Petition—Domestic Partnership* (form FL-103), *Summons* (form FL-110), and blank *Response—Domestic Partnership* (form FL-123)

c. ☐ Uniform Parentage: *Petition to Establish Parental Relationship* (form FL-200), *Summons* (form FL-210), and blank *Response to Petition to Establish Parental Relationship* (form FL-220)

d. ☐ Custody and Support: *Petition for Custody and Support of Minor Children* (form FL-260), *Summons* (form FL-210), and blank *Response to Petition for Custody and Support of Minor Children* (form FL-270)

e. ☐

(1) ☐ Completed and blank *Declaration Under Uniform Child Custody Jurisdiction and Enforcement Act (UCCJEA)* (form FL-105)

(2) ☐ Completed and blank *Declaration of Disclosure* (form FL-140)

(3) ☐ Completed and blank *Schedule of Assets and Debts* (form FL-142)

(4) ☐ Completed and blank *Income and Expense Declaration* (form FL-150)

(5) ☐ Completed and blank *Financial Statement (Simplified)* (form FL-155)

(6) ☐ *Order to Show Cause* (form FL-300), *Application for Order and Supporting Declaration* (form FL-310), and blank *Responsive Declaration to Order to Show Cause or Notice of Motion* (form FL-320)

(7) ☐ Other *(specify)*:

(To be completed by recipient)
Date this acknowledgment is signed: _____

▶

_____   _____
(TYPE OR PRINT NAME)   (SIGNATURE OF PERSON ACKNOWLEDGING RECEIPT)

Page 1 of 1

NOTICE AND ACKNOWLEDGMENT OF RECEIPT
(Family Law)

Code of Civil Procedure, §§ 415.30, 417.10
www.courtinfo.ca.gov

This page intentionally left blank.

FL-140

ATTORNEY OR PARTY WITHOUT ATTORNEY *(Name and Address)*:	TELEPHONE NO.:
ATTORNEY FOR *(Name)*:	

SUPERIOR COURT OF CALIFORNIA, COUNTY OF
STREET ADDRESS:
MAILING ADDRESS:
CITY AND ZIP CODE:
BRANCH NAME:

PETITIONER:

RESPONDENT:

DECLARATION OF DISCLOSURE	CASE NUMBER:
☐ Petitioner's ☐ Preliminary	
☐ Respondent's ☐ Final	

DO NOT FILE WITH THE COURT

Both the preliminary and the final declaration of disclosure must be served on the other party with certain exceptions. Neither disclosure is filed with the court. A declaration stating service was made of the final declaration of disclosure must be filed with the court (see form FL-141).

A preliminary declaration of disclosure but not a final declaration of disclosure is required in the case of a summary dissolution (see Family Code section 2109) or in a default judgment (see Family Code section 2110) provided the default is not a stipulated judgment or a judgment based upon a marriage settlement agreement.

A declaration of disclosure is required in a nullity or legal separation action as well as in a dissolution action.

Attached are the following:

1. ☐ A completed *Schedule of Assets and Debts* (form FL-142).

2. ☐ A completed *Income and Expense Declaration* (form FL-150 (as applicable)).

3. ☐ A statement of all material facts and information regarding valuation of all assets that are community property or in which the community has an interest *(not a form)*.

4. ☐ A statement of all material facts and information regarding obligations for which the community is liable *(not a form)*.

5. ☐ An accurate and complete written disclosure of any investment opportunity, business opportunity, or other income-producing opportunity presented since the date of separation that results from any investment, significant business, or other income-producing opportunity from the date of marriage to the date of separation *(not a form)*.

I declare under penalty of perjury under the laws of the State of California that the foregoing is true and correct.

Date:

_____   ▶   _____
(TYPE OR PRINT NAME)   (SIGNATURE)

Page 1 of 1

Form Adopted for Mandatory Use
Judicial Council of California
FL-140 [Rev. January 1, 2003]

DECLARATION OF DISCLOSURE
(Family Law)

Family Code, §§ 2102, 2104, 2105,
2106, 2112
www.courtinfo.ca.gov

This page intentionally blank.

form 7   211

FL-142

ATTORNEY OR PARTY WITHOUT ATTORNEY (Name and Address):		TELEPHONE NO.:

ATTORNEY FOR (Name):

SUPERIOR COURT OF CALIFORNIA, COUNTY OF

PETITIONER:

RESPONDENT:

SCHEDULE OF ASSETS AND DEBTS ☐ Petitioner's ☐ Respondent's	CASE NUMBER:

— INSTRUCTIONS —

List all your known community and separate assets or debts. Include assets even if they are in the possession of another person, including your spouse. If you contend an asset or debt is separate, put P (for Petitioner) or R (for Respondent) in the first column (separate property) to indicate to whom you contend it belongs.

All values should be as of the date of signing the declaration unless you specify a different valuation date with the description. For additional space, use a continuation sheet numbered to show which item is being continued.

ITEM NO.	ASSETS DESCRIPTION	SEP. PROP	DATE ACQUIRED	CURRENT GROSS FAIR MARKET VALUE	AMOUNT OF MONEY OWED OR ENCUMBRANCE
1.	REAL ESTATE (Give street addresses and attach copies of deeds with legal descriptions and latest lender's statement.)			$	$
2.	HOUSEHOLD FURNITURE, FURNISHINGS, APPLIANCES (Identify.)				
3.	JEWELRY, ANTIQUES, ART, COIN COLLECTIONS, etc. (Identify.)				

Page 1 of 4

ITEM NO.	ASSETS DESCRIPTION	SEP. PROP	DATE ACQUIRED	CURRENT GROSS FAIR MARKET VALUE	AMOUNT OF MONEY OWED OR ENCUMBRANCE
				$	$
4.	VEHICLES, BOATS, TRAILERS (Describe and attach copy of title document.)				
5.	SAVINGS ACCOUNTS (Account name, account number, bank, and branch. Attach copy of latest statement.)				
6.	CHECKING ACCOUNTS (Account name and number, bank, and branch. Attach copy of latest statement.)				
7.	CREDIT UNION, OTHER DEPOSIT ACCOUNTS (Account name and number, bank, and branch. Attach copy of latest statement.)				
8.	CASH (Give location.)				
9.	TAX REFUND				
10.	LIFE INSURANCE WITH CASH SURRENDER OR LOAN VALUE (Attach copy of declaration page for each policy.)				

SCHEDULE OF ASSETS AND DEBTS
(Family Law)

ITEM NO.	ASSETS DESCRIPTION	SEP. PROP	DATE ACQUIRED	CURRENT GROSS FAIR MARKET VALUE	AMOUNT OF MONEY OWED OR ENCUMBRANCE
				$	$
11.	STOCKS, BONDS, SECURED NOTES, MUTUAL FUNDS (Give certificate number and attach copy of the certificate or copy of latest statement.)				
12.	RETIREMENT AND PENSIONS (Attach copy of latest summary plan documents and latest benefit statement.)				
13.	PROFIT - SHARING, ANNUITIES, IRAS, DEFERRED COMPENSATION (Attach copy of latest statement.)				
14.	ACCOUNTS RECEIVABLE AND UNSECURED NOTES (Attach copy of each.)				
15.	PARTNERSHIPS AND OTHER BUSINESS INTERESTS (Attach copy of most current K-1 form and Schedule C.)				
16.	OTHER ASSETS				
17.	TOTAL ASSETS FROM CONTINUATION SHEET				
18.	TOTAL ASSETS			$	$

SCHEDULE OF ASSETS AND DEBTS
(Family Law)

ITEM NO.	DEBTS—SHOW TO WHOM OWED	SEP. PROP.	TOTAL OWING	DATE INCURRED
19. STUDENT LOANS (Give details.)			$	
20. TAXES (Give details.)				
21. SUPPORT ARREARAGES (Attach copies of orders and statements.)				
22. LOANS—UNSECURED (Give bank name and loan number and attach copy of latest statement.)				
23. CREDIT CARDS (Give creditor's name and address and the account number. Attach copy of latest statement.)				
24. OTHER DEBTS (Specify.):				
25. TOTAL DEBTS FROM CONTINUATION SHEET				
26. TOTAL DEBTS			$	

27. ☐ (Specify number):_____ pages are attached as continuation sheets.

I declare under penalty of perjury under the laws of the State of California that the foregoing is true and correct.

Date:

_____   ▶ _____
(TYPE OR PRINT NAME)   (SIGNATURE OF DECLARANT)

SCHEDULE OF ASSETS AND DEBTS
(Family Law)

FL-150

ATTORNEY OR PARTY WITHOUT ATTORNEY *(Name, State Bar number, and address)*:	FOR COURT USE ONLY
TELEPHONE NO.: E-MAIL ADDRESS *(Optional)*: ATTORNEY FOR *(Name)*:	

SUPERIOR COURT OF CALIFORNIA, COUNTY OF

STREET ADDRESS:

MAILING ADDRESS:

CITY AND ZIP CODE:

BRANCH NAME:

PETITIONER/PLAINTIFF:

RESPONDENT/DEFENDANT:

OTHER PARENT/CLAIMANT:

INCOME AND EXPENSE DECLARATION	CASE NUMBER:

1. **Employment** *(Give information on your current job or, if you're unemployed, your most recent job.)*

   Attach copies of your pay stubs for last two months (black out social security numbers).

   a. Employer:

   b. Employer's address:

   c. Employer's phone number:

   d. Occupation:

   e. Date job started:

   f. If unemployed, date job ended:

   g. I work about _____ hours per week.

   h. I get paid $ _____ gross (before taxes) ☐ per month ☐ per week ☐ per hour.

(If you have more than one job, attach an 8½-by-11-inch sheet of paper and list the same information as above for your other jobs. Write "Question 1—Other Jobs" at the top.)

2. **Age and education**

   a. My age is *(specify)*:

   b. I have completed high school or the equivalent: ☐ Yes ☐ No   If no, highest grade completed *(specify)*:

   c. Number of years of college completed *(specify)*:   ☐ Degree(s) obtained *(specify)*:

   d. Number of years of graduate school completed *(specify)*:   ☐ Degree(s) obtained *(specify)*:

   e. I have: ☐ professional/occupational license(s) *(specify)*:
      ☐ vocational training *(specify)*:

3. **Tax information**

   a. ☐ I last filed taxes for tax year *(specify year)*:

   b. My tax filing status is ☐ single ☐ head of household ☐ married, filing separately
      ☐ married, filing jointly with *(specify name)*:

   c. I file state tax returns in ☐ California ☐ other *(specify state)*:

   d. I claim the following number of exemptions (including myself) on my taxes *(specify)*:

4. **Other party's income.** I estimate the gross monthly income (before taxes) of the other party in this case at *(specify)*: $
   This estimate is based on *(explain)*:

(If you need more space to answer any questions on this form, attach an 8½-by-11-inch sheet of paper and write the question number before your answer.) Number of pages attached: _____

I declare under penalty of perjury under the laws of the State of California that the information contained on all pages of this form and any attachments is true and correct.

Date:

▶

_____   _____
(TYPE OR PRINT NAME)   (SIGNATURE OF DECLARANT)

Page 1 of 4

Form Adopted for Mandatory Use
 Judicial Council of California
 FL-150 [Rev. January 1, 2007]

INCOME AND EXPENSE DECLARATION

Family Code, §§ 2030–2032,
 2100–2113, 3552, 3620–3634,
 4050–4076, 4300–4339 <br> www.courtinfo.ca.gov

	CASE NUMBER:
PETITIONER/PLAINTIFF:	
RESPONDENT/DEFENDANT:	
OTHER PARENT/CLAIMANT:	

Attach copies of your pay stubs for the last two months and proof of any other income. Take a copy of your latest federal tax return to the court hearing. *(Black out your social security number on the pay stub and tax return.)*

5. **Income** *(For average monthly, add up all the income you received in each category in the last 12 months and divide the total by 12.)*

    Last month   Average monthly

   a. Salary or wages (gross, before taxes). . . . . $_____ _____

   b. Overtime (gross, before taxes) . . . . $_____ _____

   c. Commissions or bonuses. . . . . $_____ _____

   d. Public assistance (for example: TANF, SSI, GA/GR) ☐ currently receiving . . . . $_____ _____

   e. Spousal support ☐ from this marriage ☐ from a different marriage . . . . $_____ _____

   f. Partner support ☐ from this domestic partnership ☐ from a different domestic partnership $_____ _____

   g. Pension/retirement fund payments. . . . . $_____ _____

   h. Social security retirement (not SSI) . . . . $_____ _____

   i. Disability: ☐ Social security (not SSI) ☐ State disability (SDI) ☐ Private insurance . $_____ _____

   j. Unemployment compensation . . . . $_____ _____

   k. Workers' compensation . . . . $_____ _____

   l. Other (military BAQ, royalty payments, etc.) *(specify):* . . . . $_____ _____

6. **Investment income** *(Attach a schedule showing gross receipts less cash expenses for each piece of property.)*

   a. Dividends/interest. . . . . $_____ _____

   b. Rental property income . . . . $_____ _____

   c. Trust income. . . . . $_____ _____

   d. Other *(specify):* . . . . $_____ _____

7. **Income from self-employment, after business expenses for all businesses.** . . . . $_____ _____

   I am the ☐ owner/sole proprietor ☐ business partner ☐ other *(specify):*

   Number of years in this business *(specify):*

   Name of business *(specify):*

   Type of business *(specify):*

   Attach a profit and loss statement for the last two years or a Schedule C from your last federal tax return. Black out your social security number. If you have more than one business, provide the information above for each of your businesses.

8. ☐ **Additional income.** I received one-time money (lottery winnings, inheritance, etc.) in the last 12 months *(specify source and amount):*

9. ☐ **Change in income.** My financial situation has changed significantly over the last 12 months because *(specify):*

10. **Deductions**

    Last month

   a. Required union dues . . . . $_____

   b. Required retirement payments (not social security, FICA, 401(k), or IRA). . . . . $_____

   c. Medical, hospital, dental, and other health insurance premiums *(total monthly amount)*. . . . . $_____

   d. Child support that I pay for children from other relationships. . . . . $_____

   e. Spousal support that I pay by court order from a different marriage. . . . . $_____

   f. Partner support that I pay by court order from a different domestic partnership . . . . $_____

   g. Necessary job-related expenses not reimbursed by my employer *(attach explanation labeled "Question 10g")* . . . . . $_____

11. **Assets**

    Total

   a. Cash and checking accounts, savings, credit union, money market, and other deposit accounts . . . . $_____

   b. Stocks, bonds, and other assets I could easily sell . . . . $_____

   c. All other property, ☐ real and ☐ personal *(estimate fair market value minus the debts you owe)* . . . . $_____

PETITIONER/PLAINTIFF:	CASE NUMBER:
RESPONDENT/DEFENDANT:	
OTHER PARENT/CLAIMANT:	

12. The following people live with me:

Name	Age	How the person is related to me? *(ex: son)*	That person's gross monthly income	Pays some of the household expenses?
a.				☐ Yes ☐ No
b.				☐ Yes ☐ No
c.				☐ Yes ☐ No
d.				☐ Yes ☐ No
e.				☐ Yes ☐ No

13. Average monthly expenses   ☐ Estimated expenses   ☐ Actual expenses   ☐ Proposed needs

a. Home:

   (1) ☐ Rent or ☐ mortgage... $ _____

   If mortgage:

     (a) average principal: $ _____

     (b) average interest: $ _____

   (2) Real property taxes . . . . $ _____

   (3) Homeowner's or renter's insurance (if not included above) . . . . $ _____

   (4) Maintenance and repair . . . . $ _____

b. Health-care costs not paid by insurance. . . $ _____

c. Child care . . . . $ _____

d. Groceries and household supplies. . . . . . $ _____

e. Eating out. . . . . $ _____

f. Utilities (gas, electric, water, trash) . . . . . $ _____

g. Telephone, cell phone, and e-mail . . . .$ _____

h. Laundry and cleaning . . . . $ _____

i. Clothes . . . . $ _____

j. Education . . . . $ _____

k. Entertainment, gifts, and vacation. . . . . . . $ _____

l. Auto expenses and transportation (insurance, gas, repairs, bus, etc.) . . . . $ _____

m. Insurance (life, accident, etc.; do not include auto, home, or health insurance). . . $ _____

n. Savings and investments. . . . . $ _____

o. Charitable contributions. . . . . $ _____

p. Monthly payments listed in item 14 *(itemize below in 14 and insert total here)*. . $ _____

q. Other *(specify):* . . . . $ _____

r. **TOTAL EXPENSES** (a–q) *(do not add in the amounts in a(1)(a) and (b))* $ _____

s. **Amount of expenses paid by others** $ _____

14. Installment payments and debts not listed above

Paid to	For	Amount	Balance	Date of last payment
		$	$	
		$	$	
		$	$	
		$	$	
		$	$	
		$	$	

15. Attorney fees *(This is required if either party is requesting attorney fees.):*

a. To date, I have paid my attorney this amount for fees and costs *(specify):* $

b. The source of this money was *(specify):*

c. I still owe the following fees and costs to my attorney *(specify total owed):* $

d. My attorney's hourly rate is *(specify):* $

I confirm this fee arrangement.

Date:

_____
(TYPE OR PRINT NAME OF ATTORNEY)

▶

_____
(SIGNATURE OF ATTORNEY)

FL-150

PETITIONER/PLAINTIFF:	CASE NUMBER:
RESPONDENT/DEFENDANT:	
OTHER PARENT/CLAIMANT:	

CHILD SUPPORT INFORMATION
(NOTE: Fill out this page only if your case involves child support.)

16. **Number of children**
    a. I have *(specify number):*   children under the age of 18 with the other parent in this case.
    b. The children spend   percent of their time with me and   percent of their time with the other parent.
    (If you're not sure about percentage or it has not been agreed on, please describe your parenting schedule here.)

17. **Children's health-care expenses**
    a. ☐ I do   ☐ I do not   have health insurance available to me for the children through my job.
    b. Name of insurance company:
    c. Address of insurance company:

    d. The monthly cost for the **children's** health insurance is or would be *(specify):* $
       (Do not include the amount your employer pays.)

18. **Additional expenses for the children in this case**   Amount per month
    a. Child care so I can work or get job training. . . . . $ _____
    b. Children's health care not covered by insurance . . . . $ _____
    c. Travel expenses for visitation . . . . $ _____
    d. Children's educational or other special needs *(specify below):* . . . . $ _____

19. **Special hardships.** I ask the court to consider the following special financial circumstances

(attach documentation of any item listed here, including court orders):	Amount per month	For how many months?
a. Extraordinary health expenses not included in 18b.	$ _____	_____
b. Major losses not covered by insurance (examples: fire, theft, other insured loss)	$ _____	_____
c. (1) Expenses for my minor children who are from other relationships and are living with me	$ _____	_____

       (2) Names and ages of those children *(specify):*

       (3) Child support I receive for those children. . . . . $ _____

    The expenses listed in a, b, and c create an extreme financial hardship because *(explain):*

20. **Other information I want the court to know concerning support in my case** *(specify):*

INCOME AND EXPENSE DECLARATION

FL-141

ATTORNEY OR PARTY WITHOUT ATTORNEY *(Name, state bar number, and address):*	*FOR COURT USE ONLY*
TELEPHONE NO.: FAX NO.:	
ATTORNEY FOR *(Name):*	

SUPERIOR COURT OF CALIFORNIA, COUNTY OF
STREET ADDRESS:
MAILING ADDRESS:
CITY AND ZIP CODE:
BRANCH NAME:

PETITIONER:

RESPONDENT:

DECLARATION REGARDING SERVICE OF DECLARATION OF DISCLOSURE AND INCOME AND EXPENSE DECLARATION	CASE NUMBER:
☐ **Petitioner's** ☐ **Preliminary** ☐ **Respondent's** ☐ **Final**	

1. I am the ☐ Attorney for ☐ Petitioner ☐ Respondent in this matter.

2. ☐ Petitioner's ☐ Respondent's *Preliminary Declaration of Disclosure* and *Income and Expense Declaration* was served on: ☐ Attorney for ☐ Petitioner ☐ Respondent by: ☐ personal service ☐ mail ☐ other *(specify):*

   on *(date):*

3. ☐ Petitioner's ☐ Respondent's *Final Declaration of Disclosure* and *Income and Expense Declaration* was served on: ☐ Attorney for ☐ Petitioner ☐ Respondent by: ☐ personal service ☐ mail ☐ other *(specify):*

   on *(date):*

4. ☐ Service of the *Final Declaration of Disclosure* has been waived under Family Code section 2105, subdivision (d).

I declare under penalty of perjury under the laws of the State of California that the foregoing is true and correct.

Date:

▶

_____
(TYPE OR PRINT NAME)

_____
(SIGNATURE)

Note:
File this document with the court.
Do not file a copy of either the *Preliminary* or *Final Declaration of
***Disclosure* with this document.**

Form Adopted for Mandatory Use
Judicial Council of California
FL-141 [Rev. January 1, 2003]

**DECLARATION REGARDING SERVICE OF
DECLARATION OF DISCLOSURE
(Family Law)**

Family Code, §§ 2104, 2106, 2112
www.courtinfo.ca.gov

This page intentionally blank.

FL-155

Your name and address or attorney's name and address:	TELEPHONE NO.:	*FOR COURT USE ONLY*

ATTORNEY FOR *(Name)*:

SUPERIOR COURT OF CALIFORNIA, COUNTY OF

STREET ADDRESS:

MAILING ADDRESS:

CITY AND ZIP CODE:

BRANCH NAME:

PETITIONER/PLAINTIFF:

RESPONDENT/DEFENDANT:

OTHER PARENT:

FINANCIAL STATEMENT (SIMPLIFIED)	CASE NUMBER:

> **NOTICE: Read page 2 to find out if you qualify to use this form and how to use it.**

1. a. ☐ My only source of income is TANF, SSI, or GA/GR.
   b. ☐ I have applied for TANF, SSI, or GA/GR.
2. I am the parent of the following number of natural or adopted children from this relationship .... _____
3. a. The children from this relationship are with me this amount of time .... _____ %
   b. The children from this relationship are with the other parent this amount of time .... _____ %
   c. Our arrangement for custody and visitation is *(specify, using extra sheet if necessary)*:

4. My tax filing status is: ☐ single ☐ married filing jointly ☐ head of household ☐ married filing separately.
5. My current gross income *(before taxes)* per month is .... $ _____

Attach 1 copy of pay stubs for last 2 months here (cross out social security numbers)

This income comes from the following:

☐ Salary/wages: Amount before taxes per month........................... $ _____
☐ Retirement: Amount before taxes per month............................ $ _____
☐ Unemployment compensation: Amount per month .... $ _____
☐ Workers' compensation: Amount per month .... $ _____
☐ Social security: ☐ SSI ☐ Other   Amount per month .... $ _____
☐ Disability: Amount per month .... $ _____
☐ Interest income (from bank accounts or other): Amount per month .... $ _____

I have no income other than as stated in this paragraph.

6. I pay the following monthly expenses for the children in this case:
   a. ☐ Day care or preschool to allow me to work or go to school .... $ _____
   b. ☐ Health care not paid for by insurance .... $ _____
   c. ☐ School, education, tuition, or other special needs of the child .... $ _____
   d. ☐ Travel expenses for visitation .... $ _____

7. ☐ There are *(specify number)* _____ other minor children of mine living with me. Their monthly expenses
   that I pay are .... $ _____

8. I spend the following average monthly amounts *(please attach proof)*:
   a. ☐ Job-related expenses that are not paid by my employer *(specify reasons for expenses on separate sheet)* $ _____
   b. ☐ Required union dues .... $ _____
   c. ☐ Required retirement payments (not social security, FICA, 401k or IRA) .... $ _____
   d. ☐ Health insurance costs .... $ _____
   e. ☐ Child support I am paying for other minor children of mine who are not living with me .... $ _____
   f. ☐ Spousal support I am paying because of a court order for another relationship............. $ _____
   g. ☐ Monthly housing costs: ☐ rent or ☐ mortgage .... $ _____
      If mortgage: interest payments $ _____ real property taxes $ _____

9. Information concerning ☐ my current employment ☐ my most recent employment:
   Employer:
   Address:
   Telephone number:
   My occupation:
   Date work started:
   Date work stopped *(if applicable)*:   What was your gross income *(before taxes)* before work stopped?:

Page 1 of 2

Form Approved for Optional Use
Judicial Council of California
FL-155 [Rev. January 1, 2004]

FINANCIAL STATEMENT (SIMPLIFIED)

Family Code, § 4068(b)
www.courtinfo.ca.gov

222

10. My estimate of the other party's gross monthly income *(before taxes)* is . . . . $ _____

11. My current spouse's monthly income *(before taxes)* is . . . . $ _____

12. Other information I want the court to know concerning child support in my case *(attach extra sheet with the information)*.

13. [ ] I am attaching a copy of page 3 of form FL-150, *Income and Expense Declaration* showing my expenses.

I declare under penalty of perjury under the laws of the State of California that the information contained on all pages of this form and any attachments is true and correct.

Date:

_____ ▶ _____

(TYPE OR PRINT NAME) (SIGNATURE OF DECLARANT)

[ ] PETITIONER/PLAINTIFF [ ] RESPONDENT/DEFENDANT

INSTRUCTIONS

Step 1: Are you eligible to use this form? *If your answer is YES to any of the following questions, you may NOT use this form:*

• Are you asking for spousal support (alimony) or a change in spousal support?
• Is your spouse or former spouse asking for spousal support (alimony) or a change in spousal support?
• Are you asking the other party to pay your attorney fees?
• Is the other party asking you to pay his or her attorney fees?
• Do you receive money (income) from any source other than the following?

   • Welfare (such as TANF, GR, or GA)   • Interest
   • Salary or wages   • Workers' compensation
   • Disability   • Social security
   • Unemployment   • Retirement

• Are you self-employed?

If you are eligible to use this form and choose to do so, you do not need to complete the *Income and Expense Declaration* (form FL-150). Even if you are eligible to use this form, you may choose instead to use the *Income and Expense Declaration* (form FL-150).

Step 2: Make 2 copies of each of your pay stubs for the last two months. If you received money from other than wages or salary, include copies of the pay stub received with that money.

Privacy notice: If you wish, you may cross out your social security number if it appears on the pay stub, other payment notice or your tax return

Step 3: Make 2 copies of your most recent federal income tax form.

Step 4: Complete this form with the required information. Type the form if possible or complete it neatly and clearly in black ink. If you need additional room, please use plain or lined paper, 8½-by-11", and staple to this form.

Step 5: Make 2 copies of each side of this completed form and any attached pages.

Step 6: Serve a copy on the other party. Have someone other than yourself mail to the attorney for the other party, the other party, and the local child support agency, if they are handling the case, 1 copy of this form, 1 copy of each of your stubs for the last two months, and 1 copy of your most recent federal income tax return.

Step 7: File the original with the court. Staple this form with 1 copy of each of your pay stubs for the last two months. Take this document and give it to the clerk of the court. Check with your local court about how to submit your return.

Step 8: Keep the remaining copies of the documents for your file.

Step 9: Take the copy of your latest federal income tax return to the court hearing.

It is very important that you attend the hearings scheduled for this case. If you do not attend a hearing, the court may make an order without considering the information you want the court to consider.

FL-130

ATTORNEY OR PARTY WITHOUT ATTORNEY *(Name, State Bar number, and address)*:	FOR COURT USE ONLY
TELEPHONE NO.: FAX NO. *(Optional)*: E-MAIL ADDRESS *(Optional)*: ATTORNEY FOR *(Name)*:	

SUPERIOR COURT OF CALIFORNIA, COUNTY OF
   STREET ADDRESS:
   MAILING ADDRESS:
   CITY AND ZIP CODE:
   BRANCH NAME:

PETITIONER:

RESPONDENT:

APPEARANCE, STIPULATIONS, AND WAIVERS	CASE NUMBER:

1. **Appearance by respondent** *(you must choose one)*:
   a. ☐ By filing this form, the respondent makes a general appearance.
   b. ☐ The respondent has previously made a general appearance.
   c. ☐ The respondent is a member of the military services of the United States of America and waives all rights under the Servicemembers Civil Relief Act (50 U.S.C. Appen. § 501 et seq.). No appearance fee is required.

2. **Agreements, stipulations, and waivers** *(choose all that apply)*:
   a. ☐ The parties agree that this cause may be decided as an uncontested matter.
   b. ☐ The parties waive their rights to notice of trial, a statement of decision, a motion for new trial, and the right to appeal.
   c. ☐ This matter may be decided by a commissioner sitting as a temporary judge.
   d. ☐ We have a written agreement, or a stipulation for judgment will be submitted to the court.
   e. ☐ None of these agreements or waivers will apply unless the court approves the stipulation for judgment or incorporates the written settlement agreement into the judgment.
   f. ☐ This is a parentage case, and both parties have signed an *Advisement and Waiver of Rights Re: Establishment of Parental Relationship* (form FL-235) or its equivalent.

3. **Other** *(specify)*:

Date: _____

_____
(TYPE OR PRINT NAME)

▶ _____
(SIGNATURE OF PETITIONER)

Date: _____

_____
(TYPE OR PRINT NAME)

▶ _____
(SIGNATURE OF RESPONDENT)

Date: _____

_____
(TYPE OR PRINT NAME)

▶ _____
(SIGNATURE OF ATTORNEY FOR PETITIONER)

Date: _____

_____
(TYPE OR PRINT NAME)

▶ _____
(SIGNATURE OF ATTORNEY FOR RESPONDENT)

Page 1 of 1

APPEARANCE, STIPULATIONS, AND WAIVERS
(Family Law—Uniform Parentage—Custody and Support)

www.courtinfo.ca.gov

This page intentionally blank.

FL-165

ATTORNEY OR PARTY WITHOUT ATTORNEY (Name, State Bar number, and address):	FOR COURT USE ONLY
TELEPHONE NO.: FAX NO. (Optional):	
E-MAIL ADDRESS (Optional):	
ATTORNEY FOR (Name):	

SUPERIOR COURT OF CALIFORNIA, COUNTY OF

STREET ADDRESS:

MAILING ADDRESS:

CITY AND ZIP CODE:

BRANCH NAME:

PETITIONER:

RESPONDENT:

REQUEST TO ENTER DEFAULT	CASE NUMBER:

1. To the clerk: Please enter the default of the respondent who has failed to respond to the petition.

2. A completed Income and Expense Declaration (form FL-150) or Financial Statement (Simplified) (form FL-155)
   ☐ is attached ☐ is not attached.
   A completed Property Declaration (form FL-160) ☐ is attached ☐ is not attached
   because (check at least one of the following):
   (a) ☐ there have been no changes since the previous filing.
   (b) ☐ the issues subject to disposition by the court in this proceeding are the subject of a written agreement.
   (c) ☐ there are no issues of child, spousal, or partner support or attorney fees and costs subject to determination by the court.
   (d) ☐ the petition does not request money, property, costs, or attorney fees. (Fam. Code, § 2330.5.)
   (e) ☐ there are no issues of division of community property.
   (f) ☐ this is an action to establish parental relationship.

Date:

_____   ▶   _____
(TYPE OR PRINT NAME)   (SIGNATURE OF [ATTORNEY FOR] PETITIONER)

3. Declaration
   a. ☐ No mailing is required because service was by publication or posting and the address of the respondent remains unknown.
   b. ☐ A copy of this Request to Enter Default, including any attachments and an envelope with sufficient postage, was provided to the court clerk, with the envelope addressed as follows (address of the respondent's attorney or, if none, the respondent's last known address):

I declare under penalty of perjury under the laws of the State of California that the foregoing is true and correct.

Date:

_____   ▶   _____
(TYPE OR PRINT NAME)   (SIGNATURE OF DECLARANT)

FOR COURT USE ONLY
☐ Request to Enter Default mailed to the respondent or the respondent's attorney on (date):
☐ Default entered as requested on (date):
☐ Default not entered. Reason:
Clerk, by _____ , Deputy

Page 1 of 2

Form Adopted for Mandatory Use	REQUEST TO ENTER DEFAULT	Code of Civil Procedure, §§ 585, 587;
Judicial Council of California	(Family Law—Uniform Parentage)	Family Code, § 2335.5
FL-165 [Rev. January 1, 2005]		www.courtinfo.ca.gov

CASE NAME (Last name, first name of each party):	CASE NUMBER:

4. Memorandum of costs

    a. ☐ Costs and disbursements are waived.

    b. Costs and disbursements are listed as follows:

        (1) ☐ Clerk's fees .... $............................

        (2) ☐ Process server's fees .... $............................

        (3) ☐ Other (specify): .... $............................

        .... $............................

        .... $............................

        .... $ _____

        TOTAL .... $............................

    c. I am the attorney, agent, or party who claims these costs. To the best of my knowledge and belief, the foregoing items of cost are correct and have been necessarily incurred in this cause or proceeding.

I declare under penalty of perjury under the laws of the State of California that the foregoing is true and correct.

Date:

_____   ▶   _____
(TYPE OR PRINT NAME)   (SIGNATURE OF DECLARANT)

5. Declaration of nonmilitary status.   The respondent is not in the military service of the United States as defined in section 511 et seq. of the Servicemembers Civil Relief Act (50 U.S.C. Appen. § 501 et seq.), and is not entitled to the benefits of such act.

I declare under penalty of perjury under the laws of the State of California that the foregoing is true and correct.

Date:

_____   ▶   _____
(TYPE OR PRINT NAME)   (SIGNATURE OF DECLARANT)

REQUEST TO ENTER DEFAULT
(Family Law—Uniform Parentage)

FL-170

ATTORNEY OR PARTY WITHOUT ATTORNEY *(Name, State Bar number, and address)*:	FOR COURT USE ONLY
TELEPHONE NO.: FAX NO. *(Optional)*: E-MAIL ADDRESS *(Optional)*: ATTORNEY FOR *(Name)*:	

SUPERIOR COURT OF CALIFORNIA, COUNTY OF
STREET ADDRESS: MAILING ADDRESS: CITY AND ZIP CODE: BRANCH NAME:

PETITIONER:

RESPONDENT:

DECLARATION FOR DEFAULT OR UNCONTESTED ☐ **DISSOLUTION** ☐ **LEGAL SEPARATION**	CASE NUMBER:

(NOTE: Items 1 through 16 apply to both dissolution and legal separation proceedings.)

1. I declare that if I appeared in court and were sworn, I would testify to the truth of the facts in this declaration.

2. I agree that my case will be proven by this declaration and that I will not appear before the court unless I am ordered by the court to do so.

3. All the information in the ☐ *Petition* ☐ *Response* is true and correct.

4. **Default or uncontested** *(Check a or b.)*
   - a. ☐ The default of the respondent was entered or is being requested, and I am not seeking any relief not requested in the petition. **OR**
   - b. ☐ The parties have agreed that the matter may proceed as an uncontested matter without notice, and the agreement is attached or is incorporated in the attached settlement agreement or stipulated judgment.

5. **Settlement agreement** *(Check a or b.)*
   - a. ☐ The parties have entered into ☐ **an agreement** ☐ **a stipulated judgment** regarding their property their marriage or domestic partnership rights, including support, the original of which is or has been submitted to the court. I request that the court approve the agreement. **OR**
   - b. ☐ **There is no agreement or stipulated judgment,** and the following statements are true *(check at least one, including item (2) if a community estate exists)*:
     - (1) ☐ There are no community or quasi-community assets or community debts to be disposed of by the court.
     - (2) ☐ The community and quasi-community assets and debts are listed on the attached **completed** current *Property Declaration* (form FL-160), which includes an estimate of the value of the assets and debts that I propose to be distributed to each party. The division in the proposed *Judgment (Family Law)* (form FL-180) is a fair and equal division of the property and debts, or if there is a negative estate, the debts are assigned fairly and equitably.

6. **Declaration of disclosure** *(Check a, b, or c.)*
   - a. ☐ Both the petitioner and respondent have filed, or are filing concurrently, a *Declaration Regarding Service of Declaration of Disclosure* (form FL-141) and an *Income and Expense Declaration* (form FL-150).
   - b. ☐ This matter is proceeding by default. I am the petitioner in this action and have filed a proof of service of the preliminary *Declaration of Disclosure* (form FL-140) with the court. I hereby waive receipt of the final *Declaration of Disclosure* (form FL-140) from the respondent.
   - c. ☐ This matter is proceeding as an uncontested action. Service of the final *Declaration of Disclosure* (form FL-140) is mutually waived by both parties. A waiver provision executed by both parties under penalty of perjury is contained in the settlement agreement or proposed judgment or another, separate stipulation.

7. ☐ **Child custody** should be ordered as set forth in the proposed *Judgment (Family Law)* (form FL-180).

8. ☐ **Child visitation** should be ordered as set forth in the proposed *Judgment (Family Law)* (form FL-180).

9. **Spousal, partner, and family support** *(If a support order or attorney fees are requested, submit a completed* Income and Expense Declaration *(form FL-150) unless a current form is on file. Include your best estimate of the other party's income. Check at least one of the following.)*
   - a. ☐ I knowingly give up forever any right to receive spousal or partner support.
   - b. ☐ I ask the court to reserve jurisdiction to award spousal or partner support in the future to *(name)*:
   - c. ☐ Spousal support should be ordered as set forth in the proposed *Judgment (Family Law)* (form FL-180).
   - d. ☐ Family support should be ordered as set forth in the proposed *Judgment (Family Law)* (form FL-180).

Form Adopted for Mandatory Use Judicial Council of California FL-170 [Rev. January 1, 2007]	**DECLARATION FOR DEFAULT OR UNCONTESTED** **DISSOLUTION or LEGAL SEPARATION** **(Family Law)**	Family Code, § 2336 *www.courtinfo.ca.gov*

PETITIONER:	CASE NUMBER:
RESPONDENT:	

10. ☐ **Child support** should be ordered as set forth in the proposed *Judgment (Family Law)* (form FL-180).

11. a. I ☐ am receiving ☐ am not receiving ☐ intend to apply for public assistance for the child or children listed in the proposed order.

   b. To the best of my knowledge, the other party ☐ is ☐ is not receiving public assistance.

12. ☐ The petitioner ☐ respondent is presently receiving public assistance, and all support should be made payable to the local child support agency at the address set forth in the proposed judgment. A representative of the local child support agency has signed the proposed judgment.

13. If there are minor children, check and complete item a and item b or c:

   a. My gross (before taxes) monthly income is *(specify)*: $

   b. ☐ The estimated gross monthly income of the other party is *(specify)*: $

   c. ☐ I have no knowledge of the estimated monthly income of the other party for the following reasons *(specify)*:

   d. ☐ I request that this order be based on the ☐ petitioner's ☐ respondent's earning ability. The facts in support of my estimate of earning ability are *(specify)*:

   ☐ Continued on Attachment 13d.

14. ☐ **Parentage** of the children of the petitioner and respondent born prior to their marriage or domestic partnership should be ordered as set forth in the proposed *Judgment (Family Law)* (form FL-180). A declaration regarding parentage is attached.

15. ☐ **Attorney fees** should be ordered as set forth in the proposed *Judgment (Family Law)* (form FL-180).

16. ☐ The petitioner ☐ respondent requests restoration of his or her former name as set forth in the proposed *Judgment (Family Law)* (form FL-180).

17. There are irreconcilable differences that have led to the irremediable breakdown of the marriage or domestic partnership, and there is no possibility of saving the marriage or domestic partnership through counseling or other means.

18. This declaration may be reviewed by a commissioner sitting as a temporary judge, who may determine whether to grant this request or require my appearance under Family Code section 2336.

STATEMENTS IN THIS BOX APPLY ONLY TO DISSOLUTIONS—Items 19 through 21

19. If this is a dissolution of marriage or of a domestic partnership created in another state, the petitioner and/or the respondent has been a resident of this county for at least three months and of the state of California for at least six months continuously and immediately preceding the date of the filing of the petition for dissolution of marriage or domestic partnership.

20. I ask that the court grant the request for a judgment for dissolution of marriage or domestic partnership based upon irreconcilable differences and that the court make the orders set forth in the proposed *Judgment (Family Law)* (form FL-180) submitted with this declaration.

21. ☐ This declaration is for the termination of **marital or domestic partner status only.** I ask the court to reserve jurisdiction over all issues whose determination is not requested in this declaration.

THIS STATEMENT APPLIES ONLY TO LEGAL SEPARATIONS

22. I ask that the court grant the request for a judgment for legal separation based upon irreconcilable differences and that the court make the orders set forth in the proposed *Judgment (Family Law)* (form FL-180) submitted with this declaration.

   I understand that a judgment of legal separation does not terminate a marriage or domestic partnership and that I am still married or a partner in a domestic partnership.

---

23. ☐ Other *(specify)*:

I declare under penalty of perjury under the laws of the State of California that the foregoing is true and correct.

Date:

▶

_____
(TYPE OR PRINT NAME)

_____
(SIGNATURE OF DECLARANT)

**DECLARATION FOR DEFAULT OR UNCONTESTED
DISSOLUTION or LEGAL SEPARATION**
(Family Law)

FL-160

ATTORNEY OR PARTY WITHOUT ATTORNEY *(Name, State Bar number, and address):*	FOR COURT USE ONLY
TELEPHONE NO.: FAX NO. *(Optional):* E-MAIL ADDRESS *(Optional):* ATTORNEY FOR *(Name):*	

SUPERIOR COURT OF CALIFORNIA, COUNTY OF
STREET ADDRESS:
MAILING ADDRESS:
CITY AND ZIP CODE:
BRANCH NAME:

PETITIONER:

RESPONDENT:

☐ PETITIONER'S ☐ RESPONDENT'S ☐ COMMUNITY AND QUASI-COMMUNITY PROPERTY DECLARATION ☐ SEPARATE PROPERTY DECLARATION	CASE NUMBER:

INSTRUCTIONS

When this form is attached to the *Petition* or *Response,* values and your proposal regarding division need not be completed. Do not list community, including quasi-community, property with separate property on the same form. Quasi-community property must be so identified. For additional space, use *Continuation of Property Declaration* (form FL-161).

ITEM NO. BRIEF DESCRIPTION	GROSS FAIR MARKET VALUE	AMOUNT OF DEBT	NET FAIR MARKET VALUE	PROPOSAL FOR DIVISION Award to:	
				PETITIONER	RESPONDENT
1. REAL ESTATE	$	$	$	$	$
2. HOUSEHOLD FURNITURE, FURNISHINGS, APPLIANCES					
3. JEWELRY, ANTIQUES, ART, COIN COLLECTIONS, etc.					
4. VEHICLES, BOATS, TRAILERS					

Form Adopted for Mandatory Use
Judicial Council of California
FL-160 [Rev. January 1, 2007]

PROPERTY DECLARATION
(Family Law)

Family Code, §§ 115, 2500–2660
www.courtinfo.ca.gov

230

ITEM NO. BRIEF DESCRIPTION	GROSS FAIR MARKET VALUE	AMOUNT OF DEBT	NET FAIR MARKET VALUE	PROPOSAL FOR DIVISION Award to: PETITIONER	RESPONDENT
5. SAVINGS, CHECKING, CREDIT UNION, CASH	$	$	$	$	$
6. LIFE INSURANCE (CASH VALUE)					
7. EQUIPMENT, MACHINERY, LIVESTOCK					
8. STOCKS, BONDS, SECURED NOTES					
9. RETIREMENT, PENSION, PROFIT-SHARING, ANNUITIES					
10. ACCOUNTS RECEIVABLE, UNSECURED NOTES, TAX REFUNDS					
11. PARTNERSHIPS, OTHER BUSINESS INTERESTS					
12. OTHER ASSETS AND DEBTS					
13. TOTAL FROM CONTINUATION SHEET					
14. TOTALS					

15. ☐ A *Continuation of Property Declaration* (form FL-161) is attached and incorporated by reference.

I declare under penalty of perjury under the laws of the State of California that, to the best of my knowledge, the foregoing is a true and correct listing of assets and obligations and the amounts shown are correct.

Date:

_____
(TYPE OR PRINT NAME)

▶

_____
(SIGNATURE)

PROPERTY DECLARATION
(Family Law)

FL-161

MARRIAGE OF (Last name—first names of parties)	CASE NUMBER

☐ **PETITIONER'S**   ☐ **RESPONDENT'S**

☐ **COMMUNITY AND QUASI-COMMUNITY PROPERTY DECLARATION**
☐ **SEPARATE PROPERTY DECLARATION**

ITEM NO.	BRIEF DESCRIPTION	GROSS FAIR MARKET VALUE	AMOUNT OF DEBT	NET FAIR MARKET VALUE	PROPOSAL FOR DIVISION AWARD TO PETITIONER	RESPONDENT
		$	$	$	$	$

Page 1 of 2

Form Adopted for Mandatory Use
Judicial Council of California
FL-161 [Rev. January 1, 2003]

CONTINUATION OF PROPERTY DECLARATION
(FAMILY LAW)

Family Code, §§ 2500–2600
www.courtinfo.ca.gov

232

ITEM NO.	BRIEF DESCRIPTION	GROSS FAIR MARKET VALUE	AMOUNT OF DEBT	NET FAIR MARKET VALUE	PROPOSAL FOR DIVISION AWARD TO	
					PETITIONER	RESPONDENT
		$	$	$	$	$

FL-350

ATTORNEY OR PARTY WITHOUT ATTORNEY *(Name and Address):*	TELEPHONE NO.:	FOR COURT USE ONLY

ATTORNEY FOR *(Name):*

SUPERIOR COURT OF CALIFORNIA, COUNTY OF
STREET ADDRESS:
MAILING ADDRESS:
CITY AND ZIP CODE:
BRANCH NAME:

PETITIONER/PLAINTIFF:

RESPONDENT/DEFENDANT:

STIPULATION TO ESTABLISH OR MODIFY CHILD SUPPORT AND ORDER	CASE NUMBER:

1. a. ☐ Mother's net monthly disposable income: $
       Father's net monthly disposable income: $
      —*OR*—

   b. ☐ A printout of a computer calculation of the parents' financial circumstances is attached.

2. ☐ Percentage of time each parent has primary responsibility for the children: Mother   %   Father   %

3. a. ☐ A hardship is being experienced by the mother for: $ per month because of *(specify):*

      The hardship will last until *(date):*

   b. ☐ A hardship is being experienced by the father for: $ per month because of *(specify):*

      The hardship will last until *(date):*

4. The amount of child support payable by *(name):*   , referred to as the "obligor" below,
   as calculated under the guideline is: $ per month.

5. ☐ We agree to guideline support.

6. ☐ The guideline amount should be rebutted because of the following:

     a. ☐ We agree to child support in the amount of: $ per month; the agreement is in the best interest of the children; the needs of the children will be adequately met by the agreed amount; and application of the guideline would be unjust or inappropriate in this case.

     b. ☐ Other rebutting factors *(specify):*

7. Obligor must pay child support as follows beginning *(date):*

   a. BASIC CHILD SUPPORT

Child's name	Monthly amount	Payable to *(name)*

     Total: $ payable ☐ on the first of the month   ☐ other *(specify):*

   b. ☐ In addition obligor must pay the following:

      ☐ $ per month for child care costs to *(name):*   on *(date):*

      ☐ $ per month for health care costs not deducted from gross income
        to *(name):*   on *(date):*

      ☐ $ per month for special educational or other needs of the children
        to *(name):*   on *(date):*

      ☐ other *(specify):*

   c. **Total monthly child support** payable by obligor will be: $
     payable ☐ on the first of the month   ☐ other *(specify):*

Form Adopted for Mandatory Use
Judicial Council of California
FL-350 [Rev. July 1, 2003]

**STIPULATION TO ESTABLISH OR MODIFY
CHILD SUPPORT AND ORDER**

Family Code, § 4065
www.courtinfo.ca.gov

234

8. a. Health insurance will be maintained by *(specify name):*

    b. ☐ A health insurance coverage assignment will issue if available through employment or other group plan or otherwise available at reasonable cost. Both parents are ordered to cooperate in the presentation, collection, and reimbursement of any medical claims.

    c. Any health expenses not paid by insurance will be shared: Mother   %   Father   %

9. a. An Order/Notice to Withhold Child Support (form FL-195) will be issued.

    b. ☐ We agree that service of the earnings assignment be stayed because we have made the following alternative arrangements to ensure payment *(specify):*

10. ☐ Travel expenses for visitation will be shared: Mother   %   Father   %

11. ☐ We agree that we will promptly inform each other of any change of residence or employment, including the employer's name, address, and telephone number.

12. ☐ Other *(specify):*

13. We agree that we are fully informed of our rights under the California child support guidelines.
14. We make this agreement freely without coercion or duress.
15. The right to support

    a. ☐ has not been assigned to any county and no application for public assistance is pending.

    b. ☐ has been assigned or an application for public assistance is pending in *(county name):*

If you checked b., an attorney for the local child support agency must sign below, joining in this agreement.

Date:

    ▶

| (TYPE OR PRINT NAME) | (SIGNATURE OF ATTORNEY FOR LOCAL CHILD SUPPORT AGENCY) |

Notice: If the amount agreed to is less than the guideline amount, no change of circumstances need be shown to obtain a change in the support order to a higher amount. If the order is above the guideline, a change of circumstances will be required to modify this order. This form must be signed by the court to be effective.

Date: ▶

| (TYPE OR PRINT NAME) | (SIGNATURE OF PETITIONER) |

Date: ▶

| (TYPE OR PRINT NAME) | (SIGNATURE OF RESPONDENT) |

Date: ▶

| (TYPE OR PRINT NAME) | (SIGNATURE OF ATTORNEY FOR PETITIONER) |

     ▶

| (TYPE OR PRINT NAME) | (SIGNATURE OF ATTORNEY FOR RESPONDENT) |

THE COURT ORDERS

16. a. ☐ The guideline child support amount in item 4 is rebutted by the factors stated in item 6.

    b. Items 7 through 12 are ordered. All child support payments must continue until further order of the court, or until the child marries, dies, is emancipated, or reaches age 18. The duty of support continues as to an unmarried child who has attained the age of 18 years, is a full-time high school student, and resides with a parent, until the time the child completes the 12th grade or attains the age of 19 years, whichever first occurs. Except as modified by this stipulation, all provisions of any previous orders made in this action will remain in effect.

Date:

| | JUDGE OF THE SUPERIOR COURT |

NOTICE: Any party required to pay child support must pay interest on overdue amounts at the "legal" rate, which is currently 10 percent per year. This can be a large added amount.

MARITAL SETTLEMENT AGREEMENT (MSA)

THIS AGREEMENT is made on _____ by
_____ (Wife) and _____ (Husband).
This agreement shall become effective on the date it is approved by the court in the pending
dissolution proceeding; or on the date a final judgment is entered.

Purpose. The purpose of this agreement is to settle the parties' rights and obligations as
to their property, debts, and support.

RECITALS

This agreement is made in light of the facts stated below.

1. Marriage. The parties were married to each other on _____,
and ever since have been, and are now, husband and wife.

2. Separation. Irreconcilable differences have arisen between the parties which have led
to the irremediable breakdown of their marriage. The parties agree that no further waiting
period, marriage counseling, or conciliation efforts would save the marriage, and the parties
have filed for dissolution of their marriage. They have lived separate and apart since
_____. They now intend to live apart permanently.

3. Legal Proceedings. An action for dissolution of marriage has been filed by
☐ Wife ☐ Husband and is now pending in the Superior Court of the State of California, County
of _____ Case No. _____.

4. Children of the Marriage.
☐ No children have been born to, or adopted by, the parties during their marriage, and the
wife is not now pregnant.
☐ The minor children of the parties are as follows (name and birthdate of child(ren) under
18 years:

The surname of the child(ren) shall not be changed.

5. Social Security Identification. The Social Security numbers of the parties are as follows:
        Husband: _____
        Wife: _____

6. Health of Parties.
☐ The parties are both in good health and neither has any known illness, disability, or
physical condition which renders either incapable of gainful employment or makes either subject
to extraordinary medical or dental expenditures in the near future.
☐ Husband ☐ Wife is not in good health because _____
_____.

7. <u>Employment</u>. Husband is presently employed by _____ _____ and his sole gross monthly earnings are $_____, as shown on his wage stub attached as part of this document. Wife is presently employed by _____ and her sole gross monthly earnings are $_____, as shown on her pay stub attached as part of this document.

8. <u>Voluntariness</u>. The parties acknowledge and agree that they enter into this agreement voluntarily, free from duress, fraud, undue influence, coercion, or misrepresentation of any kind.

For valuable consideration, the parties agree as follows:

WARRANTIES

9. <u>Full Disclosure</u>. Each party expressly promises that he or she has fully disclosed all of the real and personal property belonging to each of them and all debts.

10. <u>Warranty of Values of Property</u>. The parties intend the transfers of property in this agreement to be a substantially equal division of their community property. Husband and Wife each agree that they have had sufficient opportunity to investigate the values of the property and that each warrants to the other that each has no knowledge of any fact which would affect the distribution of any property listed in this agreement.

11. <u>After Discovered Property</u>. The parties agree that any property discovered after the date of this agreement which would have been their community or quasi-community property as of the effective date of this agreement shall be divided equally between them. If one party wilfully concealed such property, that party shall be obligated to pay any costs and attorneys fees incurred by the other party to collect such after-discovered community property.

12. <u>Transfers for Adequate Consideration</u>. Each party promises that he or she has not gifted or transferred any community property without the other's knowledge and consent. Each party signs this agreement relying on these representations.

DIVISION OF PROPERTY

13. <u>Wife's Share of Community Property</u>. Husband hereby transmutes and transfers to Wife as her sole and separate property the following property (list all community property going to Wife, including family residence and other real property, attach additional page if needed and make sure you include the legal description):

14. <u>Confirmation of Wife's Separate Property</u>. Husband hereby confirms that the following property owned by Wife prior to this marriage or received by Wife by gift of inheritance during the marriage shall remain the sole and separate property of Wife (List any separate property that Wife had before her marriage and property received by gift or inheritance during her marriage):

15. <u>Husband's Share of Community Property</u>. Wife hereby transmutes and transfers to Husband as his sole and separate property the following property (list all community property going to Husband, attach additional page if needed):

16. <u>Confirmation of Husband's Separate Property</u>. Wife hereby confirms that the following property owned by Husband prior to this marriage or received by him by gift of inheritance shall remain the sole and separate property of Husband (list any separate property that Husband had before the marriage and property received by gift or inheritance during his marriage):

The division shall be effected when necessary by a transfer of title. All property is transferred subject to any debt attached to it.

FAMILY RESIDENCE

17. <u>Family Residence</u>. The family residence is commonly known as _____
_____, and its legal description is as follows:
☐ The family residence is to be sold promptly and the proceeds after all debt, taxes, selling and other related expenses are deducted are to be divided evenly between the parties.
OR
☐ The ☐ Wife ☐ Husband shall remain living in the family residence until _____
_____, at which time the home shall be sold and the proceeds after all debt, taxes, selling and other related expenses are deducted are to be divided evenly between the parties. During the time the ☐ Wife ☐ Husband remains in the home, he/she will be responsible for all mortgage payments, taxes, insurance, and general maintenance. Capital improvements if needed will be shared equally between the parties.

OR

☐ The family residence is to be disposed of as follows: _____

_____

_____.

OBLIGATIONS TO THIRD PARTIES & DIVISION OF DEBTS

18. <u>The parties agree not to incur any further debts or obligations for which the other may be liable.</u> The parties agree that any debt incurred by either after the effective date of this agreement shall be the sole responsibility of that party, and each agrees to hold the other harmless against any such debt and agrees to indemnify the other against any liability in connection with it, including court costs and attorney's fees. The court shall retain jurisdiction over this issue.

19. <u>Distribution of Debt to Wife.</u> The Wife agrees to assume, to make payment on, and to hold the Husband harmless from the following obligations, with each debt described as "community" or "separate":

a. Any loans acquired by Wife where Wife is on the account as the sole debtor, as follows (list them):

b. Any credit cards where Wife is on the account as the sole debtor, as follows (list them):

c. Other debts as follows (list them):

d. If a creditor makes an attempt to obtain satisfaction from the Husband for any obligation listed above, the Wife shall defend and fully indemnify the Husband with regard to such attempt.

20. <u>Distribution of Debt to Husband</u>. The Husband agrees to assume, to make payment on, and to hold the Wife harmless from the following obligations, with each debt described as "community" or "separate":

a. Any loans acquired by Husband where Husband is on the account as the sole debtor, as follows (list them):

b. Any credit cards where Husband is on the account as the sole debtor, as follows (list them):

c. Other debts as follows (list them):

d. If a creditor makes an attempt to obtain satisfaction from the Wife for any obligation listed above, the Husband shall defend and fully indemnify the Wife with regard to such attempt.

WAIVER

21. <u>Waiver of Rights and Respective Estates</u>: Husband and Wife agree that each party waives all right, title, claim, lien, or interest in the other's separate property, separate property income, and separate property estate, by reason of their marriage, including the following:

1. All community property, quasi-community property, and quasi-marital property rights.
2. The right to a probate family allowance.
3. The right to a probate homestead.
4. The right or claims of dower, curtesy, or any statutory substitute now or hereafter provided under the laws of the state of California. The court shall retain jurisdiction over this issue indefinitely.
5. The right to inherit separate property from the other by intestate succession.
6. The right to receive separate property which would pass from the decedent party by testamentary disposition in a Will executed before this agreement.
7. The right of election to take against the Will of the other.
8. The right to take the statutory share of an omitted spouse.
9. The right to be appointed as administrator of the deceased party's estate, or as executor of the deceased party's Will, unless appointed pursuant to a Will executed after the date of this agreement.
10. The right to have exempt property set aside in probate.
11. Any right created under federal law, including without limitation, the Retirement Equity Act of 1984.

12.   Any right, title, claim, or interest in or to the separate property, separate income, or separate estate of the other by reason of the party's marriage.

22. <u>Confirmation of Personal Belongings</u>. Certain items of personal wearing apparel, jewelry, furniture, furnishings, and other miscellaneous items have previously been divided between the parties, and the parties agree that the distribution was an equal division of such property and each confirms to the other all such property now in that party's possession.

EMPLOYEE RETIREMENT BENEFITS

23. <u>Employee Retirement Benefits</u>. We understand that retirement and pension plans are community property to the extent either party received such benefits during the time of the marriage to the date of separation. The plans are valued at _____, and we are disposing of the asset(s) as follows:_____
_____.

SPOUSAL SUPPORT, CHILD SUPPORT, CUSTODY

24. <u>Spousal Support</u>.
☐ We are aware that it is mandated that the Court reserve spousal support for long-term marriages of more than ten years, when requested by either party. We waive the right to receive spousal support now or at any time in the future. This waiver shall not be modifiable by the parties or the court for any reason whatsoever. By executing this agreement, we each agree and acknowledge that we understand that by waiving spousal support we will be forever barred from seeking spousal support at any time in the future regardless of the circumstances.
OR
☐ We waive spousal support as to each other at this time. However, the Court shall retain jurisdiction over this issue until _____(date), so that during such time either of us may petition the court for spousal support if circumstances warrant.
OR
☐ _____ shall pay to _____ for support and maintenance the sum of $_____ per month payable on the _____ of each month beginning _____. This payment shall continue until _____, or the death of either spouse, or the remarriage of the payee spouse, or further order of court, or when payee spouse receives a gross income of $_____ monthly for _____ consecutive months, or _____, whichever occurs first. This support shall be paid pursuant to a Wage and Earnings Assignment Order to be served on payor's employer immediately upon receipt of the judgment.

25. <u>Child Custody</u>. The parenting plan is as follows (pick one):
☐ The legal and physical custody of our minor children during minority is jointly awarded to both Husband and Wife; the ☐ Husband's ☐ Wife's home shall be considered the child's primary residence for purposes of school registration, insurance, and other purposes.
OR

□ The legal custody of our minor children during minority is jointly awarded to both Husband and Wife. Physical custody is awarded to □ Husband □ Wife subject to reasonable visitation by □ Husband □ Wife.

The parent who has the physical care of the children at any given time shall have the routine decision-making rights and responsibilities during such times. However, all major decisions as to health, education, and day care shall be a joint decision, unless in an emergency. Each parent shall have the right of reasonable private telephone communication with the children. The estimated time which each parent will spend with the children is ____% with Husband and _____% with Wife. If one parent wishes to travel outside California with the child(ren), he or she must obtain the written consent of the other parent. The parties must keep each other informed as to the name, address, and phone number of their respective employers. Additionally, each parent shall keep the other apprised of the child(ren)'s health care provider's name, address, phone number, and identification number, as well as his or her own personal address and phone number. Each shall also keep the other informed during visitations of any medication the child(ren) may be taking and provide such medication to the visitation parent. A Wage and Earnings Assignment Order shall be submitted to the court at the time of judgment and served on the employer of the spouse obligated to pay child support.

If a disagreement arises as to reasonable visitation, "reasonable visitation" shall mean:

(a)   Regular Visitation:

1.   On (the first and third) (the second and fourth) weekends of each month from six (6:00) p.m. Friday to six (6:00) p.m. Sunday, commencing Friday, _____, _____.

2.   The entire month of July, _____, the entire month of August the following year, and alternating July and August in subsequent years.

(b)   Holidays and Special Days:

1.   Lincoln's Birthday, _____, from seven (7:00) p.m. the day before the holiday to seven (7:00) p.m. the day of said holiday and thereafter on alternate years.

2.   Washington's Birthday, _____, from seven (7:00) p.m. the day before said holiday to seven (7:00) p.m. the day of said holiday and thereafter on alternate years.

3.   Memorial Day, _____, from seven (7:00) p.m. the day before said holiday to seven (7:00) p.m. the day of said holiday and thereafter on alternate years.

4.   Independence Day, _____, from seven (7:00) p.m. the day before said holiday to seven (7:00) p.m. the day of said holiday and thereafter on alternate years.

5.   Labor Day, _____, from seven (7:00) p.m. the day before said holiday to seven (7:00) p.m. the day of said holiday, and thereafter on alternate years.

6.   Thanksgiving Day, _____, from six (6:00) p.m. the Wednesday before said holiday to six (6:00) p.m. the Sunday after said holiday and thereafter on alternate years.

7.   Christmas, _____, the first week of the Christmas school vacation, commencing seven (7:00) p.m. the last day of school before the vacation and ending at ten (10:00) a.m. Christmas Day, and thereafter on alternate years.

8.   Christmas, _____, the second week of the Christmas school vacation, commencing ten (10:00) a.m. Christmas Day to five (5:00) p.m. New Year's Day, and thereafter on alternate years.

9.   One-half Easter school vacation defined as four (4) days, to include Easter Sunday in □ even □ odd numbered years.

10.   On the children's birthdays in the year _____, and thereafter on alternate years.

11. Every (Father's Day)(Mother's Day).
12. On (Father's)(Mother's) birthday.

26. <u>Child Support</u>. ☐ Husband ☐ Wife shall pay ☐ Husband ☐ Wife child support beginning _____ in the amount of $_____ monthly. This support shall be paid pursuant to an Order/Notice to Withhold Income for Child Support to be served on payor's employer immediately upon receipt of the judgment. This support is based on ☐ Wife ☐ Husband having physical custody of the children _____ percent of the time. Payment shall be for the benefit of the following minor children (use the computer guideline for the distribution of child support among the children if more than one):

NAME OF CHILD	DATE OF BIRTH	AMOUNT OF CHILD SUPPORT

These payments shall continue at the rates until the child marries, dies, is emancipated, reaches 19, or reaches 18 and is not a full-time high school student residing with a parent, or further order of court, whichever first occurs.

Medical, dental, orthodontia, and hospital insurance for the children is provided for by ☐ Wife ☐ Husband ☐ both through employment. Wife and Husband shall cooperate in the presentation, collection, and reimbursement of any claims, and any medical, dental, orthodontic, optometric, psychiatric, psychological, or other related expense not otherwise covered by insurance shall be shared equally by the parties. In the event such insurance terminates for whatever reason, either or both parents shall immediately replace it and share the costs.

As additional support, child care costs to enable the custody parent to work shall be shared between the parents equally until the child is at an age where child care is unnecessary.

☐ Costs for special needs or travel expenses for visitation shall be paid as follows:

_____

_____

☐ Wife ☐ Husband shall be entitled to claim the following child(ren) as dependents for income   tax   purposes:

_____.

☐ We are aware that the child support is less than the guideline amount of approximately $_____. We therefore state:

1. We agree that we are fully informed of our rights concerning child support;
2. We make this agreement freely without coercion or duress;
3. This agreement is in the best interests of the children involved;
4. The needs of the children will be adequately met by the stipulated amount;
5. The right to support has not been assigned to the county pursuant to Section 11477 of the Welfare and Institutions Code and no public assistance application is pending.

INCOME TAX RETURNS

27. <u>Tax Refunds or Deficiencies</u>. If at any time after the effective date of this agreement any federal or state income tax deficiency is assessed against either of us for any year in which we filed joint returns, the liability shall be shared equally. If any refund shall become due for any federal or state income tax previously paid by us for any year in which we filed a joint return, the refund shall be divided between us. Any refund from overpayment of estimated taxes is not a "refund" for the purposes of this paragraph, and shall be the separate property of the party paying the overage.

28. <u>Tax Deficiencies</u>. Each party shall bear one-half of all liabilities for income tax, including interest and penalties, assessed on all joint income tax returns previously filed by the parties or resulting from a failure to file returns for prior years.

29. <u>Notices</u>. Each party, or the representative of the party's estate, will immediately send the other party a copy of any communication or notice he or she receives from the state or federal taxing authorities which relates to a joint return formerly filed by the parties.

30. <u>Property Transfer Provisions</u>. The parties agree that neither know of any transfer of property which should result in any income tax consequences to either party other than as stated in this agreement.

GENERAL PROVISIONS

31. <u>Freedom From Interference</u>. Each party may lawfully continue to live apart from the other as though he or she were unmarried and free from the other's direct and indirect control. Each party may engage in any employment or business of his/her choosing, entirely free of the other party's interference.

32. <u>Freedom From Harassment</u>. Each party agrees not to annoy, harass, embarrass, or interfere with the other in any way and agrees not to interfere with property that the other now owns or will later acquire.

33. <u>Further Acts to Implement Agreement</u>. On the demand of the other party, each party will promptly execute any document or perform any other act reasonably necessary to implement the terms of this agreement. A party who fails to comply with this provision will pay all attorney's fees and other expenses resulting from noncompliance.

34. <u>Release of All Claims</u>. Except as provided in this agreement, each party releases the other from all claims, liabilities, debts, obligations, actions, and causes of action that have been or will be asserted or incurred. This release does not apply to any obligation incurred under this agreement, under any document executed pursuant to the agreement, or under any order issued incident to the agreement. The release is binding on each party's heirs, executors, administrators, and assigns.

35. <u>Effect of Reconciliation</u>. Any reconciliation between the parties after they execute this agreement will have no effect on the agreement unless the parties modify or cancel it in a writing signed by both parties.

36. <u>Breach</u>. If any provision of this agreement is breached, the non-breaching party has a right to remedy the breach. If the breach involves an amount of money that is due, the non-breaching party has the right to collect the money as well as legal interest on it. Should an action for breach be brought and proved, the breaching party will pay all reasonable attorney's fees and other expenses that the non-breaching party has incurred in bringing the action. Either party's failure to insist upon the strict performance of any provision of this agreement will not be construed as a waiver of the provision, which will continue in full force. No breach or claimed breach will impair any rights or obligations that the parties have under the agreement.

37. <u>Waiver of Final Declaration of Disclosure and Declaration as to Preliminary Declaration of Disclosure</u>. Each of us waives the final Declaration of Disclosure, and we have complied with Family Code section 2104, and the preliminary Declarations of Disclosure have been completed and exchanged. We have completed and exchanged a current income and expense statement. This waiver is knowingly, intelligently, and voluntarily entered into by each of us and we understand that by signing below we may be affecting the ability to have the judgment set aside as provided by law.

38. <u>Governing Law</u>. This agreement shall be interpreted according to the laws of the State of California.

39. <u>Parties and Persons Bound</u>. This agreement shall bind the parties to the agreement and their respective heirs, assigns, representatives, executors and administrators, and any other successors in interest.

40. <u>Costs of Enforcement</u>. If either party be required to bring any action to enforce this agreement or any court order made after merger of any provision of this agreement in the judgment, the prevailing party shall be entitled to recover costs and reasonable attorney fees.

41. <u>Execution of Instruments</u>. The parties agree that each will execute and deliver to the other upon request any legal instrument or title document which may be necessary to carry out this agreement including, but not limited to, the division of property or confirmation of property set forth in this agreement.

42. <u>Execution Formalities</u>. The parties agree that upon their signing of this agreement, their signatures shall be acknowledged by a notary public. This agreement, or final judgment of dissolution into which this agreement has been merged, may be recorded at any time by either party in any place.

43. <u>Modification, Revocation or Termination</u>. This agreement may be amended or revoked only by a writing expressly referring to this agreement and signed by both Husband and Wife. Each of the parties waives the right to claim in the future that this agreement was modified, canceled, or superseded by oral agreement or conduct.

44. <u>Invalidity; Severability</u>. If any provision or condition of this agreement is held by a court as invalid, void or unenforceable, the remainder of the provisions shall remain in full force and effect.

45. <u>Entire Agreement</u>. The parties intend this agreement to be a final and complete settlement of all of their rights and obligations arising out of their marriage.

46. <u>Merger of Agreement</u>. If either party obtains a judgment of dissolution of marriage, this agreement shall be incorporated into the judgment and be a part of it, or otherwise filed with court pursuant to local court procedure. The parties shall ask the court to approve the agreement as fair and to order each of them to comply with all of its provisions.

DATE:_____

_____
Husband

DATE:_____

_____
Wife

State of California   )
) s.s.
County of _____)

On _____, before me, _____, Notary Public, personally appeared _____, ☐ personally known to me or ☐ proved to me on the basis of satisfactory evidence to be the person whose name is subscribed to the within instrument and acknowledged to me that he executed the same in his authorized capacity, and that by his signature on the instrument the person or the entity upon behalf of which the person acted, executed the instrument.

WITNESS my hand and official seal.

_____
Notary Public

State of California   )
) s.s.
County of _____)

On _____, before me, _____, Notary Public, personally appeared _____, ☐ personally known to me or ☐ proved to me on the basis of satisfactory evidence to be the person whose name is subscribed to the within instrument and acknowledged to me that she executed the same in her authorized capacity, and that by her signature on the instrument the person or the entity upon behalf of which the person acted, executed the instrument.

WITNESS my hand and official seal.

_____
Notary Public

FL-180

ATTORNEY OR PARTY WITHOUT ATTORNEY *(Name, State Bar number, and address)*:	*FOR COURT USE ONLY*
TELEPHONE NO.: FAX NO. *(Optional)*: E-MAIL ADDRESS *(Optional)*: ATTORNEY FOR *(Name)*:	

SUPERIOR COURT OF CALIFORNIA, COUNTY OF
  STREET ADDRESS:
  MAILING ADDRESS:
  CITY AND ZIP CODE:
  BRANCH NAME:

MARRIAGE OF
  PETITIONER:

  RESPONDENT:

JUDGMENT	CASE NUMBER:

☐ **DISSOLUTION**   ☐ **LEGAL SEPARATION**   ☐ **NULLITY**
     ☐ **Status only**
     ☐ **Reserving jurisdiction over termination of**
        marital or domestic partnership status
     ☐ **Judgment on reserved issues**
 Date marital or domestic partnership status ends:	

1. ☐ This judgment ☐ contains personal conduct restraining orders ☐ modifies existing restraining orders.
    The restraining orders are contained on page(s)   of the attachment. They expire on *(date)*:

2. This proceeding was heard as follows: ☐ Default or uncontested ☐ By declaration under Family Code section 2336
    ☐ Contested
  a. Date: Dept.:   Room:
  b. Judicial officer *(name)*:   ☐ Temporary judge
  c. ☐ Petitioner present in court   ☐ Attorney present in court *(name)*:
  d. ☐ Respondent present in court   ☐ Attorney present in court *(name)*:
  e. ☐ Claimant present in court *(name)*:   ☐ Attorney present in court *(name)*:
  f. ☐ Other *(specify name)*:

3. The court acquired jurisdiction of the respondent on *(date)*:
  a. ☐ The respondent was served with process.
  b. ☐ The respondent appeared.

THE COURT ORDERS, GOOD CAUSE APPEARING
4. a. ☐ Judgment of dissolution is entered. Marital or domestic partnership status is terminated and the parties are restored to the
        status of single persons
      (1) ☐ on *(specify date)*:
      (2) ☐ on a date to be determined on noticed motion of either party or on stipulation.
  b. ☐ Judgment of legal separation is entered.
  c. ☐ Judgment of nullity is entered. The parties are declared to be single persons on the ground of *(specify)*:

  d. ☐ This judgment will be entered nunc pro tunc as of *(date)*:
  e. ☐ Judgment on reserved issues.
  f. The ☐ petitioner's ☐ respondent's former name is restored to *(specify)*:
  g. ☐ Jurisdiction is reserved over all other issues, and all present orders remain in effect except as provided below.
  h. ☐ This judgment contains provisions for child support or family support. Each party must complete and file with the court a
      Child Support Case Registry Form (form FL-191) within 10 days of the date of this judgment. The parents must notify the
      court of any change in the information submitted within 10 days of the change, by filing an updated form. The *Notice*
      of Rights and Responsibilities—Health Care Costs and Reimbursement Procedures and Information Sheet on Changing a
      Child Support Order (form FL-192) is attached.

Form Adopted for Mandatory Use
 Judicial Council of California
 FL-180 [Rev. January 1, 2007]

JUDGMENT
(Family Law)

Family Code, §§ 2024, 2340,
 2343, 2346 <br> www.courtinfo.ca.gov

CASE NAME (Last name, first name of each party):	CASE NUMBER:

4. (Cont'd.)

  i. ☐ A settlement agreement between the parties is attached.

  j. ☐ A written stipulation for judgment between the parties is attached.

  k. ☐ The children of this marriage or domestic partnership.

     (1) ☐ The children of this marriage or domestic partnership are:

        Name   Birthdate

     (2) ☐ Parentage is established for children of this relationship born prior to the marriage or domestic partnership.

  l. ☐ Child custody and visitation are ordered as set forth in the attached

     (1) ☐ settlement agreement, stipulation for judgment, or other written agreement.

     (2) ☐ *Child Custody and Visitation Order Attachment* (form FL-341).

     (3) ☐ *Stipulation and Order for Custody and/or Visitation of Children* (form FL-355).

     (4) ☐ other (specify):

  m. ☐ Child support is ordered as set forth in the attached

     (1) ☐ settlement agreement, stipulation for judgment, or other written agreement.

     (2) ☐ *Child Support Information and Order Attachment* (form FL-342).

     (3) ☐ *Stipulation to Establish or Modify Child Support and Order* (form FL-350).

     (4) ☐ other (specify):

  n. ☐ Spousal or partner support is ordered as set forth in the attached

     (1) ☐ settlement agreement, stipulation for judgment, or other written agreement.

     (2) ☐ *Spousal, Partner, or Family Support Order Attachment* (form FL-343).

     (3) ☐ other (specify):

     NOTICE: It is the goal of this state that each party will make reasonable good faith efforts to become self-supporting as provided for in Family Code section 4320. The failure to make reasonable good faith efforts may be one of the factors considered by the court as a basis for modifying or terminating spousal or partner support.

  o. ☐ Property division is ordered as set forth in the attached

     (1) ☐ settlement agreement, stipulation for judgment, or other written agreement.

     (2) ☐ *Property Order Attachment to Judgment* (form FL-345).

     (3) ☐ other (specify):

  p. ☐ Other (specify):

Each attachment to this judgment is incorporated into this judgment, and the parties are ordered to comply with each attachment's provisions.

Jurisdiction is reserved to make other orders necessary to carry out this judgment.

Date:

_____
JUDICIAL OFFICER

☐ SIGNATURE FOLLOWS LAST ATTACHMENT

5. Number of pages attached: _____

NOTICE

Dissolution or legal separation may automatically cancel the rights of a spouse or domestic partner under the other spouse's or domestic partner's will, trust, retirement plan, power of attorney, pay-on-death bank account, transfer-on-death vehicle registration, survivorship rights to any property owned in joint tenancy, and any other similar thing. It does not automatically cancel the rights of a spouse or domestic partner as beneficiary of the other spouse's or domestic partner's life insurance policy. You should review these matters, as well as any credit cards, other credit accounts, insurance policies, retirement plans, and credit reports, to determine whether they should be changed or whether you should take any other actions.

A debt or obligation may be assigned to one party as part of the dissolution of property and debts, but if that party does not pay the debt or obligation, the creditor may be able to collect from the other party.

An earnings assignment may be issued without additional proof if child, family, partner, or spousal support is ordered.

Any party required to pay support must pay interest on overdue amounts at the "legal rate," which is currently 10 percent.

FL-192

NOTICE OF RIGHTS AND RESPONSIBILITIES

Health-Care Costs and Reimbursement Procedures

IF YOU HAVE A CHILD SUPPORT ORDER THAT INCLUDES A PROVISION FOR THE REIMBURSEMENT OF A PORTION OF THE CHILD'S OR CHILDREN'S HEALTH-CARE COSTS AND THOSE COSTS ARE NOT PAID BY INSURANCE, THE LAW SAYS:

1. Notice. You must give the other parent an itemized statement of the charges that have been billed for any health-care costs not paid by insurance. You must give this statement to the other parent within a reasonable time, but no more than 30 days after those costs were given to you.

2. Proof of full payment. If you have already paid all of the uninsured costs, you must (1) give the other parent proof that you paid them and (2) ask for reimbursement for the other parent's court-ordered share of those costs.

3. Proof of partial payment. If you have paid only your share of the uninsured costs, you must (1) give the other parent proof that you paid your share, (2) ask that the other parent pay his or her share of the costs directly to the health-care provider, and (3) give the other parent the information necessary for that parent to be able to pay the bill.

4. Payment by notified parent. If you receive notice from a parent that an uninsured health-care cost has been incurred, you must pay your share of that cost within the time the court orders; or if the court has not specified a period of time, you must make payment (1) within 30 days from the time you were given notice of the amount due, (2) according to any payment schedule set by the health-care provider, (3) according to a schedule agreed to in writing by you and the other parent, or (4) according to a schedule adopted by the court.

5. Disputed charges. If you dispute a charge, you may file a motion in court to resolve the dispute, but only if you pay that charge before filing your motion.

If you claim that the other party has failed to reimburse you for a payment, or the other party has failed to make a payment to the provider after proper notice has been given, you may file a motion in court to resolve the dispute. The court will presume that if uninsured costs have been paid, those costs were reasonable. The court may award attorney fees and costs against a party who has been unreasonable.

6. Court-ordered insurance coverage. If a parent provides health-care insurance as ordered by the court, that insurance must be used at all times to the extent that it is available for health-care costs.

a. **Burden to prove.** The party claiming that the coverage is inadequate to meet the child's needs has the burden of proving that to the court.

b. **Cost of additional coverage.** If a parent purchases health-care insurance in addition to that ordered by the court, that parent must pay all the costs of the additional coverage. In addition, if a parent uses alternative coverage that costs more than the coverage provided by court order, that parent must pay the difference.

7. Preferred health providers. If the court-ordered coverage designates a preferred health-care provider, that provider must be used at all times consistent with the terms of the health insurance policy. When any party uses a health-care provider other than the preferred provider, any health-care costs that would have been paid by the preferred health provider if that provider had been used must be the sole responsibility of the party incurring those costs.

INFORMATION SHEET ON CHANGING A CHILD SUPPORT ORDER

General Information

The court has just made a child support order in your case. This order will remain the same unless a party to the action requests that the support be changed (modified). An order for child support can be modified only by filing a motion to change child support and serving each party involved in your case. If both parents and the local child support agency (if it is involved) agree on a new child support amount, you can complete, have all parties sign, and file with the court *Stipulation to Establish or Modify Child Support and Order* (form FL-350) or *Stipulation and Order (Governmental)* (form FL-625).

When a Child Support Order May Be Modified

The court takes several things into account when ordering the payment of child support. First, the number of children is considered. Next, the net incomes of both parents are determined, along with the percentage of time each parent has physical custody of the children. The court considers both parties' tax filing status and may consider hardships, such as a child of another relationship. An existing order for child support may be modified when the net income of one of the parents changes significantly, the parenting schedule changes significantly, or a new child is born.

Examples

- You have been ordered to pay $500 per month in child support. You lose your job. You will continue to owe $500 per month, plus 10 percent interest on any unpaid support, unless you file a motion to modify your child support to a lower amount and the court orders a reduction.
- You are currently receiving $300 per month in child support from the other parent, whose net income has just increased substantially. You will continue to receive $300 per month unless you file a motion to modify your child support to a higher amount and the court orders an increase.
- You are paying child support based upon having physical custody of your children 30 percent of the time. After several months it turns out that you actually have physical custody of the children 50 percent of the time. You may file a motion to modify child support to a lower amount.

How to Change a Child Support Order

To change a child support order, you must file papers with the court. *Remember:* You must follow the order you have now.

What forms do I need?

If you are asking to change a child support order open with the local child support agency, you must fill out one of these forms:
- FL-680, *Notice of Motion (Governmental)* or FL-683 *Order to Show Cause (Governmental)* **and**
- FL-684, *Request for Order and Supporting Declaration (Governmental)*

If you are asking to change a child support order that is **not** open with the local child support agency, you must fill out one of these forms:
- FL-301, *Notice of Motion* or FL-300, *Order to Show Cause* **and**
- FL-310, *Application for Order and Supporting Declaration* **or**
- FL-390, *Notice of Motion and Motion for Simplified Modification of Order for Child, Spousal, or Family Support*

You must also fill out one of these forms:
- FL-150, *Income and Expense Declaration* **or** FL-155, *Financial Statement (Simplified)*

What if I am not sure which forms to fill out?

Talk to the family law facilitator at your court.

After you fill out the forms, file them with the court clerk and ask for a hearing date. Write the hearing date on the form.
The clerk will ask you to pay a filing fee. If you cannot afford the fee, fill out these forms, too:
- Form FW-001, *Application for Waiver of Court Fees and Costs*
- Form FW-003, *Order on Application for Waiver of Court Fees and Costs*

You must serve the other parent. If the local child support agency is involved, serve it too.
This means someone 18 or over—**not you**—must serve the other parent copies of your filed court forms at least **16 court days** before the hearing. Add **5 calendar days** if you serve by mail within California (see Code of Civil Procedure section 1005 for other situations). **Court days** are weekdays when the court is open for business (Monday through Friday except court holidays). **Calendar days** include all days of the month, including weekends and holidays. To determine court and calendar days, go to
www.courtinfo.ca.gov/selfhelp/courtcalendars/.

The server must also serve blank copies of these forms:
- FL-320, *Responsive Declaration to Order to Show Cause or Notice of Motion* **and** FL-150, *Income and Expense Declaration,* **or**
- FL-155, *Financial Statement (Simplified)*
Then the server fills out and signs a *Proof of Service* (form FL-330 or FL-335). Take this form to the clerk and file it.

Go to your hearing and ask the judge to change the support. Bring your tax returns from the last two years and your last two months' pay stubs. The judge will look at your information, listen to both parents, and make an order. After the hearing, fill out:
- FL-340, *Findings and Order After Hearing* **and**
- FL-342, *Child Support Information and Order Attachment*

Need help?

Contact the family law facilitator in your county or call your county's bar association and ask for an experienced family lawyer.

NOTICE OF RIGHTS AND RESPONSIBILITES
Health-Care Costs and Reimbursement Procedures

FL-190

ATTORNEY OR PARTY WITHOUT ATTORNEY *(Name, State Bar number, and address):*	*FOR COURT USE ONLY*
TELEPHONE NO.: FAX NO. *(Optional):* E-MAIL ADDRESS *(Optional):* ATTORNEY FOR *(Name):*	

SUPERIOR COURT OF CALIFORNIA, COUNTY OF

STREET ADDRESS:

MAILING ADDRESS:

CITY AND ZIP CODE:

BRANCH NAME:

PETITIONER:

RESPONDENT:

NOTICE OF ENTRY OF JUDGMENT	CASE NUMBER:

You are notified that the following judgment was entered on *(date):*

1. ☐ Dissolution
2. ☐ Dissolution—status only
3. ☐ Dissolution—reserving jurisdiction over termination of marital status or domestic partnership
4. ☐ Legal separation
5. ☐ Nullity
6. ☐ Parent-child relationship
7. ☐ Judgment on reserved issues
8. ☐ Other *(specify):*

Date:

Clerk, by _____, Deputy

—NOTICE TO ATTORNEY OF RECORD OR PARTY WITHOUT ATTORNEY—

Under the provisions of Code of Civil Procedure section 1952, if no appeal is filed the court may order the exhibits destroyed or otherwise disposed of after 60 days from the expiration of the appeal time.

STATEMENT IN THIS BOX APPLIES ONLY TO JUDGMENT OF DISSOLUTION

Effective date of termination of marital or domestic partnership status *(specify):*

WARNING: Neither party may remarry or enter into a new domestic partnership until the effective date of the termination of marital or domestic partnership status, as shown in this box.

CLERK'S CERTIFICATE OF MAILING

I certify that I am not a party to this cause and that a true copy of the *Notice of Entry of Judgment* was mailed first class, postage fully prepaid, in a sealed envelope addressed as shown below, and that the notice was mailed

at *(place):* _____, California,   on *(date):* _____

Date:

Clerk, by _____, Deputy

⌐ Name and address of petitioner or petitioner's attorney ⌐	⌐ Name and address of respondent or respondent's attorney ⌐

Page 1 of 1

Form Adopted for Mandatory Use
 Judicial Council of California
 FL-190 [Rev. January 1, 2005]

NOTICE OF ENTRY OF JUDGMENT
(Family Law—Uniform Parentage—Custody and Support)

Family Code, §§ 2338, 7636, 7637 <br> www.courtinfo.ca.gov

This page intentionally blank.

FL-435

ATTORNEY OR PARTY WITHOUT ATTORNEY (Name, State Bar number, and address):	FOR COURT USE ONLY
TELEPHONE NO.: FAX NO. (Optional): E-MAIL ADDRESS (Optional): ATTORNEY FOR (Name):	

SUPERIOR COURT OF CALIFORNIA, COUNTY OF

STREET ADDRESS:

MAILING ADDRESS:

CITY AND ZIP CODE:

BRANCH NAME:

PETITIONER/PLAINTIFF:

RESPONDENT/DEFENDANT:

OTHER PARENT:

EARNINGS ASSIGNMENT ORDER FOR SPOUSAL OR PARTNER SUPPORT ☐ Modification	CASE NUMBER:

TO THE PAYOR: This is a court order. You must withhold a portion of the earnings of   (specify obligor's name and birthdate):

and pay as directed below.   (An explanation of this order is printed on page 2 of this form.)

THE COURT ORDERS

1. You must pay part of the earnings of the employee or other person who has been ordered to pay support, as follows:
    a. ☐ $ per month current spousal or partner support
    b. ☐ $ per month spousal or partner support arrearages
    c. Total deductions per month: $

2. ☐ The payments ordered under item 1a must be paid to (name, address):

3. ☐ The payments ordered under item 1b must be paid to (name, address):

4. The payments ordered under item 1 must continue until further written notice from the payee or the court.

5. ☐ This order modifies an existing order. The amount you must withhold may have changed.   The existing order continues in effect until this modification is effective.

6. This order affects all earnings that are payable beginning as soon as possible but not later than 10 days after you receive it.

7. You must give the obligor a copy of this order and the blank Request for Hearing Regarding Earnings Assignment (form FL-450) within 10 days.

8. ☐ Other (specify):

9. For the purposes of this order, spousal or partner support arrearages are set at: $ as of (date):

Date:

_____
JUDICIAL OFFICER

Form Adopted for Mandatory Use
 Judicial Council of California
 FL-435 [Rev. January 1, 2005]

**EARNINGS ASSIGNMENT ORDER FOR SPOUSAL
 OR PARTNER SUPPORT
 (Family Law)**

Family Code, §§ 299(d), 5208;
 Code of Civil Procedure, § 706.031;
 15 U.S.C. §§ 1672–1673 <br> www.courtinfo.ca.gov

INSTRUCTIONS FOR EARNINGS ASSIGNMENT ORDER

1. DEFINITION OF IMPORTANT WORDS IN THE EARNINGS ASSIGNMENT ORDER

   a. Earnings:
      (1) Wages, salary, bonuses, vacation pay, retirement pay, and commissions paid by an employer;
      (2) Payments for services of independent contractors;
      (3) Dividends, interest, rents, royalties, and residuals;
      (4) Patent rights and mineral or other natural resource rights;
      (5) Any payments due as a result of written or oral contracts for services or sales, regardless of title;
      (6) Payments due for workers' compensation temporary benefits, or payments from a disability or health insurance policy or program; and
      (7) Any other payments or credits due, regardless of source.

   b. Earnings assignment order: a court order issued in every court case in which one person is ordered to pay for the support of another person. This order has priority over any other orders such as garnishments or earnings withholding orders.

      Earnings should not be withheld for any other order until the amounts necessary to satisfy this order have been withheld in full. However, an Order/Notice to Withhold Income for Child Support for child support or family support has priority over this order for spousal or partner support.

   c. Obligor: any person ordered by a court to pay support. The obligor is named before item 1 in the order.

   d. Obligee: the person or governmental agency to whom the support is to be paid.

   e. Payor: the person or entity, including an employer, that pays earnings to an obligor.

2. INFORMATION FOR ALL PAYORS. Withhold money from the earnings payable to the obligor as soon as possible but no later than 10 days after you receive the Earnings Assignment Order for Spousal or Partner Support. Send the withheld money to the payee(s) named in items 2 and 3 of the order within 10 days of the pay date. You may deduct $1 from the obligor's earnings for each payment you make.

   When sending the withheld earnings to the payee, state the date on which the earnings were withheld. You may combine amounts withheld for two or more obligors in a single payment to each payee, and identify what portion of that payment is for each obligor.

   You will be liable for any amount you fail to withhold and can be cited for contempt of court.

3. SPECIAL INSTRUCTIONS FOR PAYORS WHO ARE EMPLOYERS

   a. State and federal laws limit the amount you can withhold and pay as directed by this order. This limitation applies only to earnings defined above in item 1a(1) and are usually half the obligor's disposable earnings.

      Disposable earnings are different from gross pay or take-home pay. Disposable earnings are earnings left after subtracting the money that state or federal law requires an employer to withhold. Generally these required deductions are (1) federal income tax, (2) social security, (3) state income tax, (4) state disability insurance, and (5) payments to public employees' retirement systems.

      After the obligor's disposable earnings are known, withhold the amount required by the order, but never withhold more than 50 pe rcent of the disposable earnings unless the court order specifies a higher percentage. Federal law prohibits withholding more than 65 percent of disposable earnings of an employee in any case.

      If the obligor has more than one assignment for support, add together the amounts of support due for all the assignments. If 50 percent of the obligor's net disposable earnings will not pay in full all of the assignments for support, prorate it first among all of the current support assignments in the same proportion that each assignment bears to the total current support owed. Apply any remainder to the assignments for arrearage support in the same proportion that each assignment bears to the total arrearage owed. If you have any questions, please   contact the office or person who sent this form to you.   This office or person's name appears in the upper left-hand corner   of the order.

   b. If the employee's pay period differs from the period specified in the order, prorate the amount ordered withheld so that part of it is withheld from each of the obligor's paychecks.

   c. If the obligor stops working for you, notify the office that sent you this form of that, no later than the date of the next payment, by first-class mail. Give the obligor's last known address and, if known, the name and address of any new employer.

   d. California law prohibits you from firing, refusing to hire, or taking any disciplinary action against any employee ordered to pay support through an earnings assignment. Such action can lead to a $500 civil penalty per employee.

4. INFORMATION FOR ALL OBLIGORS. You should have received a Request for Hearing Regarding Earnings Assignment (form FL-450) with this Earnings Assignment Order for Spousal or Partner Support. If not, you may get one from either the court clerk or the family law facilitator. If you want the court to stop or modify your earnings assignment, you must file (by hand delivery or mail) an original copy of the form with the court clerk within 10 days of the date you received this order. Keep a copy of the form for your records.

   If you think your support order is wrong, you can ask for a modification of the order or, in some cases, you can have the order set aside and have a new order issued. You can talk to an attorney or get information from the family law facilitator about this.

5. SPECIAL INFORMATION FOR THE OBLIGOR WHO IS AN EMPLOYEE. State law requires you to notify the payees named in items 2 and 3 of the order if you change your employment. You must provide the name and address of your new employer.

EARNINGS ASSIGNMENT ORDER FOR SPOUSAL
OR PARTNER SUPPORT
(Family Law)

FL-120

ATTORNEY OR PARTY WITHOUT ATTORNEY (Name, State Bar number, and address):	FOR COURT USE ONLY
TELEPHONE NO.: FAX NO. (Optional):	
E-MAIL ADDRESS (Optional):	
ATTORNEY FOR (Name):	

SUPERIOR COURT OF CALIFORNIA, COUNTY OF

    STREET ADDRESS:

    MAILING ADDRESS:

    CITY AND ZIP CODE:

    BRANCH NAME:

MARRIAGE OF

    PETITIONER:

    RESPONDENT:

RESPONSE ☐ and REQUEST FOR	CASE NUMBER:
☐ Dissolution of Marriage	
☐ Legal Separation	
☐ Nullity of Marriage ☐ AMENDED	

1. RESIDENCE (Dissolution only) ☐ Petitioner ☐ Respondent   has been a resident of this state for at least six months and of this county for at least three months immediately preceding the filing of the Petition for Dissolution of Marriage.

2. STATISTICAL FACTS
   a. Date of marriage:
   b. Date of separation:
   c. Time from date of marriage to date of separation (specify):
     Years: Months:

3. DECLARATION REGARDING MINOR CHILDREN (include children of this relationship born prior to or during the marriage or adopted during the marriage):
   a. ☐ There are no minor children.
   b. ☐ The minor children are:

Child's name	Birthdate	Age	Sex

    ☐ Continued on Attachment 3b.
   c. If there are minor children of the Petitioner and Respondent, a completed Declaration Under Uniform Child Custody Jurisdiction and Enforcement Act (UCCJEA) (form FL-105) must be attached.
   d. ☐ A completed voluntary declaration of paternity regarding minor children born to the Petitioner and Respondent prior to the marriage is attached.

4. SEPARATE PROPERTY
   Respondent requests that the assets and debts listed ☐ in Property Declaration (form FL-160) ☐ in Attachment 4
   ☐ below   be confirmed as separate property.

Item	Confirm to

NOTICE: You may redact (black out) social security numbers fr   om any written material filed with the court in this case other than a form used to collect child or spousal support.

Form Adopted for Mandatory Use
Judicial Council of California
FL-120 [Rev. January 1, 2005]

RESPONSE—MARRIAGE
(Family Law)

Family Code, § 2020
www.courtinfo.ca.gov.

MARRIAGE OF (last name, first name of parties):	CASE NUMBER:

5. DECLARATION REGARDING COMMUNITY AND QUASI-COMMUNITY ASSETS AND DEBTS AS CURRENTLY KNOWN
   a. ☐ There are no such assets or debts subject to disposition by the court in this proceeding.
   b. ☐ All such assets and debts are listed ☐ in Property Declaration (form FL-160) ☐ in Attachment 5b.
   ☐ below (specify):

6. ☐ Respondent contends that the parties were never legally married.

7. ☐ Respondent denies the grounds set forth in item 6 of the petition.

8. Respondent requests
   a. ☐ dissolution of the marriage based on
      (1) ☐ irreconcilable differences. (Fam. Code, § 2310(a).)
      (2) ☐ incurable insanity. (Fam. Code, § 2310(b).)
   b. ☐ legal separation of the parties based on
      (1) ☐ irreconcilable differences. (Fam. Code, § 2310(a).)
      (2) ☐ incurable insanity. (Fam. Code, § 2310(b).)
   c. ☐ nullity of void marriage based on
      (1) ☐ incestuous marriage. (Fam. Code, § 2200.)
      (2) ☐ bigamous marriage. (Fam. Code, § 2201.)
   d. ☐ nullity of voidable marriage based on
      (1) ☐ respondent's age at time of marriage. (Fam. Code, § 2210(a).)
      (2) ☐ prior existing marriage. (Fam. Code, § 2210(b).)
      (3) ☐ unsound mind. (Fam. Code, § 2210(c).)
      (4) ☐ fraud. (Fam. Code, § 2210(d).)
      (5) ☐ force. (Fam. Code, § 2210(e).)
      (6) ☐ physical incapacity. (Fam. Code, § 2210(f).

9. Respondent requests that the court grant the above relief and make injunctive (including restraining) and other orders as follows:

	Petitioner	Respondent	Joint	Other
a. Legal custody of children to	☐	☐	☐	☐
b. Physical custody of children to	☐	☐	☐	☐
c. Child visitation be granted to	☐	☐		☐

   As requested in form: ☐ FL-311 ☐ FL-312 ☐ FL-341(C) ☐ FL-341(D) ☐ FL-341(E) ☐ Attachment 9c.
   d. ☐ Determination of parentage of any children born to the Petitioner and Respondent prior to the marriage.
   e. Attorney fees and costs payable by .... ☐ ☐
   f. Spousal support payable to (wage assignment will be issued) .... ☐ ☐
   g. ☐ Terminate the court's jurisdiction (ability) to award spousal support to Petitioner.
   h. ☐ Property rights be determined.
   i. ☐ Respondent's former name be restored to (specify):
   j. ☐ Other (specify):

   ☐ Continued on Attachment 9j.

10. Child support– If there are minor children born to or adopted by the Petitioner and Respondent before or during this marriage, the court will make orders for the support of the children upon request and submission of financial forms by the requesting party. An earnings assignment may be issued without further notice. Any party required to pay support must pay interest on overdue amounts at the "legal" rate, which is currently 10 percent.

I declare under penalty of perjury under the laws of the State of California that the foregoing is true and correct.

Date:

▶

_____   _____
(TYPE OR PRINT NAME)   (SIGNATURE OF RESPONDENT)

Date:

▶

_____   _____
(TYPE OR PRINT NAME)   (SIGNATURE OF ATTORNEY FOR RESPONDENT)

The original response must be filed in the court with proof of service of a copy on Petitioner.

RESPONSE—MARRIAGE
(Family Law)

FL-123

ATTORNEY OR PARTY WITHOUT ATTORNEY *(Name, State Bar number, and address)*:	FOR COURT USE ONLY
TELEPHONE NO.: FAX NO. *(Optional)*:	
E–MAIL ADDRESS *(Optional)*:	
ATTORNEY FOR *(Name)*:	

SUPERIOR COURT OF CALIFORNIA, COUNTY OF
STREET ADDRESS:
MAILING ADDRESS:
CITY AND ZIP CODE:
BRANCH NAME:

DOMESTIC PARTNERSHIP OF
PETITIONER:

RESPONDENT:

RESPONSE ☐ **and REQUEST FOR**	CASE NUMBER:
☐ **Dissolution of Domestic Partnership**	
☐ **Legal Separation of Domestic Partnership**	
☐ **Nullity of Domestic Partnership** ☐ **AMENDED**	

1. STATISTICAL FACTS
   a. Date of registration of domestic partnership:
   b. Date of separation:
   c. Time from date of registration of domestic partnership to date of separation *(specify)*:   Years   Months

2. RESIDENCE (Partnerships established out of state only)
   a. ☐ Our domestic partnership was established in another state *(specify state)*:
   b. ☐ Petitioner ☐ Respondent has been a resident of this state of California for at least six months and of this county for at least three months immediately preceding the filing of this *Petition for Dissolution of Domestic Partnership.*

3. DECLARATION REGARDING MINOR CHILDREN *(include children of this relationship born prior to or during this domestic partnership or adopted during this domestic partnership)*:
   a. ☐ There are no minor children.
   b. ☐ The minor children are:

Child's name	Birthdate	Age	Sex

   ☐ Continued on Attachment 3b.
   c. If there are minor children of the petitioner and the respondent, a completed *Declaration Under Uniform Child Custody Jurisdiction and Enforcement Act (UCCJEA)* (form FL-105) must be attached.

4. SEPARATE PROPERTY
   Respondent requests that the assets and debts listed ☐ in *Property Declaration* (form FL-160) ☐ in Attachment 4
   ☐ below   be confirmed as separate property.

Item	Confirm to

NOTICE: You may redact (black out) social security numbers from any written material filed with the court in this case other than a form used to collect child or partner support.

Form Adopted for Mandatory Use
Judicial Council of California
FL-123 [New January 1, 2005]

RESPONSE—DOMESTIC PARTNERSHIP
(Family Law)

Page 1 of 2
Family Code, §§ 299, 2020
www.courtinfo.ca.gov

DOMESTIC PARTNERSHIP OF (Last name, first name of each party):	CASE NUMBER:

5. DECLARATION REGARDING COMMUNITY AND QUASI-COMMUNITY ASSETS AND DEBTS AS CURRENTLY KNOWN
   a. ☐ There are no such assets or debts subject to disposition by the court in this proceeding.
   b. ☐ All such assets and debts are listed ☐ in *Property Declaration* (form FL-160) ☐ in Attachment 5b.
       ☐ below *(specify):*

6. ☐ **Respondent contends** that there is not a valid domestic partnership or equivalent.

7. ☐ **Respondent denies** the grounds set forth in item 6 of the petition.

8. **Respondent requests**
   a. ☐ dissolution of the domestic partnership based on   d. ☐ nullity of voidable domestic partnership based on
     (1) ☐ irreconcilable differences. (Fam. Code, § 2310(a).)   (1) ☐ respondent's age at time of domestic
     (2) ☐ incurable insanity. (Fam. Code, § 2310(b).)   partnership. (Fam. Code, § 2210(a).)
   b. ☐ legal separation of the domestic partners based on   (2) ☐ prior existing marriage or domestic
     (1) ☐ irreconcilable differences. (Fam. Code, § 2310(a).)   partnership. (Fam. Code, § 2210(b).)
     (2) ☐ incurable insanity. (Fam. Code, § 2310(b).)   (3) ☐ unsound mind. (Fam. Code, § 2210(c).)
   c. ☐ nullity of void domestic partnership based on   (4) ☐ fraud. (Fam. Code, § 2210(d).)
     (1) ☐ incest. (Fam. Code, § 2200.)   (5) ☐ force. (Fam. Code, § 2210(e).)
     (2) ☐ bigamy. (Fam. Code, § 2201.)   (6) ☐ physical incapacity. (Fam. Code, § 2210(f).)

9. **Respondent requests** that the court grant the above relief and make injunctive (including restraining) and other orders as follows:

	Petitioner	Respondent	Joint	Other
a. Legal custody of children to	☐	☐	☐	☐
b. Physical custody of children to	☐	☐	☐	☐
c. Child visitation granted to	☐	☐		☐

     As requested in form: ☐ FL-311 ☐ FL-312 ☐ FL-341(C) ☐ FL-341(D) ☐ FL-341(E) ☐ Attachment 9c.

	Petitioner	Respondent		
d. ☐ Determination of parentage of any children born to the petitioner and respondent prior to the domestic partnership.				
e. Attorney fees and costs payable by	☐	☐		
f. Partner support payable to	☐	☐		

   g. ☐ Terminate court's jurisdiction (ability) to award partner support to the petitioner.
   h. ☐ Property rights be determined.
   i. ☐ Respondent's former name be restored to *(specify):*
   j. ☐ Other *(specify):*

     ☐ Continued on Attachment 9j.

10. **Child support** –If there are minor children who were born to or adopted by the petitioner and the respondent before or during this domestic partnership, the court will make orders for the support of the children upon request and submission of financial forms by the requesting party. An earnings assignment may be issued without further notice. Any party required to pay support must pay interest on overdue amounts at the "legal" rate, which is currently 10 percent.

I declare under penalty of perjury under the laws of the State of California that the foregoing is true and correct.

Date: _____

_____   ▶ _____
(TYPE OR PRINT NAME)   (SIGNATURE OF RESPONDENT)

Date: _____

_____   ▶ _____
(TYPE OR PRINT NAME)   (SIGNATURE OF ATTORNEY FOR RESPONDENT)

The original response must be filed in the court with proof of service of a copy on petitioner.

FL-800

ATTORNEY OR PARTY WITHOUT ATTORNEY *(Name, State Bar number and address)*:	FOR COURT USE ONLY
TELEPHONE NO.: FAX NO. *(Optional)*: E-MAIL ADDRESS *(Optional)*: ATTORNEY FOR *(Name)*:	

SUPERIOR COURT OF CALIFORNIA, COUNTY OF
   STREET ADDRESS:
   MAILING ADDRESS:
   CITY AND ZIP CODE:
   BRANCH NAME:

MARRIAGE OF
   HUSBAND:

   WIFE:

JOINT PETITION FOR SUMMARY DISSOLUTION OF MARRIAGE	CASE NUMBER:

We petition for a summary dissolution of marriage and declare that all the following conditions exist on the date this petition is filed with the court:

1. We have read and understand the *Summary Dissolution Information* booklet (form FL-810).

2. We were married on *(date)*:
   (A summary dissolution of your marriage will not be granted if you file this petition more than five years after the date of your marriage.)

3. One of us has lived in California for at least six months and in the county of filing for at least three months preceding the date of filing.

4. There are no minor children who were born of our relationship before or during our marriage or adopted by us during our marriage. The wife, to her knowledge, is not pregnant.

5. Neither of us has an interest in any real property anywhere. **(You may have a lease for a residence in which one of you lives. It must terminate within a year from the date of filing this petition. The lease must not include an option to purchase.)**

6. Except for obligations with respect to automobiles, on obligations incurred by either or both of us during our marriage, we owe no more than $5,000.

7. The total fair market value of community property assets, not including what we owe on those assets and not including automobiles, is less than $33,000.

8. Neither of us has separate property assets, not including what we owe on those assets and not including automobiles, in excess of $33,000.

9. We have each filled out and given the other an *Income and Expense Declaration* (form FL-150).

10. We have each filled out and given the other copies of the worksheets on pages 8, 10, and 12 of the *Summary Dissolution Information* booklet (form FL-810) used in determining the value and division of our property. We have told each other in writing about any investment, business, or other income-producing opportunities that came up after we were separated based on investments made or work done during the marriage and before our separation. This meets the requirements of preliminary declaration of disclosure.

11. *(Check whichever statement is true.)*
    a. ☐ We have no community assets or liabilities.
    b. ☐ We have signed an agreement listing and dividing all our community assets and liabilities and have signed all the papers necessary to carry out our agreement. A copy of our agreement is attached to this petition.

12. Irreconcilable differences have caused the irremediable breakdown of our marriage, and each of us wishes to have the court dissolve our marriage without our appearing before a judge.

13. ☐ The wife desires to have her former name restored. Her former name is *(specify name)*:

    ☐ The husband desires to have his former name restored. His former name is *(specify name)*:

Form Adopted for Mandatory Use Judicial Council of California FL-800 [Rev. January 1, 2006]	**JOINT PETITION FOR SUMMARY DISSOLUTION OF MARRIAGE** (Family Law—Summary Dissolution)	Family Code, §§ 2109, 2400–2406 *www.courtinfo.ca.gov*

FL-800

HUSBAND:	CASE NUMBER:
WIFE:	

14. Upon entry of judgment of summary dissolution of marriage, we each give up our rights to appeal and to move for a new trial.

15. **Each of us forever gives up any right to spousal support from the other.**

16. We agree that this matter may be determined by a commissioner sitting as a temporary judge.

17. **Mailing address of husband**
    Name:
    Address:

    City:
    State:
    Zip Code:

18. **Mailing address of wife**
    Name:
    Address:

    City:
    State:
    Zip Code:

I declare under penalty of perjury under the laws of the State of California that the foregoing and all attached documents are true and correct.

Date:

▶ _____
(SIGNATURE OF HUSBAND)

I declare under penalty of perjury under the laws of the State of California that the foregoing and all attached documents are true and correct.

Date:

▶ _____
(SIGNATURE OF WIFE)

You have a right to revoke this petition any time before a request for judgment is filed. You will remain married until one of you files for and obtains a judgment of dissolution. You may not request a judgment of dissolution sooner than six months from the date this petition is filed.

NOTICE: Dissolution may automatically cancel the rights of a spouse under the other spouse's will, trust, retirement benefit plan, power of attorney, pay on death bank account, transfer on death vehicle registration, survivorship rights to any property owned in joint tenancy, and any other similar thing. It does not automatically cancel the rights of a spouse as beneficiary of the other spouse's life insurance policy. You should review these matters, as well as any credit cards, other credit accounts, insurance polices, and credit reports to determine whether they should be changed or whether you should take any other actions. However, some changes may require agreement of your spouse or a court order. (See Family Code sections 231–235.)

**JOINT PETITION FOR SUMMARY
DISSOLUTION OF MARRIAGE**
(Family Law—Summary Dissolution)

FL-820

ATTORNEY OR PARTY WITHOUT ATTORNEY *(Name and address):* TELEPHONE NO. : FAX NO. *(Optional):* ATTORNEY FOR *(Name):*	*FOR COURT USE ONLY*

SUPERIOR COURT OF CALIFORNIA, COUNTY OF
　STREET ADDRESS:
　MAILING ADDRESS:
　CITY AND ZIP CODE:
　BRANCH NAME:

MARRIAGE OF PETITIONERS
　HUSBAND:

　WIFE:

REQUEST FOR JUDGMENT, JUDGMENT OF DISSOLUTION OF MARRIAGE, AND NOTICE OF ENTRY OF JUDGMENT	CASE NUMBER:

1. The *Joint Petition for Summary Dissolution of Marriage* (form FL-800) was filed on *(date):*
2. No notice of revocation has been filed and the parties have not become reconciled.
3. I request that judgment of dissolution of marriage be
　a. ☐　entered to be effective now.
　b. ☐　entered to be effective (nunc pro tunc) as of *(date):*
　　　　for the following reason:

I declare under penalty of perjury under the laws of the State of California that the foregoing is true and correct.
Date:

_____　　　▶　_____
　　　(TYPE OR PRINT NAME)　　　　　　　　　　　(SIGNATURE OF HUSBAND OR WIFE)

4. ☐　Husband, ☐　Wife,　who did **not** request his or her own former name be restored when he or she signed the joint
　　　　petition, now requests that it be restored. The applicant's former name is:

Date:

_____　　　▶　_____
　　　(TYPE OR PRINT NAME)　　　　　　　(SIGNATURE OF PARTY WISHING TO HAVE HIS OR HER NAME RESTORED)

(For Court Use Only)
JUDGMENT OF DISSOLUTION OF MARRIAGE

5. THE COURT ORDERS
　a. A judgment of dissolution of marriage will be entered, and the parties are restored to the status of unmarried persons.
　b. ☐　The judgment of dissolution of marriage will be entered nunc pro tunc as of *(date):*
　c. ☐　Wife's former name is restored *(specify):*
　d. ☐　Husband's former name is restored *(specify):*

　e. Husband and wife must comply with any agreement attached to the petition.

Date:
　　　　　　　　　　　　　　　　　　　_____
　　　　　　　　　　　　　　　　　　　　JUDGE OF THE SUPERIOR COURT

NOTICE: Dissolution may automatically cancel the rights of a spouse under the other spouse's will, trust, retirement benefit plan, power of attorney, pay on death bank account, transfer on death vehicle registration, survivorship rights to any property owned in joint tenancy, and any other similar thing. It does not automatically cancel the rights of a spouse as beneficiary of the other spouse's life insurance policy. You should review these matters, as well as any credit cards, other credit accounts, insurance policies, retirement benefit plans, and credit reports to determine whether they should be changed or whether you should take any other actions.

Page 1 of 2

262

HUSBAND:	CASE NUMBER:
WIFE:	

NOTICE OF ENTRY OF JUDGMENT

6. You are notified that a judgment of dissolution of marriage was entered on *(date):*

Date: _____ Clerk, by _____ , Deputy

CLERK'S CERTIFICATE OF MAILING

I certify that I am not a party to this cause and that a true copy of the *Notice of Entry of Judgment* was mailed first class, postage fully prepaid, in a sealed envelope addressed as shown below, and that the notice was mailed

at *(place):*   California,

on *(date):*

Date: _____ Clerk, by _____ , Deputy

HUSBAND'S ADDRESS   WIFE'S ADDRESS

FL-820 [Rev. January 1, 2003]

REQUEST FOR JUDGMENT, JUDGMENT OF DISSOLUTION OF MARRIAGE, AND NOTICE OF ENTRY OF JUDGMENT
(Family Law—Summary Dissolution)

Page 2 of 2

FL-830

ATTORNEY OR PARTY WITHOUT ATTORNEY *(Name and Address)*:	TELEPHONE NO.:	*FOR COURT USE ONLY*

ATTORNEY FOR *(Name)*:

SUPERIOR COURT OF CALIFORNIA, COUNTY OF

STREET ADDRESS:

MAILING ADDRESS:

CITY AND ZIP CODE:

BRANCH NAME:

MARRIAGE OF

PETITIONER:

RESPONDENT:

NOTICE OF REVOCATION OF PETITION FOR SUMMARY DISSOLUTION	CASE NUMBER:

Notice is given that the undersigned terminates the summary dissolution proceedings and revokes the *Joint Petition for Summary Dissolution of Marriage* (form FL-800) filed on *(date):*

I declare under penalty of perjury under the laws of the State of California that the foregoing is true and correct.

Date:

▶

_____   _____
(TYPE OR PRINT NAME)   (SIGNATURE OF DECLARANT)

COMPLETE THIS NOTICE, EXCEPT FOR THE PLACE AND DATE OF MAILING AND CLERK'S NAME. SUBMIT THE ORIGINAL AND TWO COPIES TO THE COUNTY CLERK'S OFFICE. IF NO REQUEST FOR JUDGMENT HAS BEEN FILED, THE CLERK WILL NOTIFY YOU THAT THIS NOTICE OF REVOCATION HAS BEEN FILED BY COMPLETING THE CERTIFICATE BELOW.

CLERK'S CERTIFICATE OF MAILING

I certify that I am not a party to this cause and that a copy of the foregoing was mailed first class postage prepaid, in a sealed envelope as shown below, and that the mailing of the foregoing and execution of this certificate occurred at
(place):   California, on

(Date):   Clerk, by _____ , Deputy

Name and address of husband   Name and address of wife

NOTICE

IF THE CLERK'S CERTIFICATE OF MAILING ABOVE HAS BEEN DATED AND SIGNED BY THE CLERK, THIS SUMMARY DISSOLUTION PROCEEDING IS ENDED. YOU ARE STILL MARRIED.

Form Adopted for Mandatory Use
Judicial Council of California
FL-830 [Rev. January 1, 2003]

**NOTICE OF REVOCATION OF PETITION
FOR SUMMARY DISSOLUTION**
(Family Law—Summary Dissolution)

Page 1 of 1
Family Code, § 2402
www.courtinfo.ca.gov.

This page intentionally blank.

_____
(name)

_____
(street address)

_____
(city   state   zip)

_____
(phone number)

_____
(date)

MEMORANDUM OF REQUEST FOR MILITARY SERVICE STATUS

TO: U.S. Coast Guard Commander, GPIM-2, Locators
2100 2nd St., S.W.,
Washington, DC 20593

AFMPC/RMIQL, Attn: Air Force Locator
Randolph AFB, TX 78150-6001

Department of Navy, Bureau of Navy Personnel
2 Navy Annex
Washington, DC 20370-5000

CMC MMSB-10, HQ USMC, Bldg. 2008
Quantico, VA 22134-5002

Surgeon General, U.S. Public Health Service, Div. of Comm., Off. Personnel
5600 Fishers Land
Rockville, MD 20857

Army World Wide Locator, U.S. Army Enlisted Records Center
Fort Benjamin Harrison, IN 46249-5601

Commander, U.S. Army Personnel Center, Officer Locator Branch, Attn: Locators
200 Stovall Street
Alexandria, VA 22332

RE: _____   _____
                [Party]   [Soc. Sec. #]

This case involves a family matter. It is imperative that a determination be made whether the above named individual, who has an interest in these proceedings, is presently in the military service of the United States, and the date of induction and discharge, if any. This information is necessary to comply with §581 of the Soldier's and Sailor's Civil Relief Act of 1940, as amended. Please supply a certification of verification as soon as possible. My check in enclosed for your search fees. Self-addressed, stamped envelopes are enclosed.

Very truly yours,

_____
(signature)

This page intentionally blank.

ATTORNEY OR PARTY WITHOUT ATTORNEY *(Name, State Bar number, and address)*:	FOR COURT USE ONLY
TELEPHONE NO.: FAX NO. *(Optional)*: E-MAIL ADDRESS *(Optional)*: ATTORNEY FOR *(Name)*:	

SUPERIOR COURT OF CALIFORNIA, COUNTY OF
STREET ADDRESS:
MAILING ADDRESS:
CITY AND ZIP CODE:
BRANCH NAME:

PLAINTIFF/PETITIONER:

DEFENDANT/RESPONDENT:

DECLARATION	CASE NUMBER:

I declare under penalty of perjury under the laws of the State of California that the foregoing is true and correct.

Date:

_____
(TYPE OR PRINT NAME)

_____
(SIGNATURE OF DECLARANT)

☐ Attorney for ☐ Plaintiff ☐ Petitioner ☐ Defendant
☐ Respondent ☐ Other *(Specify):*

DECLARATION

This page intentionally blank.

SHORT TITLE: CASE NUMBER

1

2

3

4

5

6

7

8

9

10

11

12

13

14

15

16

17

18

19

20

21

22

23

24

25

26   *(Required for verified pleading)* The items on this page stated on information and belief are *(specify item numbers, **not** line numbers)*.

27
| This page may be used with any Judicial Council form or any other paper filed with the court. |

Page _____

Form Approved by the
Judicial Council of California
MC-020 [New January 1, 1987]

ADDITIONAL PAGE
Attach to Judicial Council Form or Other Court Paper

CRC 201, 501

This page intentionally blank.

FL-335

ATTORNEY OR PARTY WITHOUT ATTORNEY OR GOVERNMENTAL AGENCY (under Family Code, §§ 17400, 17406) *(Name, state bar number, and address):*	*FOR COURT USE ONLY*
TELEPHONE NO.: FAX NO.:	
ATTORNEY FOR *(Name):*	

SUPERIOR COURT OF CALIFORNIA, COUNTY OF

STREET ADDRESS:

MAILING ADDRESS:

CITY AND ZIP CODE:

BRANCH NAME:

PETITIONER/PLAINTIFF:

RESPONDENT/DEFENDANT:

OTHER PARENT:

PROOF OF SERVICE BY MAIL	CASE NUMBER:

NOTICE: To serve temporary restraining orders you must use personal service (see form FL-330).

1. I am at least 18 years of age, not a party to this action, and I am a resident of or employed in the county where the mailing took place.

2. My residence or business address is:

3. I served a copy of the following documents *(specify):*

   by enclosing them in an envelope AND
   a. ☐ **depositing** the sealed envelope with the United States Postal Service with the postage fully prepaid.
   b. ☐ **placing** the envelope for collection and mailing on the date and at the place shown in item 4 following our ordinary business practices. I am readily familiar with this business's practice for collecting and processing correspondence for mailing. On the same day that correspondence is placed for collection and mailing, it is deposited in the ordinary course of business with the United States Postal Service in a sealed envelope with postage fully prepaid.

4. The envelope was addressed and mailed as follows:
   a. Name of person served:
   b. Address:

   c. Date mailed:
   d. Place of mailing *(city and state):*

5. I declare under penalty of perjury under the laws of the State of California that the foregoing is true and correct.

Date:

_____   _____
(TYPE OR PRINT NAME)   (SIGNATURE OF PERSON COMPLETING THIS FORM)

Page 1 of 2

Form Approved for Optional Use
Judicial Council of California
FL-335 [Rev. January 1, 2003]

PROOF OF SERVICE BY MAIL

Code of Civil Procedure, §§ 1013, 1013a
www.courtinfo.ca.gov

INFORMATION SHEET FOR PROOF OF SERVICE BY MAIL

Use these instructions to complete the *Proof of Service by Mail* (form FL-335).

A person at least 18 years of age or older must serve the documents. There are two ways to serve documents: (1) personal delivery and (2) by mail. See the *Proof of Personal Service* (form FL-330) if the documents are being personally served. The person who serves the documents must complete a proof of service form for the documents being served. **You cannot serve documents if you are a party to the action.**

INSTRUCTIONS FOR THE PERSON WHO SERVES THE DOCUMENTS (TYPE OR PRINT IN BLACK INK)

You must complete a proof of service for each package of documents you serve. For example, if you serve the Respondent and the Other Parent, you must complete two proofs of service, one for the Respondent and one for the Other Parent.

Complete the top section of the proof of service forms as follows:
First box, left side: In this box print the name, address, and phone number of the person for whom you are serving the documents.
Second box, left side: Print the name of the county in which the legal action is filed and the court's address in this box. Use the same address for the court that is on the documents you are serving.
Third box, left side: Print the names of the Petitioner/Plaintiff, Respondent/Defendant, and Other Parent in this box. Use the same names listed on the documents you are serving.
First box, top of form, right side: Leave this box blank for the court's use.
Second box, right side: Print the case number in this box. This number is also stated on the documents you are serving.

You cannot serve a temporary restraining order by mail. You must serve those documents by personal service.

1. You are stating that you are at least 18 years old and that you are not a party to this action. You are also stating that you either live in or are employed in the county where the mailing took place.
2. Print your home or business address.
3. List the name of each document that you mailed (the exact names are listed on the bottoms of the forms).
   a. Check this box if you put the documents in the regular U.S. mail.
   b. Check this box if you put the documents in the mail at your place of employment.
4. a. Print the name you put on the envelope containing the documents.
   b. Print the address you put on the envelope containing the documents.
   c. Write in the date that you put the envelope containing the documents in the mail.
   d. Write in the city and state you were in when you mailed the envelope containing the documents.
5. You are stating under penalty of perjury that the information you have provided is true and correct.

Print your name, fill in the date, and sign the form.

If you need additional assistance with this form, contact the Family Law Facilitator in your county.

— *THIS FORM MUST BE KEPT CONFIDENTIAL* —

FW-001

ATTORNEY OR PARTY WITHOUT ATTORNEY *(Name, state bar number, and address)*:	

TELEPHONE NO.:   FAX NO. *(Optional)*:

E-MAIL ADDRESS *(Optional)*:

ATTORNEY FOR *(Name)*:

NAME OF COURT:

STREET ADDRESS:

MAILING ADDRESS:

CITY AND ZIP CODE:

BRANCH NAME:

PLAINTIFF / PETITIONER:

DEFENDANT / RESPONDENT:

APPLICATION FOR **WAIVER OF COURT FEES AND COSTS**	CASE NUMBER:

I request a court order so that I do not have to pay court fees and costs.

1.   a. ☐   I am *not* able to pay any of the court fees and costs.

      b. ☐   I am able to pay *only* the following court fees and costs *(specify)*:

2.   My current street or mailing address is *(if applicable, include city or town, apartment no., if any, and zip code)*:

3.   a. My occupation, employer, and employer's address are *(specify)*:

      b. My spouse's occupation, employer, and employer's address are *(specify)*:

4. ☐   I am receiving financial assistance under one or more of the following programs:

      a. ☐   **SSI and SSP:** Supplemental Security Income and State Supplemental Payments Programs

      b. ☐   **CalWORKs:** California Work Opportunity and Responsibility to Kids Act, implementing TANF, Temporary Assistance for Needy Families (formerly AFDC)

      c. ☐   **Food Stamps:** The Food Stamp Program

      d. ☐   **County Relief, General Relief (G.R.), or General Assistance (G.A.)**

5.   *If you checked box 4, you must check and complete* **one of the three boxes below,** *unless you are a defendant in an unlawful detainer action. Do not check more than one box.*

      a. ☐   *(Optional)* My Medi-Cal number is *(specify)*:

      b. ☐   *(Optional)* My social security number is *(specify)*:

           ☐☐☐ - ☐☐ - ☐☐☐☐   and my date of birth is *(specify)*:

           [Federal law does not require that you give your social security number. However, if you don't give your social security number, you must check box c and attach documents to verify the benefits checked in item 4.]

      c. ☐   I am attaching documents to verify receipt of the benefits checked in item 4, if requested by the court.
           [See Form FW-001-INFO, **Information Sheet on Waiver of Court Fees and Costs,** *available from the clerk's office, for a list of acceptable documents.]*

[If you checked box 4 above, skip items 6 and 7, and sign at the bottom of this side.]

6. ☐   My total gross monthly household income is less than the amount shown on the *Information Sheet on Waiver of Court Fees and Costs* available from the clerk's office.

[if you checked box 6 above, skip item 7, complete items 8, 9a, 9d, 9f, and 9g on the back of this form, and sign at the bottom of this side.]

7. ☐   My income is not enough to pay for the common necessaries of life for me and the people in my family whom I support and also pay court fees and costs. *[If you check this box, you must complete the back of this form.]*

WARNING: You must immediately tell the court if you become able to pay court fees or costs during this action. You may be ordered to appear in court and answer questions about your ability to pay court fees or costs.

I declare under penalty of perjury under the laws of the State of California that the information on both sides of this form and all attachments are true and correct.

Date:

▶

_____   _____

(TYPE OR PRINT NAME)   *(Financial information on reverse)*   (SIGNATURE)

Form Adopted for Mandatory Use
Judicial Council of California
FW-001 [Rev. July 1, 2007]

APPLICATION FOR WAIVER OF COURT FEES AND COSTS
(Fee Waiver)

Government Code,
§ 68511.3
www.courtinfo.ca.gov

FW-001

PLAINTIFF/PETITIONER:	CASE NUMBER:
DEFENDANT/RESPONDENT:	

FINANCIAL INFORMATION

8. ☐ My pay changes considerably from month to month. [*If you check this box, each of the amounts reported in item 9 should be your average for the past 12 months.*]

9. **MY MONTHLY INCOME**

a. My gross monthly pay is: . . . . $ _____

b. **My payroll deductions are** *(specify purpose and amount)*:

   (1) _____ $ _____
   (2) _____ $ _____
   (3) _____ $ _____
   (4) _____ $ _____

My TOTAL payroll deduction amount is: $ _____

c. My monthly take-home pay is

   (a. minus b.): . . . . $ _____

d. Other money I get each month is *(specify source and amount;* include spousal support, child support, parental support, support from outside the home, scholarships, retirement or pensions, social security, disability, unemployment, military basic allowance for quarters *(BAQ),* veterans payments, dividends, interest or royalty, trust income, annuities, net business income, net rental income, reimbursement of job-related expenses, and net gambling or lottery winnings):

   (1) _____ $ _____
   (2) _____ $ _____
   (3) _____ $ _____
   (4) _____ $ _____

The TOTAL amount of other money is: $ _____
(If more space is needed, attach page labeled Attachment 9d.)

e. **MY TOTAL MONTHLY INCOME IS**

   (c. plus d.): . . . . $ _____

f. Number of persons living in my home: _____
Below list all the persons living in your home, including your spouse, who depend in whole or in part on you for support, or on whom you depend in whole or in part for support:

	Name	Age	Relationship	Gross Monthly Income
(1)	_____	___	_____	$ _____
(2)	_____	___	_____	$ _____
(3)	_____	___	_____	$ _____
(4)	_____	___	_____	$ _____
(5)	_____	___	_____	$ _____

The TOTAL amount of other money is: $ _____
(If more space is needed, attach page labeled Attachment 9f.)

g. **MY TOTAL GROSS MONTHLY HOUSEHOLD INCOME IS**

   (a. plus d. plus f): . . . . $ _____

10. **I own or have an interest in the following property:**

a. Cash . . . . $ _____

b. Checking, savings, and credit union accounts (list *banks*):

   (1) _____ $ _____
   (2) _____ $ _____
   (3) _____ $ _____
   (4) _____ $ _____

c. Cars, other vehicles, and boats *(list make, year, fair market value (FMV), and loan balance of each):*

	Property	FMV	Loan Balance
(1)	_____	$ _____	$ _____
(2)	_____	$ _____	$ _____
(3)	_____	$ _____	$ _____

d. Real estate *(list address, estimated fair market value (FMV), and loan balance of each property):*

	Property	FMV	Loan Balance
(1)	_____	$ _____	$ _____
(2)	_____	$ _____	$ _____
(3)	_____	$ _____	$ _____

e. Other personal property — jewelry, furniture, furs, stocks, bonds, etc. *(list separately):*

   $ _____

11. **My monthly expenses not already listed in item 9b above are the following:**

a. Rent or house payment & maintenance $ _____
b. Food and household supplies . . . . $ _____
c. Utilities and telephone . . . . $ _____
d. Clothing . . . . $ _____
e. Laundry and cleaning . . . . $ _____
f. Medical and dental payments . . . . $ _____
g. Insurance (life, health, accident, etc.) . . $ _____
h. School, child care . . . . $ _____
i. Child, spousal support (prior marriage) . . $ _____
j. Transportation and auto expenses (insurance, gas, repair) . . . . $ _____
k. Installment payments *(specify purpose and amount):*

   (1) _____ $ _____
   (2) _____ $ _____
   (3) _____ $ _____

The TOTAL amount of monthly installment payments is: . . . . $ _____

l. Amounts deducted due to wage assignments and earnings withholding orders: $ _____

m. Other expenses *(specify):*

   (1) _____ $ _____
   (2) _____ $ _____
   (3) _____ $ _____
   (4) _____ $ _____
   (5) _____ $ _____

The TOTAL amount of other monthly expenses is: . . . . $ _____

n. **MY TOTAL MONTHLY EXPENSES ARE**

   (add a. through m.): . . . . $ _____

12. Other facts that support this application are *(describe unusual medical needs, expenses for recent family emergencies, or other unusual circumstances or expenses to help the court understand your budget; if more space is needed, attach page labeled Attachment 12):*

WARNING: You must immediately tell the court if you become able to pay court fees or costs during this action. You may be ordered to appear in court and answer questions about your ability to pay court fees or costs.

FW-002

ATTORNEY OR PARTY WITHOUT ATTORNEY (Name and Address):	TELEPHONE NO.:	FOR COURT USE ONLY

ATTORNEY FOR (Name):

NAME OF COURT AND BRANCH. IF ANY:
 STREET ADDRESS:
 MAILING ADDRESS:
CITY AND ZIP CODE:

PLAINTIFF:

DEFENDANT:

APPLICATION FOR WAIVER OF ADDITIONAL COURT FEES AND COSTS	CASE NUMBER:

1. I was granted a waiver of court fees and costs in this case on (date) ....

2. a. ☐ My financial status has **not changed** since I filed my original application.

   b. ☐ My financial status **has changed** since I filed my original application AND a new application is attached.

3. I ask the court to extend my waiver of fees to cover the following additional court fees and costs:

   a. ☐ Jury fees and expenses.

   b. ☐ Court appointed interpreters' fees for witnesses.

   c. ☐ Witness fees of peace officers whose attendance is necessary for reasons shown below.

   d. ☐ Reporters' fees for attendance at hearings and trials held more than sixty days after the date of the original application as shown above.

   e. ☐ Witness fees for court appointed experts.

   f. ☐ Other *(specify):*

4. These additional services are needed because *(use additional sheet if necessary):*

I declare under penalty of perjury under the laws of the State of California that the foregoing is true and correct and that this declaration is executed on (date): .... at (place) ....

....
(Type or print name)

_____
(Signature)

Page 1 of 1

Form Adopted for Mandatory Use
Judicial Council of California
FW-002 [Rev. January 1, 2007]

**APPLICATION FOR WAIVER OF ADDITIONAL
COURT FEES AND COSTS
(Fee Waiver)**

Government Code § 68511.3
www.courtinfo.ca.gov

INFORMATION SHEET ON WAIVER
OF COURT FEES AND COSTS
(California Rules of Court, rules 3.50–3.63)

If you have been sued or if you wish to sue someone, and if you cannot afford to pay court fees and costs, you may not have to pay them if:

1. You are receiving **financial assistance** under one or more of the following programs:
   - SSI and SSP (Supplemental Security Income and State Supplemental Payments Programs)
   - CalWORKs (California Work Opportunity and Responsibility to Kids Act, implementing TANF, Temporary Assistance for Needy Families, formerly AFDC, Aid to Families with Dependent Children Program)
   - The Food Stamp Program
   - County Relief, General Relief (G.R.), or General Assistance (G.A.)

   If you are claiming eligibility for a waiver of court fees and costs because you receive financial assistance under one or more of these programs, and you did not provide your Medi-Cal number or your social security number and birthdate, you must produce documentation confirming benefits from a public assistance agency or one of the following documents, unless you are a defendant in an unlawful detainer action:

PROGRAM	VERIFICATION
SSI/SSP	Medi-Cal Card or Notice of Planned Action or SSI Computer-Generated Printout or Bank Statement Showing SSI Deposit or "Passport to Services"
CalWORKs/TANF (formerly known as AFDC)	Medi-Cal Card or Notice of Action or Income and Eligibility Verification Form or Monthly Reporting Form or Electronic Benefit Transfer Card or "Passport to Services"
Food Stamp Program	Notice of Action or Food Stamp ID Card or "Passport to Services"
General Relief/General Assistance	Notice of Action or Copy of Check Stub or County Voucher

–OR –

2. Your total gross **monthly household income** is equal to or less than the following amounts:

NUMBER IN FAMILY	FAMILY INCOME
1	$ 1,063.54
2	1,426.04
3	1,788.54
4	2,151.04
5	2,513.54

NUMBER IN FAMILY	FAMILY INCOME
6	$ 2,876.04
7	3,238.54
8	3,601.54
Each additional	362.50

–OR–

3. Your income is not enough to pay for the common **necessaries** of life for yourself and the people you support and also pay court fees and costs.

To apply, fill out the Application for Waiver of Court Fees and Costs (form FW-001) available from the clerk's office. If you claim no income, you may be required to file a declaration under penalty of perjury. Prison and jail inmates may be required to pay up to the full amount of the filing fee.

If you have any questions and cannot afford an attorney, you may wish to consult the legal aid office, legal services office, or lawyer referral service in your county (listed in the Yellow Pages under "Attorneys").

If you are asking for review of the decision of an administrative body under Code of Civil Procedure section 1094.5 (administrative mandate), you may ask for a transcript of the administrative proceedings at the expense of the administrative body.

Page 1 of 1

Form Adopted for Mandatory Use
Judicial Council of California
FW-001-INFO [Rev. February 6, 2007]

**INFORMATION SHEET ON WAIVER OF
COURT FEES AND COSTS
(Fee Waiver)**

Government Code, § 68511.3;
Cal. Rules of Court, rules 3.50–3.63
www.courtinfo.ca.gov

FL-300

ATTORNEY OR PARTY WITHOUT ATTORNEY *(Name, State Bar number, and address)*:	FOR COURT USE ONLY

TELEPHONE NO.:   FAX NO. *(Optional)*:

E-MAIL ADDRESS *(Optional)*:

ATTORNEY FOR *(Name)*:

SUPERIOR COURT OF CALIFORNIA, COUNTY OF

STREET ADDRESS:

MAILING ADDRESS:

CITY AND ZIP CODE:

BRANCH NAME:

PETITIONER/PLAINTIFF:

RESPONDENT/DEFENDANT:

ORDER TO SHOW CAUSE ☐ **MODIFICATION**	CASE NUMBER:
☐ **Child Custody** ☐ Visitation ☐ **Injunctive Order**	
☐ **Child Support** ☐ Spousal Support ☐ **Other** *(specify)*:	
☐ **Attorney Fees and Costs**	

1. TO *(name)*:

2. YOU ARE ORDERED TO APPEAR IN THIS COURT AS FOLLOWS TO GIVE ANY LEGAL REASON WHY THE RELIEF SOUGHT IN THE ATTACHED APPLICATION SHOULD NOT BE GRANTED. **If child custody or visitation is an issue in this proceeding, Family Code section 3170 requires mediation before or concurrently with the hearing listed below.**

   a. Date: Time: ☐ Dept.:   ☐ Room:

   b. The address of the court is ☐ same as noted above ☐ other *(specify)*:

   c. ☐ The parties are ordered to attend custody mediation services as follows:

3. THE COURT FURTHER ORDERS that a completed *Application for Order and Supporting Declaration* (form FL-310), a **blank** *Responsive Declaration* (form FL-320), and the following documents be served with this order:

   a. (1) ☐ Completed *Income and Expense Declaration* (form FL-150) and a **blank** *Income and Expense Declaration*
      (2) ☐ Completed *Financial Statement (Simplified)* (form FL-155) and a **blank** *Financial Statement (Simplified)*
      (3) ☐ Completed *Property Declaration* (form FL-160) and a **blank** *Property Declaration*
      (4) ☐ Points and authorities
      (5) ☐ Other *(specify)*:

   b. ☐ Time for ☐ service ☐ hearing   is shortened. Service must be on or before *(date)*:
      Any responsive declaration must be served on or before *(date)*:

   c. ☐ You are ordered to comply with the temporary orders attached.

   d. ☐ Other *(specify)*:

Date:

_____
JUDICIAL OFFICER

NOTICE: If you have children from this relationship, the court is required to order payment of child support based on the incomes of both parents. The amount of child support can be large. It normally continues until the child is 18. You should supply the court with information about your finances. Otherwise, the child support order will be based on the information supplied by the other parent.

You do not have to pay any fee to file declarations in response to this order to show cause (including a completed Income and Expense Declaration (form FL-150) or Financial Statement *(Simplified)* (form FL-155) that will show your finances). In the absence of an order shortening time, the original of the responsive declaration must be filed with the court and a copy served on the other party at least nine court days before the hearing date. Add five calendar days if you serve by mail within California. (See Code of Civil Procedure 1005 for other situations.) To determine court and calendar days, go to *www.courtinfo.ca.gov/selfhelp/courtcalendars/*.

 Requests for Accommodations
Assistive listening systems, computer-assisted real-time captioning, or sign language interpreter services are available if you ask at least five days before the proceeding. Contact the clerk's office or go to *www.courtinfo.ca.gov/forms* for *Request for Accommodations by Persons With Disabilities and Response* (Form MC-410). (Civil Code, § 54.8.)

Page 1 of 1

Form Adopted for Mandatory Use
Judicial Council of California
FL-300 [Rev. January 1, 2007]

ORDER TO SHOW CAUSE

Family Code, §§ 215, 270 et seq., 3000 et seq., 3500 et seq., 4300
www.courtinfo.ca.gov

This page intentionally blank.

PETITIONER:	CASE NUMBER:
RESPONDENT:	

APPLICATION FOR ORDER AND SUPPORTING DECLARATION
—THIS IS NOT AN ORDER—

☐ Petitioner ☐ Respondent ☐ Claimant   requests the following orders:

1. ☐ CHILD CUSTODY   ☐ **To be ordered pending the hearing**

   a. <u>Child</u> *(name, age)*

   b. <u>Legal custody to</u>
   (person who makes decisions
   about health, education, etc.) *(name)*

   c. <u>Physical custody to</u>
   (person with whom child lives.)
   (name)

   ☐ Modify existing order
   (1) filed on *(date):*
   (2) ordering *(specify):*

   ☐ As requested in form ☐ FL-311 ☐ FL-312 ☐ FL-341(C) ☐ FL-341(D) ☐ FL-341(E)

2. ☐ CHILD VISITATION   ☐ **To be ordered pending the hearing**

   a. As requested in: (1) ☐ Attachment 2a (2) ☐ Form FL-311 (3) ☐ Other *(specify):*

   b. ☐ Modify existing order
   (1) filed on *(date):*
   (2) ordering *(specify):*

   c. ☐ One or more domestic violence restraining/protective orders are now in effect. *(Attach a copy of the orders if you have one.)* The orders are from the following court or courts *(specify county and state):*

   (1) ☐ Criminal: County/state: _____   (3) ☐ Juvenile: County/state: _____
   Case No. *(if known):* _____   Case No. *(if known):* _____

   (2) ☐ Family: County/state: _____   (4) ☐ Other: County/state: _____
   Case No. *(if known):* _____   Case No. *(if known):* _____

3. ☐ CHILD SUPPORT *(An earnings assignment order may be issued.)*

   a. <u>Child</u> *(name, age)*

   b. <u>Monthly amount</u> (if not by guideline)
   $

   c. ☐ Modify existing order
   (1) filed on *(date):*
   (2) ordering *(specify):*

4. ☐ SPOUSAL OR PARTNER SUPPORT *(An earnings assignment order may be issued.)*
   a. ☐ Amount requested *(monthly):* $ c. ☐ Modify existing order
   b. ☐ Terminate existing order   (1) filed on *(date):*
   (1) filed on *(date):*   (2) ordering *(specify):*
   (2) ordering *(specify):*

5. ☐ ATTORNEY FEES AND COSTS   a. ☐ Fees: $ b. ☐ Costs: $

NOTE: To obtain domestic violence restraining orders, you must use the forms *Request for Order (Domestic Violence Prevention)* (form DV-100) and *Temporary Restraining Order and Notice of Hearing (Domestic Violence Prevention)* (form DV-110).

Form Adopted for Mandatory Use
Judicial Council of California
FL-310 [Rev. January 1, 2007]

APPLICATION FOR ORDER AND SUPPORTING DECLARATION

Family Code, §§ 2045, 6224, 6226,
6320–6326, 6380–6383
www.courtinfo.ca.gov

PETITIONER:	CASE NUMBER:
RESPONDENT:	

6. ☐ PROPERTY RESTRAINT ☐ **To be ordered pending the hearing**

    a. The ☐ petitioner ☐ respondent ☐ claimant is restrained from transferring, encumbering, hypothecating, concealing, or in any way disposing of any property, real or personal, whether community, quasi-community, or separate, except in the usual course of business or for the necessities of life.

        ☐ The applicant will be notified at least five business days before any proposed extraordinary expenditures, and an accounting of such will be made to the court.

    b. ☐ Both parties are restrained and enjoined from cashing, borrowing against, canceling, transferring, disposing of, or changing the beneficiaries of any insurance or other coverage, including life, health, automobile, and disability, held for the benefit of the parties or their minor children.

    c. ☐ Neither party may incur any debts or liabilities for which the other may be held responsible, other than in the ordinary course of business or for the necessities of life.

7. ☐ PROPERTY CONTROL ☐ **To be ordered pending the hearing**

    a. ☐ The petitioner ☐ respondent is given the exclusive temporary use, possession, and control of the following property that we own or are buying (specify):

    b. ☐ The petitioner ☐ respondent is ordered to make the following payments on liens and encumbrances coming due while the order is in effect:

        Debt   Amount of payment   Pay to

8. ☐ **I request** that time for service of the *Order to Show Cause* and accompanying papers be shortened so that these documents may be served no less than (specify number):   days before the time set for the hearing. I need to have the order shortening time because of the facts specified in the attached declaration.

9. ☐ OTHER RELIEF (specify):

10. ☐ FACTS IN SUPPORT of relief requested and change of circumstances for any modification are (specify):
    ☐ contained in the attached declaration.

I declare under penalty of perjury under the laws of the State of California that the foregoing is true and correct.

Date:

▶

_____   _____
(TYPE OR PRINT NAME)   (SIGNATURE OF APPLICANT)

FL-311

PETITIONER/PLAINTIFF:	CASE NUMBER:
RESPONDENT/DEFENDANT:	

CHILD CUSTODY AND VISITATION APPLICATION ATTACHMENT

TO ☐ *Findings and Order After Hearing* ☐ *Judgment*

☐ *Stipulation and Order for Custody and/or Visitation of Children*

☐ *Other (specify):*

1. ☐ **Custody.** Custody of the minor children of the parties is requested as follows:

Child's name	Date of birth	Legal custody to	Physical custody to
		(person who makes decisions about health, education, etc.)	(person with whom the child lives)

☐ Joint legal custody   ☐ Joint physical custody

2. ☐ **Visitation**

   a. ☐ Reasonable right of visitation to the party without physical custody **(not appropriate in cases involving domestic violence)**

   b. ☐ See the attached _____-page document dated *(specify date):*

   c. ☐ The parties will go to mediation at *(specify location):*

   d. ☐ No visitation

   e. ☐ Visitation for the ☐ petitioner ☐ respondent   will be as follows:

   (1) ☐ **Weekends starting** *(date):*

   (The first weekend of the month is the first weekend with a Saturday.)

   ☐ 1st ☐ 2nd ☐ 3rd ☐ 4th ☐ 5th   weekend of the month

   from _____ at _____ ☐ a.m. ☐ p.m.
         (day of week)   *(time)*

   to _____ at _____ ☐ a.m. ☐ p.m.
         (day of week)   *(time)*

   (a) ☐ The parents will alternate the fifth weekends, with the ☐ petitioner ☐ respondent having the initial fifth weekend, which starts *(date):*

   (b) ☐ The petitioner will have fifth weekends in ☐ odd ☐ even   months.

   (2) ☐ **Alternate weekends starting** *(date):*

   The ☐ petitioner ☐ respondent   will have the children with him or her during the period

   from _____ at _____ ☐ a.m. ☐ p.m.
         (day of week)   *(time)*

   to _____ at _____ ☐ a.m. ☐ p.m.
         (day of week)   *(time)*

   (3) ☐ **Weekdays starting** *(date):*

   The ☐ petitioner ☐ respondent   will have the children with him or her during the period

   from _____ at _____ ☐ a.m. ☐ p.m.
         (day of week)   *(time)*

   to _____ at _____ ☐ a.m. ☐ p.m.
         (day of week)   *(time)*

   (4) ☐ **Other** *(specify days and times as well as any additional restrictions):*

☐ See Attachment 2e(4).

Page 1 of 2

Form Approved for Optional Use
Judicial Council of California
FL-311 [Rev. January 1, 2005]

CHILD CUSTODY AND VISITATION APPLICATION ATTACHMENT

Family Code, § 6200 et seq.
www.courtinfo.ca.gov

This page intentionally blank.

FL-305

PETITIONER/PLAINTIFF:	CASE NUMBER:
RESPONDENT/DEFENDANT:	

TEMPORARY ORDERS
Attachment to Order to Show Cause (FL-300)

1. ☐ PROPERTY RESTRAINT

   a. ☐ Petitioner ☐ Respondent is restrained from transferring, encumbering, hypothecating, concealing, or in any way disposing of any property, real or personal, whether community, quasi-community, or separate, except in the usual course of business or for the necessities of life.

   ☐ The other party is to be notified of any proposed extraordinary expenditures and an accounting of such is to be made to the court.

   b. ☐ Both parties are restrained and enjoined from cashing, borrowing against, canceling, transferring, disposing of, or changing the beneficiaries of any insurance or other coverage including life, health, automobile, and disability held for the benefit of the parties or their minor child or children.

   c. ☐ Neither party may incur any debts or liabilities for which the other may be held responsible, other than in the ordinary course of business or for the necessities of life.

2. ☐ PROPERTY CONTROL

   a. ☐ Petitioner ☐ Respondent is given the exclusive temporary use, possession, and control of the following property the parties own or are buying (specify):

   b. ☐ Petitioner ☐ Respondent is ordered to make the following payments on liens and encumbrances coming due while the order is in effect:

Debt	Amount of payment	Pay to

3. ☐ MINOR CHILDREN

   a. ☐ Petitioner ☐ Respondent will have the temporary physical custody, care, and control of the minor children of the parties, ☐ subject to the other party's rights of visitation as follows:

   b. ☐ Petitioner ☐ Respondent must not remove the minor child or children of the parties
   (1) ☐ from the State of California.
   (2) ☐ from the following counties (specify):
   (3) ☐ other (specify):

   c. ☐ Child abduction prevention orders are attached (see form FL-341(B)).

   d. (1) Jurisdiction: This court has jurisdiction to make child custody orders in this case under the Uniform Child Custody Jurisdiction and Enforcement Act (part 3 of the California Family Code, commencing with § 3400).
   (2) Notice and opportunity to be heard: The responding party was given notice and an opportunity to be heard as provided by the laws of the State of California.
   (3) Country of habitual residence: The country of habitual residence of the child or children is
   ☐ the United States of America ☐ other (specify):
   (4) Penalties for violating this order: If you violate this order you may be subject to civil or criminal penalties, or both.

4. ☐ OTHER ORDERS (specify):

Date: _____

_____
JUDGE OF THE SUPERIOR COURT

5. **The date of the court hearing is** (insert date when known):

CLERK'S CERTIFICATE

[SEAL]   I certify that the foregoing is a true and correct copy of the original on file in my office.

Date: _____   Clerk, by _____, Deputy

Page 1 of 1

Form Adopted for Mandatory Use
Judicial Council of California
FL-305 [Rev. July 1, 2003]

TEMPORARY ORDERS

Family Code, §§ 2045, 6224, 6226, 6302
6320–6326, 6380–6383
www.courtinfo.ca.gov

This page intentionally blank.

FL-330

ATTORNEY OR PARTY WITHOUT ATTORNEY OR GOVERNMENTAL AGENCY (under Family Code, §§ 17400, 17406) *(Name, state bar number, and address):*	FOR COURT USE ONLY
TELEPHONE NO.: FAX NO.:	
ATTORNEY FOR *(Name):*	

SUPERIOR COURT OF CALIFORNIA, COUNTY OF

STREET ADDRESS:

MAILING ADDRESS:

CITY AND ZIP CODE:

BRANCH NAME:

PETITIONER/PLAINTIFF:

RESPONDENT/DEFENDANT:

OTHER PARENT:

PROOF OF PERSONAL SERVICE	CASE NUMBER:

1. I am at least 18 years old, not a party to this action, and not a protected person listed in any of the orders.
2. Person served *(name):*
3. I served copies of the following documents *(specify):*

4. By personally delivering copies to the person served, as follows:
   a. Date: b. Time:
   c. Address:

5. I am
   a. ☐ not a registered California process server.
   b. ☐ a registered California process server.
   c. ☐ an employee or independent contractor of a registered California process server.
   d. ☐ exempt from registration under Bus. & Prof. Code section 22350(b).
   e. ☐ a California sheriff or marshal.

6. My name, address, and telephone number, and, if applicable, county of registration and number *(specify):*

7. ☐ I declare under penalty of perjury under the laws of the State of California that the foregoing is true and correct.
8. ☐ I am a California sheriff or marshal and I certify that the foregoing is true and correct.

Date:

▶

_____   _____
(TYPE OR PRINT NAME OF PERSON WHO SERVED THE PAPERS)   (SIGNATURE OF PERSON WHO SERVED THE PAPERS)

Page 1 of 2

Form Approved for Optional Use Judicial Council of California FL-330 [Rev. January 1, 2003]	**PROOF OF PERSONAL SERVICE**	Code of Civil Procedure, § 1011 www.courtinfo.ca.gov

INFORMATION SHEET FOR PROOF OF PERSONAL SERVICE

Use these instructions to complete the *Proof of Personal Service* (form FL-330).

A person at least 18 years of age or older must serve the documents. There are two ways to serve documents: (1) personal delivery and (2) by mail. See the *Proof of Service by Mail* (form FL-335) if the documents are being served by mail. The person who serves the documents must complete a proof of service form for the documents being served. **You cannot serve documents if you are a party to the action.**

INSTRUCTIONS FOR THE PERSON WHO SERVES THE DOCUMENTS (TYPE OR PRINT IN BLACK INK)

You must complete a proof of service for each package of documents you serve. For example, if you serve the Respondent and the Other Parent, you must complete two proofs of service, one for the Respondent and one for the Other Parent.

Complete the top section of the proof of service forms as follows:
First box, left side: In this box print the name, address, and phone number of the person for whom you are serving the documents.
Second box, left side: Print the name of the county in which the legal action is filed and the court's address in this box. Use the same address for the court that is on the documents you are serving.
Third box, left side: Print the names of the Petitioner/Plaintiff, Respondent/Defendant, and Other Parent in this box. Use the same names listed on the documents you are serving.
First box, top of form, right side: Leave this box blank for the court's use.
Second box, right side: Print the case number in this box. This number is also stated on the documents you are serving.

1. You are stating that you are over the age of 18 and that you are neither a party of this action nor a protected person listed in any of the orders.
2. Print the name of the party to whom you handed the documents.
3. List the name of each document that you delivered to the party.
4. a. Write in the date that you delivered the documents to the party.
    b. Write in the time of day that you delivered the documents to the party.
    c. Print the address where you delivered the documents.
5. Check the box that applies to you. If you are a private person serving the documents for a party, check box "a."
6. Print your name, address, and telephone number. If applicable, include the county in which you are registered as a process server and your registration number.
7. You must check this box if you are not a California sheriff or marshal. You are stating under penalty of perjury that the information you have provided is true and correct.
8. Do not check this box unless you are a California sheriff or marshal.

Print your name, fill in the date, and sign the form.

If you need additional assistance with this form, contact the Family Law Facilitator in your county.

PROOF OF PERSONAL SERVICE

FL-340

ATTORNEY OR PARTY WITHOUT ATTORNEY *(Name and address)*	FOR COURT USE ONLY
TELEPHONE NO.: FAX NO. *(optional):*	
ATTORNEY FOR *(Name):*	

SUPERIOR COURT OF CALIFORNIA, COUNTY OF
STREET ADDRESS:
MAILING ADDRESS:
CITY AND ZIP CODE:
BRANCH NAME:

PETITIONER/PLAINTIFF:

RESPONDENT/DEFENDANT:

OTHER:

FINDINGS AND ORDER AFTER HEARING	CASE NUMBER:

1. This proceeding was heard
   on *(date):*   at *(time):*   in Dept.:   Room:
   by Judge *(name):*   ☐ Temporary Judge

   ☐ Petitioner/plaintiff present   ☐ Attorney present *(name):*
   ☐ Respondent/defendant present   ☐ Attorney present *(name):*
   ☐ Other present   ☐ Attorney present *(name):*
   On the order to show cause or motion filed *(date):*   by *(name):*

2. **THE COURT ORDERS**

3. Custody and visitation: ☐ As attached on form FL-341   ☐ Not applicable

4. Child support: ☐ As attached on form FL-342   ☐ Not applicable

5. Spousal or family support: ☐ As attached on form FL-343   ☐ Not applicable

6. Property orders: ☐ As attached on form FL-344   ☐ Not applicable

7. Other orders: ☐ As attached   ☐ Not applicable

8. ☐ Attorney fees *(specify amount):* $
   Payable to *(name and address):*

   Payable ☐ forthwith   ☐ other *(specify):*

9. All other issues are reserved until further order of court.

Date: ▶ _____
                                              JUDICIAL OFFICER

Approved as conforming to court order.

▶ _____

SIGNATURE OF ATTORNEY FOR   ☐ PETITIONER / PLAINTIFF ☐ RESPONDENT / DEFENDANT

Form Adopted for Mandatory Use
Judicial Council of California
FL-340 [Rev. July 1, 2003]

FINDINGS AND ORDER AFTER HEARING
(Family Law—Custody and Support—Uniform Parentage)

www.courtinfo.ca.gov

This page intentionally blank.

Name:

Address:

Phone:

Fax:

Attorney for _____

In Propria Persona

SUPERIOR COURT OF THE STATE OF CALIFORNIA

COUNTY OF _____

_____ DIVISION

Marriage of:)   CASE NO. _____
)
PETITIONER: _____)   EX PARTE APPLICATION FOR
)   PUBLICATION OF SUMMONS
)   ORDER; DECLARATION OF
RESPONDENT: _____)   PETITIONER IN SUPPORT
)   THEREOF; MEMORANDUM OF
)   POINTS AND AUTHORITIES
)
)   DATE: _____
)   TIME: _____
_____)   DEPT: _____

Application is hereby made by Petitioner _____ for an order directing the service of the Summons—Family Law on Respondent _____ by publication in the _____ newspaper, a newspaper of general circulation most likely to give notice to Respondent, pursuant to California Code of Civil Procedure 415.50.

A copy of the Summons—Family Law and the petition and other papers could not be served on Respondent because after reasonable diligence Respondent could not be located and served by any of the methods in California Code of Civil Procedure Sections 415.10 through 415.40.

The petition for dissolution of marriage in this matter was filed on _____.

This application is supported by the declaration of Petitioner _____
_____immediately following at the top of the next page.

DATED: _____   _____
                                     (Petitioner's signature)

                                     _____
                                     (Petitioner's printed name)

DECLARATION OF _____
IN SUPPORT OF APPLICATION FOR ORDER
FOR PUBLICATION OF SUMMONS—FAMILY LAW

I, _____, am the Petitioner in this matter. I declare that I have personal knowledge of the facts herein and would and could testify competently to them if called upon to do so, except for those matters which are stated on information and belief, and as to those matters I believe them to be true.

I have tried to serve Respondent _____ ever since _____. I filed the petition for dissolution of marriage in this matter on _____.

The _____ newspaper is a newspaper of general circulation most likely to give notice to the Respondent because:

_____
_____
_____.

I have made the following unsuccessful attempts to serve Respondent with the Summons—Family Law, Petition, a blank Response, and completed and blank Confidential Counseling Statements:

_____
_____
_____
_____
_____
_____
_____
_____.

In addition, I have unsuccessfully tried to locate Respondent by the following methods (certified mail, return receipt requested; records; persons who may have information; any other method):

_____
_____
_____
_____
_____
_____
_____.

I am unaware of any other reasonable source of information or informant that would have facts leading me to locate Respondent.

I declare under penalty of perjury under the laws of the State of California that the above is true and correct. Signed at _____, on _____, _____.

_____
Petitioner

This page intentionally blank.

SUPERIOR COURT OF THE STATE OF CALIFORNIA
COUNTY OF _____
_____ DIVISION

Marriage of:)   CASE NO. _____
)
PETITIONER: _____   )   ORDER FOR PUBLICATION
)   OF SUMMONS—FAMILY LAW
)
RESPONDENT: _____   )
)
_____   )

     After consideration of the application of Petitioner _____ and the other evidence submitted for an order for publication of Summons—Family Law for service on Respondent _____, and it satisfactorily appearing therefrom that the Respondent _____ cannot be served with reasonable diligence in any manner specified in California Code of Civil Procedure sections 415.10 through 415.40, and it also appearing that a good cause of action exists against Respondent, or that Respondent is a necessary party to this action, or that Respondent claims an interest in property subject to this action that is subject to the jurisdiction of this court;

     IT IS HEREBY ORDERED THAT service of said Summons—Family Law in this action be made upon Respondent _____ by publication thereof in the _____, a newspaper of general circulation published in _____, hereby designated as the newspaper most likely to give notice to said Respondent and that publication be made at least once a week for four successive weeks;

     IT IS FURTHER ORDERED THAT, a copy of the Summons—Family Law, Petition, Confidential Counseling Statement, and blank Response Response and Confidential Counseling Statement forms, and the Order for Publication be forthwith mailed to Respondent _____ in the event the address is ascertained before the time herein prescribed for publication of Summons—Family Law expires.

DATED: _____

_____
JUDGE OF THE SUPERIOR COURT

This page intentionally blank.

FL-191

ATTORNEY OR PARTY WITHOUT ATTORNEY *(Name, State Bar number, and address)*:	COURT PERSONNEL: *STAMP DATE RECEIVED HERE*
TELEPHONE NO.: FAX NO. *(Optional)*: E-MAIL ADDRESS *(Optional)*: ATTORNEY FOR *(Name)*:	**DO NOT FILE**

SUPERIOR COURT OF CALIFORNIA, COUNTY OF
STREET ADDRESS:
MAILING ADDRESS:
CITY AND ZIP CODE:
BRANCH NAME:

PETITIONER/PLAINTIFF:

RESPONDENT/DEFENDANT:

OTHER PARENT:

CHILD SUPPORT CASE REGISTRY FORM ☐ Mother ☐ First form completed ☐ Father ☐ Change to previous information	CASE NUMBER:

THIS FORM WILL NOT BE PLACED IN THE COURT FILE. IT WILL BE MAINTAINED IN A CONFIDENTIAL FILE WITH THE STATE OF CALIFORNIA.

Notice: Pages 1 and 2 of this form must be completed and delivered to the court along with the court order for support. Pages 3 and 4 are instructional only and do not need to be delivered to the court. If you did not file the court order, you must complete this form and deliver it to the court within 10 days of the date on which you received a copy of the support order. Any later change to the information on this form must be delivered to the court on another form within 10 days of the change. It is important that you keep the court informed in writing of any changes of your address and telephone number.

1. Support order information *(this information is on the court order you are filing or have received)*.
   a. Date order filed:
   b. ☐ Initial child support or family support order   ☐ Modification
   c. Total monthly base current child or family support amount ordered for children listed below, plus any monthly amount ordered payable on past-due support:

   Child Support: Family Support: Spousal Support:
   (1) ☐ Current $ ☐ Current $ ☐ Current $
       base child   ☐ Reserved order   base family   ☐ Reserved order   spousal   ☐ Reserved order
       support: ☐ $0 (zero) order   support: ☐ $0 (zero) order   support: ☐ $0 (zero) order

   (2) ☐ Additional $ ☐ Additional $
       monthly   monthly
       support: support:

   (3) ☐ Total $ ☐ Total $ ☐ Total $
       past-due   past-due   past-due
       support: support: support:

   (4) ☐ Payment $ ☐ Payment $ ☐ Payment $
       on past-   on past-   on past-
       due support: due support: due support:

   (5) Wage withholding was ☐ ordered   ☐ ordered but stayed until *(date)*:

2. Person required to pay child or family support *(name)*:
   Relationship to child *(specify)*:

3. Person or agency to receive child or family support payments *(name)*:
   Relationship to child *(if applicable)*:

TYPE OR PRINT IN INK

Form Adopted for Mandatory Use
Judicial Council of California
FL-191 [Rev. July 1, 2005]

CHILD SUPPORT CASE REGISTRY FORM

Family Code, § 4014
www.courtinfo.ca.gov

296

PETITIONER/PLAINTIFF:	CASE NUMBER:
RESPONDENT/DEFENDANT:	
OTHER PARENT:	

4. The child support order is for the following children:

Child's name	Date of birth	Social security number
a.		
b.		
c.		

☐ Additional children are listed on a page attached to this document.

You are required to complete the following information about yourself. You are not required to provide information about the other person, but you are encouraged to provide as much as you can. This form is confidential and will not be filed in the court file. It will be maintained in a confidential file with the State of California.

5. Father's name:

   a. Date of birth:

   b. Social security number:

   c. Street address:

     City, state, zip code:

   d. Mailing address:

     City, state, zip code:

   e. Driver's license number:

     State:

   f. Telephone number:

   g. ☐ Employed ☐ Not employed ☐ Self-employed

     Employer's name:

     Street address:

     City, state, zip code:

     Telephone number:

6. Mother's name:

   a. Date of birth:

   b. Social security number:

   c. Street address:

     City, state, zip code:

   d. Mailing address:

     City, state, zip code:

   e. Driver's license number:

     State:

   f. Telephone number:

   g. ☐ Employed ☐ Not employed ☐ Self-employed

     Employer's name:

     Street address:

     City, state, zip code:

     Telephone number:

7. ☐ A restraining order, protective order, or nondisclosure order due to domestic violence is in effect.

   a. The order protects: ☐ Father ☐ Mother ☐ Children

   b. From: ☐ Father ☐ Mother

   c. The restraining order expires on (date):

I declare under penalty of perjury under the laws of the State of California that the foregoing is true and correct.

Date:

▶

_____   _____
(TYPE OR PRINT NAME)   (SIGNATURE OF PERSON COMPLETING THIS FORM)

INFORMATION SHEET FOR CHILD SUPPORT CASE REGISTRY FORM
(Do NOT deliver this Information Sheet to the court clerk.)

Please follow these instructions to complete the *Child Support Case Registry Form* (form FL-191) if you do not have an attorney to represent you. Your attorney, if you have one, should complete this form.

Both parents must complete a *Child Support Case Registry Form.* The information on this form will be included in a national database that, among other things, is used to locate absent parents. When you file a court order, you must deliver a completed form to the court clerk along with your court order. If you did not file a court order, you must deliver a completed form to the court clerk **WITHIN 10 DAYS** of the date you received a copy of your court order. If any of the information you provide on this form changes, you must complete a new form and deliver it to the court clerk within 10 days of the change. The address of the court clerk is the same as the one shown for the superior court on your order. This form is confidential and will not be filed in the court file. It will be maintained in a confidential file with the State of California.

INSTRUCTIONS FOR COMPLETING THE *CHILD SUPPORT CASE REGISTRY FORM* (TYPE OR PRINT IN INK):

If the top section of the form has already been filled out, skip down to number 1 below. If the top section of the form is blank, you must provide this information.

<u>Page 1, first box, top of form, left side</u>: Print your name, address, telephone number, fax number, and e-mail address, if any, in this box. Attorneys must include their State Bar identification numbers.

<u>Page 1, second box, top of form, left side</u>: Print the name of the county and the court's address in this box. Use the same address for the court that is on the court order you are filing or have received.

<u>Page 1, third box, top of form, left side</u>: Print the names of the petitioner/plaintiff, respondent/defendant, and other parent in this box. Use the same names listed on the court order you are filing or have received.

<u>Page 1, fourth box, top of form, left side</u>: Check the box indicating whether you are the mother or the father. If you are the attorney for the mother, check the box for mother. If you are the attorney for the father, check the box for father. Also, if this is the first time you have filled out this form, check the box by "First form completed." If you have filled out form FL-191 before, and you are changing any of the information, check the box by "Change to previous information."

<u>Page 1, first box, right side</u>: Leave this box blank for the court's use in stamping the date of receipt.

<u>Page 1, second box, right side</u>: Print the court case number in this box. This number is also shown on the court papers.

Instructions for numbered paragraphs:

1. a. Enter the date the court order was filed. This date is shown in the "COURT PERSONNEL: STAMP DATE RECEIVED HERE" box on page 1 at the top of the order on the right side. If the order has not been filed, leave this item blank for the court clerk to fill in.

   b. If the court order you filed or received is the first child or family support order for this case, check the box by "Initial child support or family support order." If this is a change to your order, check the box by "Modification."

   c. Information regarding the amount and type of support ordered and wage withholding is on the court order you are filing or have received.

      (1) If your order provides for any type of current support, check all boxes that describe that support. For example, if your order provides for both child and spousal support, check both of those boxes. If there is an amount, put it in the blank provided. If the order says the amount is reserved, check the "Reserved order" box. If the order says the amount is zero, check the "$0 (zero) order" box. Do not include child care, special needs, uninsured medical expenses, or travel for visitation here These amounts will go in (2). Do NOT complete the Child Support Case Registry form if you receive spousal support only.

      (2) If your order provides for a set monthly amount to be paid as additional support for such needs as child care, special needs, uninsured medical expenses or travel for visitation check the box in Item 2 and enter the monthly amount. For example, if your order provides for base child support and in addition the paying parent is required to pay $300 per month, check the box in item 2 underneath the "Child Support" column and enter $300. Do NOT check this box if your order provides only for a payment of a percentage, such as 50% of the childcare.

(3) If your order determined the amount of past due support, check the box in Item 3 that states the type of past due support and enter the amount. For example, if the court determined that there was $5000 in past due child support and $1000 in past due spousal support, you would check the box in item 3 in the "Child Support" column and enter $5000 and you would also check the box in item 3 in the "Spousal Support" column and enter $1000.

(4) If your order provides for a specific dollar amount to be paid towards any past due support, check the box in Item 4 that states the type of past due support and enter the amount. For example, the court ordered $350 per month to be paid on the past due child support, you would check the box in Item 4 in the "Child Support" column and enter $350.

(5) Check the "ordered" box if wage withholding was ordered with no conditions. Check the box "ordered but stayed until" if wage withholding was ordered but is not to be deducted until a later date. If the court delayed the effective date of the wage withholding, enter the specific date. Check only one box in this item.

2. a. Write the name of the person who is supposed to pay child or family support.
   b. Write the relationship of that person to the child.

3. a. Write the name of the person or agency supposed to receive child or family support payments.
   b. Write the relationship of that person to the child.

4. List the full name, date of birth, and social security number for each child included in the support order. If there are more than five children included in the support order, check the box below item 4e and list the remaining children with dates of birth and social security numbers on another sheet of paper. Attach the other sheet to this form.

The local child support agency is required, under section 466(a)(13) of the Social Security Act, to place in the records pertaining to child support the social security number of any individual who is subject to a divorce decree, support order, or paternity determination or acknowledgment. This information is mandatory and will be kept on file at the local child support agency.

Top of page 2, box on left side: Print the names of the petitioner/plaintiff, respondent/defendant, and other parent in this box. Use the same names listed on page 1.

Top of page 2, box on right side: Print your court case number in this box. Use the same case number as on page 1, second box, right side.

You are required to complete information about yourself. If you know information about the other person, you may also fill in what you know about him or her.

5. If you are the father in this case, list your full name in this space. See instructions for a–g under item 6 below.

6. If you are the mother in this case, list your full name in this space.

   a. List your date of birth.
   b. Write your social security number.
   c. List the street address, city, state, and zip code where you live.
   d. List the street address, city, state, and zip code where you want your mail sent, if different from the address where you live.
   e. Write your driver's license number and the state where it was issued.
   f. List the telephone number where you live.
   g. Indicate whether you are employed, not employed, self-employed, or by checking the appropriate box. If you are employed, write the name, street address, city, state, zip code, and telephone number where you work.

7. If there is a restraining order, protective order, or nondisclosure order, check this box.

   a. Check the box beside each person who is protected by the restraining order.
   b. Check the box beside the parent who is restrained.
   c. Write the date the restraining order expires. See the restraining order, protective order, or nondisclosure order for this date.

If you are in fear of domestic violence, you may want to ask the court for a restraining order, protective order, or nondisclosure order.

You must type or print your name, fill in the date, and sign the *Child Support Case Registry Form* under penalty of perjury. When you sign under penalty of perjury, you are stating that the information you have provided is true and correct.

CHILD SUPPORT CASE REGISTRY FORM

INFORMATION SHEET
SIMPLIFIED WAY TO CHANGE CHILD, SPOUSAL, OR FAMILY SUPPORT

New laws make it easier for a person to ask the court to raise or lower the amount paid for child, spousal, or family support.

How to Ask for a Change

1. Get copies of these forms:
    *   *Notice of Motion and Motion for Simplified Modification of Order for Child, Spousal, or Family Support ("Notice of Motion")* (form FL-390).
    *   *Responsive Declaration to Motion for Simplified Modification for Child, Spousal, or Family Support* (form FL-392).
    *   *Findings and Order After Hearing* (form FL-340) and *Child Support Information and Order Attachment (form FL-342)*.
    *   *Financial Statement (Simplified)* (form FL-155) or *Income and Expense Declaration* (form FL-150).
    The court clerk's office, the office of the family law facilitator, or the local child support agency can tell you where to get these forms. You can get them at the Judicial Council website: *www.courtinfo.ca.gov*

2. Fill out and sign the form *Notice of Motion*. **Check with your local court clerk's office or the office of the family law facilitator to see if the forms must be typewritten.**

3. Fill out the form *Financial Statement (Simplified)*, if you are allowed to use the form. See the instructions on the back side of the form to see if you qualify; otherwise you must fill out the *Income and Expense Declaration*. You must attach copies of your most recent W-2 form(s) and three most recent paycheck stubs, to the form *Financial Statement (Simplified)* or the form *Income and Expense Declaration*.

4. You must schedule a hearing date with your court clerk's office before filing and serving these papers. You must enter the hearing date in item 1 of the *Notice of Motion*.

5. Make at least three copies of these forms after you have completed them:
    *   *Notice of Motion and Motion for Simplified Modification of Order for Child, Spousal, or Family Support* (form FL-390).
    *   *Financial Statement (Simplified)* (form FL-155) or *Income and Expense Declaration* (form FL-150).

6. You must have one copy of each of the following papers served on the local child support agency **and on the other party,** if the other party is not the county:
    *   Your *Notice of Motion and Motion for Simplified Modification of Order for Child, Spousal, or Family Support* (form FL-390).
    *   Your *Financial Statement (Simplified)* (form FL-155) or *Income and Expense Declaration* (form FL-150).
    *   A blank *Responsive Declaration to Motion for Simplified Modification of Order for Child, Spousal, or Family Support* (form FL-392).
    *   A blank *Financial Statement (Simplified)* (form FL-155) or *Income and Expense Declaration* (form FL-150). *Information Sheet—How to Oppose a Request to Change Child, Spousal, or Family Support* (form FL-393).

    For instructions on how to serve these papers properly, see the information box on the Proof of Service, found on the reverse of the *Notice of Motion* (form FL-390). Whoever serves the papers should fill out and must sign the Proof of Service.

7. Take the original of each of the completed forms to the court clerk's office for filing. If you or your attorney have not filed any other papers in the case, you must do one or more of the following:
    *   Pay a first appearance filing fee to the court clerk when you go to file these papers (you can find out what the amount of the fee is from the court clerk's office or the office of the family law facilitator); or
    *   Pay a fee to file this motion with the court clerk, even if you or your attorney have already filed papers in this case; or
    *   Apply for a fee waiver. For more information on how to request a waiver of the filing fees, get the form *Information Sheet on Waiver of Court Fees and Costs* (form FW-001-INFO).

Form Approved for Optional Use
Judicial Council of California
FL-391 [Rev. July 1, 2007]

INFORMATION SHEET—SIMPLIFIED WAY TO CHANGE CHILD, SPOUSAL, OR FAMILY SUPPORT

Family Code, § 3680
www.courtinfo.ca.gov

Using an Attorney

If you use this method to modify support, you may hire an attorney to represent you in court, or you may represent yourself. If you hire an attorney, you will have to pay the cost. The court will not provide you with a free attorney.

If the county is the other party, and if one of the parties is receiving welfare benefits, or if one of the parties has asked the local child support agency to enforce support, a representative from the local child support agency will be present at the hearing.

REMEMBER: The local child support agency does not represent any individual in this lawsuit, including the child, the child's mother, or the child's father.

Agreeing to Support Before the Hearing

A court hearing may not be necessary to modify the current support order, if you are able to reach an agreement with the other party. Note that if an agreement is reached with the other party, you must prepare an order and submit it to the court for the judge's signature and file the order with the court clerk's office. If one of the parties is receiving welfare benefits or the local child support agency is enforcing the support order, the local child support agency must sign the agreement before it is filed with the court.

Hearing

Even if neither the local child support agency nor the other party has filed a response to your *Notice of Motion,* the judge may still require a hearing. Make sure you bring with you a copy of your *Notice of Motion* (form FL-390), *Financial Statement (Simplified)* (form FL-155) or *Income and Expense Declaration* (form FL-150), your most recent federal and state income tax returns and W-2 form(s), and three most recent paycheck stubs. The other party has a right to see your financial information, and you have the right to see the other party's financial information.

Court Order

Once the judge makes a decision, you may be required to prepare the form *Findings and Order After Hearing* (form FL-340) with the *Child Support Information and Order Attachment* (form FL-342). If the support order has changed, you may required to prepare a modified *Order/Notice to Withhold Income for Child Support* (FL-195). You will not have to prepare these documents if the local child support agency is involved. If you have prepared these documents yourself, you must make sure that they are signed by the judge. Check with the court clerk's office or the office of the family law facilitator for the proper procedure. After the *Order/Notice to Withhold Income for Child Support* (FL-195) is signed by the judge and filed, it must be served on the noncustodial parent's employer, on the other party, and on the local child support agency if the local child support agency is involved in the case.

**INFORMATION SHEET—SIMPLIFIED WAY TO CHANGE
CHILD, SPOUSAL, OR FAMILY SUPPORT**

FL-341

PETITIONER/PLAINTIFF:	CASE NUMBER:
RESPONDENT/DEFENDANT:	

CHILD CUSTODY AND VISITATION ORDER ATTACHMENT

TO ☐ *Findings and Order After Hearing* ☐ *Judgment*

☐ *Stipulation and Order for Custody and/or Visitation of Children*

☐ *Other (specify):*

1. ☐ **Custody.** Custody of the minor children of the parties is awarded as follows:

Child's name	Date of birth	Legal custody to (person who makes decisions about health, education, etc.)	Physical custody to (person with whom the child lives)

2. ☐ **Visitation**

   a. ☐ Reasonable right of visitation to the party without physical custody **(not appropriate in cases involving domestic violence)**

   b. ☐ See the attached _____-page document dated *(specify date):*

   c. ☐ The parties will go to mediation at *(specify location):*

   d. ☐ No visitation

   e. ☐ Visitation for the ☐ petitioner ☐ respondent will be as follows:

      (1) ☐ **Weekends starting** *(date):*

         (The first weekend of the month is the first weekend with a Saturday.)

         ☐ 1st ☐ 2nd ☐ 3rd ☐ 4th ☐ 5th weekend of the month

         from _____ at _____ ☐ a.m. ☐ p.m.
               (day of week)   *(time)*

         to _____ at _____ ☐ a.m. ☐ p.m.
               (day of week)   *(time)*

         (a) ☐ The parents will alternate the fifth weekends, with the ☐ petitioner ☐ respondent having the initial fifth weekend, which starts *(date):*

         (b) ☐ The petitioner will have fifth weekends in ☐ odd ☐ even months.

      (2) ☐ **Alternate weekends starting** *(date):*

         The ☐ petitioner ☐ respondent will have the children with him or her during the period

         from _____ at _____ ☐ a.m. ☐ p.m.
               (day of week)   *(time)*

         to _____ at _____ ☐ a.m. ☐ p.m.
               (day of week)   *(time)*

      (3) ☐ **Weekdays starting** *(date):*

         The ☐ petitioner ☐ respondent will have the children with him or her during the period

         from_____ at _____ ☐ a.m. ☐ p.m.
               (day of week)   *(time)*

         to _____ at _____ ☐ a.m. ☐ p.m.
               (day of week)   *(time)*

      (4) ☐ **Other** *(specify days and times as well as any additional restrictions):*

☐ See Attachment 2e(4).

Page 1 of 2

Form Approved for Optional Use
Judicial Council of California
FL-341 [Rev. July 1, 2006]
CHILD CUSTODY AND VISITATION ORDER ATTACHMENT
Family Code, §§ 3020, 3022, 3025,
3040–3043, 3048, 3100, 6340, 7604
www.courtinfo.ca.gov

FL-34

| PETITIONER/PLAINTIFF: | CASE NUMBER: |
| RESPONDENT/DEFENDANT: | |

3. ☐ **The court acknowledges** that criminal protective orders in case number *(specify):*
   in *(specify court):*   relating to the parties in this case are in effect
   under Penal Code section 136.2, are current, and have priority of enforcement.

4. ☐ **Supervised visitation.** Until ☐ further order of the court ☐ other *(specify):*
   the ☐ petitioner ☐ respondent will have supervised visitation with the minor children according to the schedul
   set forth on page 1. (**You must attach form FL-341(A).)**

5. ☐ **Transportation for visitation**
   a. ☐ Transportation **to** the visits will be provided by the ☐ petitioner ☐ respondent
      ☐ other *(specify):*
   b. ☐ Transportation **from** the visits will be provided by the ☐ petitioner ☐ respondent
      ☐ other *(specify):*
   c. ☐ Drop-off of the children will be at *(address):*
   d. ☐ Pick-up of the children will be at *(address):*
   e. ☐ The children will be driven only by a licensed and insured driver. The car or truck must have legal child restraint
      devices.
   f. ☐ During the exchanges, the parent driving the children will wait in the car and the other parent will wait in his or
      her home while the children go between the car and the home.
   g. ☐ Other *(specify):*

6. ☐ **Travel with children.** The ☐ petitioner ☐ respondent ☐ other *(name):*
   must have written permission from the other parent or a court order to take the children out of
   a. ☐ the state of California.
   b. ☐ the following counties *(specify):*
   c. ☐ other places *(specify):*

7. ☐ **Child abduction prevention.** There is a risk that one of the parents will take the children out of California without the other
   parent's permission. Form FL-341(B) is attached and must be obeyed.

8. ☐ **Holiday schedule.** The children will spend holiday time as listed in the attached ☐ form FL-341(C)
   ☐ other *(specify):*

9. ☐ **Additional custody provisions.** The parents will follow the additional custody provisions listed in the attached
   ☐ form FL-341(D) ☐ other *(specify):*

10. ☐ **Joint legal custody.** The parents will share joint legal custody as listed in the attached ☐ form FL-341(E)
    ☐ other *(specify):*

11. ☐ **Other** *(specify):*

12. **Jurisdiction.** This court has jurisdiction to make child custody orders in this case under the Uniform Child Custody Jurisdiction ar
    Enforcement Act (part 3 of the California Family Code, commencing with section 3400).

13. **Notice and opportunity to be heard.** The responding party was given notice and an opportunity to be heard, as provided by the
    laws of the State of California.

14. **Country of habitual residence.** The country of habitual residence of the child or children in this case is
    ☐ the United States ☐ other *(specify):*

15. **Penalties for violating this order.** If you violate this order, you may be subject to civil or criminal penalties, or both.

CHILD CUSTODY AND VISITATION ORDER ATTACHMENT

FL-341(A)

PETITIONER / PLAINTIFF:	CASE NUMBER:
RESPONDENT / DEFENDANT:	

SUPERVISED VISITATION ORDER
Attachment to *Child Custody and Visitation Order Attachment* (form FL-341)

1. Evidence has been presented in support of a request that the contact of ☐ Petitioner ☐ Respondent with the child(ren) be supervised based upon allegations of
   ☐ abduction of child(ren) ☐ physical abuse ☐ drug abuse ☐ neglect
   ☐ sexual abuse ☐ domestic violence ☐ alcohol abuse ☐ other *(specify):*

   ☐ Petitioner ☐ Respondent disputes these allegations and the court reserves the findings on these issues pending further investigation and hearing or trial.

2. The court finds, under Family Code section 3100, that the best interest of the child(ren) requires that visitation by
   ☐ Petitioner ☐ Respondent must, until further order of the court, be limited to contact supervised by the person(s) set forth in item 6 below pending further investigation and hearing or trial.

THE COURT MAKES THE FOLLOWING ORDERS
3. **CHILD(REN) TO BE SUPERVISED**

Child's name	Birth date	Age	Sex

4. **TYPE**
   a. ☐ Supervised visitation   b. ☐ Supervised exchange only   c. ☐ Therapeutic visitation

5. **SUPERVISED VISITATION PROVIDER**
   a. ☐ Professional (individual provider or supervised visitation center)   b. ☐ Nonprofessional

6. **AUTHORIZED PROVIDER**

Name	Address	Telephone

   ☐ Any other mutually agreed-upon third party as arranged.

7. **DURATION AND FREQUENCY OF VISITS** *(see form FL-341 for specifics of visitation):*

8. **PAYMENT RESPONSIBILITY**   Petitioner: _____%   Respondent: _____%

9. ☐ Petitioner will contact professional provider or supervised visitation center no later than *(date):*
   ☐ Respondent will contact professional provider or supervised visitation center no later than *(date):*

10. **THE COURT FURTHER ORDERS**

Date: _____

_____
JUDICIAL OFFICER

Form Adopted for Mandatory Use
Judicial Council of California
FL-341(A) [Rev. January 1, 2003]

SUPERVISED VISITATION ORDER

Family Code, §§ 3100, 3031
www.courtinfo.ca.gov

This page intentionally blank.

FL-341(B)

PETITIONER:	CASE NUMBER:
RESPONDENT:	

CHILD ABDUCTION PREVENTION ORDER ATTACHMENT

TO ☐ *Child Custody and Visitation Order Attachment* (form FL-341(A)) ☐ Other *(specify):*

1. **The court finds there is a risk that** *(specify name of parent):* **will take the child without permission because that parent** *(check all that apply):*

   a. ☐ has violated—or threatened to violate—a custody or visitation order in the past.

   b. ☐ does not have strong ties to California.

   c. ☐ has done things that make it easy for him or her to take the children away without any permission, such as *(check all that apply):*

      ☐ quit a job.   ☐ sold his or her home.

      ☐ closed a bank account.   ☐ ended a lease.

      ☐ sold or gotten rid of assets. ☐ hidden or destroyed documents.

      ☐ applied for a passport, birth certificate, or school or medical records.

      ☐ Other *(specify):*

   d. ☐ has a history of *(check all that apply):*

      ☐ domestic violence.

      ☐ child abuse.

      ☐ not cooperating with the other parent in parenting.

   e. ☐ has a criminal record.

   f. ☐ has family or emotional ties to another country, state, or foreign country.
      (NOTE: If item "f" is checked, at least one other factor must be checked, too.)

THE COURT ORDERS, to prevent the parent in item 1 from taking the children without permission:

2. ☐ **Supervised visitation.** Terms of visitation are *(check one):*

   ☐ as specified on attached form FL-341(A) ☐ as follows:

3. ☐ **The parent in item 1 must post a bond for $**   . The terms of the bond are *(specify):*

4. ☐ **The parent in item 1 must not move from the following locations with the children** without permission in writing from the other parent or a court order:

   ☐ Current residence ☐ Current school district *(specify):*

   ☐ This county   ☐ Other *(specify):*

5. ☐ **The parent in item 1 must not travel with the children** out of *(check all that apply):*

   ☐ this county.   ☐ the United States.

   ☐ California.   ☐ other *(specify):*

6. ☐ **The parent in item 1 must register this order** in the state of *(specify):*   before the children can travel to that state for visits.

7. ☐ **The parent in item 1 must not apply for a passport or any other document,** such as a visa or birth certificate, that can be used for travel, and must turn in the following documents *(specify):*

Form Adopted for Mandatory Use
Judicial Council of California
FL-341(B) [Rev. January 1, 2005]
CHILD ABDUCTION PREVENTION ORDER ATTACHMENT
Family Code, § 3048; 42 U.S.C § 11601
www.courtinfo.ca.gov

306

8. ☐ **The parent in item 1 must give the other parent the following *before* traveling with the children:**

    ☐ The children's travel itinerary

    ☐ Copies of round-trip airline tickets

    ☐ Addresses and telephone numbers where the children can be reached at all times

    ☐ An open airline ticket for the other parent in case the children are not returned

    ☐ Other *(specify):*

9. ☐ **The parent in item 1 must notify the embassy or consulate** of *(specify country):*   of
this order and provide the court with proof of that notification within *(specify number):*   days.

10. ☐ **The parent in item 1 must get a custody and visitation order** equivalent to the most recent U.S. order before the children may travel to that country for visits. The court recognizes that foreign orders may be changed or enforced according to the laws of that country.

11. ☐ **Enforcing the order.** The court authorizes any law enforcement officer to enforce this order. In this county, contact the Child Abduction Unit of the Office of the District Attorney at *(phone number and address):*

12. ☐ **Other** *(specify):*

13. This order is valid in other states and in any country that has signed the Hague Convention on Child Abduction.

NOTICE TO AUTHORITIES IN OTHER STATES AND COUNTRIES

This court has jurisdiction to make child custody orders under California's Uniform Child Custody Jurisdiction and Enforcement Act (California Fam. Code, § 3400 et seq.) and the Hague Convention on Civil Aspects of International Child Abduction (42 U.S.C. § 11601 et seq.). If jurisdiction is based on other factors, they are listed in item 12 above.

Date: _____

                                          _____

                                              JUDICIAL OFFICER

FL-341(C)

PETITIONER:	CASE NUMBER:
RESPONDENT:	

CHILDREN'S HOLIDAY SCHEDULE ATTACHMENT

TO ☐ **Petition or Application for Order** ☐ **Findings and Order After Hearing or Judgment**
☐ **Stipulation and Order for Custody and/or Visitation of Children**

1. **Holiday parenting.** The following table shows the holiday parenting schedules. Write "Pet" or "Resp" to specify each parent's years—odd, even, or both ("every year")—and under "Time" specify the starting and ending days and times.

Holiday	Time (from when to when) *(Unless otherwise noted, all single-day holidays start at ___ a.m. and end at ___ p.m.)*	Every Year *Petitioner/ Respondent*	Even Years *Petitioner/ Respondent*	Odd Years *Petitioner/ Respondent*
January 1 (New Year's Day)				
Martin Luther King's Birthday (weekend)				
Lincoln's Birthday				
President's Day (weekend)				
Spring Break, first half				
Spring Break, second half				
Mother's Day				
Memorial Day (weekend)				
Father's Day				
July 4th				
Labor Day (weekend)				
Columbus Day (weekend)				
Halloween				
Veteran's Day (weekend)				
Thanksgiving Day				
Thanksgiving weekend				
Winter Break, first half				
Winter Break, second half				
New Year's Eve				
Child's birthday				
Mother's birthday				
Father's birthday				
Breaks for year-round schools				
Summer Break, first half				
Summer Break, second half				
Other (specify):				

☐ Any three-day weekend not specified above will be spent with the parent who would normally have that weekend.
☐ Other (specify):

2. **Vacations.** The ☐ petitioner ☐ respondent may take a vacation of up to (specify number): ☐ days
☐ weeks with the children the following number of times per year (specify): ___ . They must notify the other parent in writing of their vacation plans a minimum of (specify number): ___ days in advance and provide the other parent with a basic itinerary that includes dates of leaving and returning, destinations, flight information, and telephone numbers for emergency purposes.
☐ The other parent has (specify number): ___ days to respond if there is a problem with the schedule.
   a. ☐ This vacation may be outside California.
   b. ☐ Any vacation outside ☐ California ☐ the United States requires prior written consent of the other parent or a court order.
   c. ☐ Other (specify):

Form Approved for Optional Use
Judicial Council of California
FL-341(C) [Rev. January 1, 2005]

CHILDREN'S HOLIDAY SCHEDULE ATTACHMENT

Family Code, §§ 3003, 3083
www.courtinfo.ca.gov

This page intentionally blank.

FL-341(D)

PETITIONER:	CASE NUMBER:
RESPONDENT:	

ADDITIONAL PROVISIONS—PHYSICAL CUSTODY ATTACHMENT

TO ☐ Petition or Application for Order   ☐ Findings and Order After Hearing or Judgment
☐ Stipulation and Order for Custody and/or Visitation of Children

1. ☐ **Notification of parent's current address.** Each parent must notify the other parent of his or her current address and telephone number within *(specify number):*   days of any change in his or her
   a. address for ☐ residence ☐ mailing ☐ work.
   b. telephone/message number at ☐ home ☐ work ☐ the children's schools.

   Neither parent may use such information for the purpose of harassing, annoying, or disturbing the peace of the other or invading the other's privacy. If a parent has an address with the State of California's Safe at Home confidential address program, no residence or work address is needed.

2. ☐ **Notification of proposed move of child.** Each parent must notify the other parent *(specify number):*   days prior to any planned change in residence of the children. The notification must state, to the extent known, the planned address of the children, including the county and state of the new residence. The notification must be sent by certified mail, return receipt requested.

3. ☐ **Child care**
   a. ☐ The children must not be left alone without age-appropriate supervision.
   b. ☐ The parents must let each other know the name, address, and phone number of the children's regular child-care providers.

4. ☐ **Right of first option of child care.** In the event either parent requires child care for *(specify number):*   hours or more while the children are in his or her custody, the other parent must be given first opportunity, with as much prior notice as possible, to care for the children before other arrangements are made. Unless specifically agreed or ordered by the court, this order does not include regular child care needed when a parent is working.

5. ☐ **Canceled parenting time**
   a. ☐ If the noncustodial parent fails to arrive at the appointed time and fails to notify the custodial parent that he or she will be late, then the custodial parent need wait for only *(specify number):*   minutes before considering the visitation canceled.
   b. ☐ In the event a noncustodial parent is unable to exercise visitation on a given occasion, he or she must notify the custodial parent at the earliest possible opportunity.
   c. ☐ The custodial parent must give the noncustodial parent as much notice as possible if the children are ill and unable to participate in scheduled time with the other parent. ☐ A doctor's excuse is required.

6. ☐ **Phone contact between parents and children**
   a. ☐ The children may have telephone access to the parents ☐ and the parents may have telephone access to the children   at reasonable times, for reasonable durations.
   b. ☐ The scheduled phone contact between parents and the children is *(specify):*
   c. ☐ Neither parent nor any other third party may listen to or monitor the calls.

7. ☐ **No negative comments.** Neither parent will make or allow others to make negative comments about the other parent or the other parent's past or present relationships, family, or friends within hearing distance of the children.

8. ☐ **No use of children as messengers.** The parents will communicate directly with each other on matters concerning the children and may not use the children as messengers between them.

9. ☐ **Alcohol or substance abuse.** The ☐ petitioner ☐ respondent   may not consume alcoholic beverages, narcotics, or restricted dangerous drugs (except by prescription) within *(specify number):*   hours prior to or during periods of time with the children ☐ and may not permit any third party to do so in the presence of the children.

10. ☐ **No exposure to cigarette smoke.** The children will not be exposed to secondhand cigarette smoke while in the home or car of either parent.

Page 1 of 2

PETITIONER:	CASE NUMBER:
RESPONDENT:	

11. ☐ **No interference with schedule of other parent without that parent's consent.** Neither parent will schedule activities for the children during the other parent's scheduled parenting time without the other parent's prior agreement.

12. ☐ **Third-party contact**
   a. ☐ The children will have no contact with *(specify name):*
   b. ☐ The children must not be left alone in the presence of *(specify name):*

13. ☐ **Children's clothing and belongings**
   a. ☐ Each parent will maintain clothing for the children so that the children do not have to make the exchanges with additional clothing.
   b. ☐ The children will be returned to the other parent with the clothing and other belongings they had when they arrived.

14. ☐ **Log book.** The parents will maintain a "log book" and make sure that the book is sent with the children between their two homes. Using businesslike notes (no personal comments), parents will record information related to the health, education, and welfare issues that arise during the time the children are with them.

15. ☐ **Terms and conditions of order may be changed.** The terms and conditions of this order may be added to or changed as the needs of the children and parents change. Such changes will be in writing, dated and signed by both parents; each parent will retain a copy. If the parents want a change to be a court order, it must be filed with the court in the form of a court document.

16. ☐ **Other** *(specify):*

ADDITIONAL PROVISIONS—PHYSICAL CUSTODY ATTACHMENT

FL-341(E)

PETITIONER:	CASE NUMBER:
RESPONDENT:	

JOINT LEGAL CUSTODY ATTACHMENT

TO ☐ **Petition or Application for Order**   ☐ **Findings and Order After Hearing or Judgment**
☐ **Stipulation and Order for Custody and/or Visitation of Children**

1. The parents will have joint legal custody of the minor children.

2. In exercising joint legal custody, the parents will share in the responsibility and confer in good faith on matters concerning the health, education, and welfare of the children. The parents must confer in making decisions on the following matters:

   a. ☐ Enrollment in or leaving a particular private or public school or daycare center

   b. ☐ Participation in particular religious activities or institutions

   c. ☐ Beginning or ending of psychiatric, psychological, or other mental health counseling or therapy

   d. ☐ Selection of a doctor, dentist, or other health professional (except in emergency situations)

   e. ☐ Participation in extracurricular activities

   f. ☐ Out-of-country or out-of-state travel

   g. ☐ Other (specify):

   In all other matters in exercising joint legal custody, the parents may act alone, as long as the action does not conflict with any orders concerning the physical custody of the children.

3. If a parent does not obtain the required consent of the other parent to the decisions checked in item 2:
   a. He or she may be subject to civil or criminal penalties.
   b. The court may change the legal and physical custody of the minor children.
   c. ☐ Other consequences (specify):

4. ☐ **Special decision-making designation**
   a. The ☐ petitioner ☐ respondent   will be responsible for making decisions regarding the following issues (specify):

   b. ☐ Each parent will have access to the children's school, medical, and dental records and the right to consult with professionals who are providing services to the children.

5. ☐ **Health-care notification**
   a. ☐ Each parent must notify the other of the name and address of each health practitioner who examines or treats the children; such notification must be made within (specify number):   days of the commencement of the first such treatment or examination.

   b. ☐ Each parent is authorized to take any and all actions necessary to protect the health and welfare of the children, including but not limited to consent to emergency surgical procedures or treatment. The parent authorizing such emergency treatment must notify the other parent as soon as possible of the emergency situation and of all procedures or treatment administered to the children.

   c. ☐ Both parents are required to administer any prescribed medications for the children.

6. ☐ **School notification.** Each parent will be designated as a person the children's school will contact in the event of an emergency.

7. ☐ **Name.** Neither parent will change the last name of the children or have a different name used on the children's medical, school, or other records without the written consent of the other parent.

8. ☐ Other (specify):

Page 1 of 1

Form Approved for Optional Use
Judicial Council of California
FL-341(E) [Rev. January 1, 2005]

JOINT LEGAL CUSTODY ATTACHMENT

Family Code, § 3003, 3083
www.courtinfo.ca.gov

This page intentionally blank.

FL-355

ATTORNEY OR PARTY WITHOUT ATTORNEY *(Name, State Bar number, and address):*	TELEPHONE NO.:	FOR COURT USE ONLY

TELEPHONE NO: FAX NO. *(Optional):*

E-MAIL ADDRESS *(Optional):*

ATTORNEY FOR *(Name):*

SUPERIOR COURT OF CALIFORNIA, COUNTY OF

STREET ADDRESS:

MAILING ADDRESS:

CITY AND ZIP CODE:

BRANCH NAME:

PETITIONER:

RESPONDENT:

OTHER:

STIPULATION AND ORDER FOR CUSTODY AND/OR VISITATION OF CHILDREN ☐ MODIFICATION	CASE NUMBER:

The parties signing this stipulation agree that:

1. This court has jurisdiction over the minor children because California is the children's home state.

2. The habitual residence of the children is the United States of America.

3. **The parties acknowledge they were advised that any violation of this order may result in civil or criminal penalties, or both.**

4. a. The parties stipulate that the attached document, dated *(specify):*   and consisting of *(number):*   pages is their custody and visitation agreement and request that it be made an order of the court, or

   b. The parties stipulate that the attached forms

   ☐ FL-341 ☐ FL-341(A) ☐ FL-341(B) ☐ FL-341(C) ☐ FL-341(D) ☐ FL-341(E)

   are their agreement regarding custody and/or visitation of their children and request that they be made an order of the court.

Each party declares under penalty of perjury under the laws of the State of California that the foregoing is true and correct.

Date:

Date: _____   ▶ _____
     (TYPE OR PRINT NAME)   (SIGNATURE OF PETITIONER)

Date: _____   ▶ _____
     (TYPE OR PRINT NAME)   (SIGNATURE OF RESPONDENT)

Date: _____   ▶ _____
     (TYPE OR PRINT NAME)   (SIGNATURE OF ATTORNEY FOR PETITIONER)

Date: _____   ▶ _____
     (TYPE OR PRINT NAME)   (SIGNATURE OF ATTORNEY FOR RESPONDENT)

Date: _____   ▶ _____
     (TYPE OR PRINT NAME)   (SIGNATURE OF OTHER)

_____   _____
     (TYPE OR PRINT NAME)   (SIGNATURE OF ATTORNEY FOR OTHER)

FINDINGS AND ORDER

THE COURT FINDS:

1. This court has jurisdiction over the minor children because California is the children's home state.
2. The habitual residence of the children is the United States of America.
3. Both parties have been advised that any violation of this order may result in civil or criminal penalties, or both.

THE COURT ORDERS:

1. The agreement of the parties regarding custody and visitation ☐ as set forth in the attached document dated *(specify):* and consisting of *(number):*   pages or ☐ set forth in the attached forms:

   ☐ FL-341 ☐ FL-341(A) ☐ FL-341(B) ☐ FL-341(C) ☐ FL-341(D) ☐ FL-341(E)

   is adopted as the order of the court and fully incorporated by reference herein.

Date: _____

_____
JUDICIAL OFFICER

Page 1 of 1

This page intentionally blank.

FL-342

PETITIONER/PLAINTIFF: RESPONDENT/DEFENDANT: OTHER PARENT:	CASE NUMBER:

CHILD SUPPORT INFORMATION AND ORDER ATTACHMENT

Attachment to ☐ **Findings and Order After Hearing** ☐ **Restraining Order After Hearing (CLETS)**
☐ **Judgment** ☐ **Other**

THE COURT USED THE FOLLOWING INFORMATION IN DETERMINING THE AMOUNT OF CHILD SUPPORT:

1. ☐ A printout of a computer calculation and findings is attached and incorporated in this order for all required items not filled out below.

2. ☐ **Income**

	Gross monthly income	Net monthly income	Receiving TANF/CalWORKS
a. Each parent's monthly income is as follows: petitioner/plaintiff:	$	$	☐
respondent/defendant:	$	$	☐
other parent:	$	$	☐

   b. Imputation of income. The court finds that the ☐ petitioner/plaintiff ☐ respondent/defendant
   ☐ other parent has the capacity to earn:

   $ _____ per: _____ and has based the support order upon this imputed income.

3. ☐ **Children of This Relationship**

   a. Number of children who are the subjects of the support order *(specify)*:

   b. Approximate percentage of time spent with: petitioner/plaintiff _____ %
   respondent/defendant _____ %
   other parent _____ %

4. ☐ **Hardships**

   Hardships for the following have been allowed in calculating child support:

	petitioner/plaintiff	respondent/defendant	other parent	Approximate ending time for the hardship
a. ☐ Other minor children:	$	$	$	
b. ☐ Extraordinary medical expenses:	$	$	$	
c. ☐ Catastrophic losses:	$	$	$	

THE COURT ORDERS

5. ☐ **Low-Income Adjustment**

   a. ☐ The low-income adjustment applies.

   b. ☐ The low-income adjustment does not apply because *(specify reasons)*:

6. ☐ **Child Support**

   a. **Base child support**

   ☐ Petitioner/plaintiff ☐ Respondent/defendant ☐ Other parent must pay child support beginning
   (date): _____ and continuing until further order of the court, or until the child marries, dies, is emancipated, reaches age 19, or reaches age 18 and is not a full-time high school student, whichever occurs first, as follows:

Child's name	Date of birth	Monthly amount	Payable to *(name)*

   Payable ☐ on the 1st of the month ☐ one-half on the 1st and one-half on the 15th of the month
   ☐ other *(specify)*:

   b. ☐ **Mandatory additional child support**

   (1) ☐ Child-care costs related to employment or reasonably necessary job training.

   ☐ Petitioner/plaintiff must pay: _____ % of total or ☐ $ _____ per month child-care costs.
   ☐ Respondent/defendant must pay: _____ % of total or ☐ $ _____ per month child-care costs.
   ☐ Other parent must pay: _____ % of total or ☐ $ _____ per month child-care costs.
   ☐ Costs to be paid as follows *(specify)*:

THIS IS A COURT ORDER.

Form Adopted for Mandatory Use
Judicial Council of California
FL-342 [Rev. July 1, 2005]

CHILD SUPPORT INFORMATION AND ORDER ATTACHMENT

Family Code, §§ 4055–4069
www.courtinfo.ca.gov

PETITIONER/PLAINTIFF:	CASE NUMBER:
RESPONDENT/DEFENDANT:	
OTHER PARENT:	

THE COURT FURTHER ORDERS

6. b. **Mandatory additional child support** *(continued)*

    (2) ☐ Reasonable uninsured health-care costs for the children

        ☐ Petitioner/plaintiff must pay: % of total or ☐ $ per month.

        ☐ Respondent/defendant must pay: % of total or ☐ $ per month.

        ☐ Other parent must pay: % of total or ☐ $ per month.

        ☐ Costs to be paid as follows *(specify)*:

    c. ☐ **Additional child support**

        (1) ☐ Costs related to the educational or other special needs of the children

          ☐ Petitioner/plaintiff must pay: % of total or ☐ $ per month.

          ☐ Respondent/defendant must pay: % of total or ☐ $ per month.

          ☐ Other parent must pay: % of total or ☐ $ per month.

          ☐ Costs to be paid as follows *(specify)*:

        (2) ☐ Travel expenses for visitation

          ☐ Petitioner/plaintiff must pay: % of total or ☐ $ per month.

          ☐ Respondent/defendant must pay: % of total or ☐ $ per month.

          ☐ Other parent must pay: % of total or ☐ $ per month.

          ☐ Costs to be paid as follows *(specify)*:

> **Total child support per month: $**

7. **Health-Care Expenses**

    a. Health insurance coverage for the minor children of the parties must be maintained by the

      ☐ petitioner/plaintiff   ☐ respondent/defendant   ☐ other parent   if available at no or reasonable cost through their respective places of employment or self-employment. Both parties are ordered to cooperate in the presentation, collection, and reimbursement of any health-care claims.

    b. ☐ Health insurance is not available to the ☐ petitioner/plaintiff ☐ respondent/defendant ☐ other parent at a reasonable cost at this time.

    c. ☐ The party providing coverage must assign the right of reimbursement to the other party.

8. **Earnings Assignment**

    An *Order/Notice to Withhold Income for Child Support* (form FL-195) must issue. **Note:** The payor of child support is responsible for the payment of support directly to the recipient until support payments are deducted from the payor's wages, and for any support not paid by the assignment.

9. ☐ **Non-Guideline Order**

    This order does not meet the child support guideline set forth in Family Code section 4055. A *Non-Guideline Child Support Findings Attachment* (form FL-342(A)) is attached.

10. ☐ **Employment Search Order (Family Code, § 4505)**

    ☐ Petitioner/plaintiff ☐ Respondent/defendant ☐ Other parent   is ordered to seek employment with the following terms and conditions:

11. **Other Orders** *(specify)*:

12. **Required Attachments**

    A *Notice of Rights and Responsibilities—Health Care Costs and Reimbursement Procedures* and *Information Sheet on Changing a Child Support Order* (form FL-192) must be attached and is incorporated into this order.

13. **Child Support Case Registry Form**

    Both parties must complete and file with the court a *Child Support Case Registry Form* (form FL-191) within 10 days of the date of this order. Thereafter, the parties must notify the court of any change in the information submitted within 10 days of the change by filing an updated form.

> **NOTICE: Any party required to pay child support must pay interest on overdue amounts at the legal rate, which is currently 10 percent per year.**

THIS IS A COURT ORDER.

   CHILD SUPPORT INFORMATION AND ORDER ATTACHMENT

FL-342(A)

PETITIONER/PLAINTIFF:	CASE NUMBER:
RESPONDENT/DEFENDANT:	

NON-GUIDELINE CHILD SUPPORT FINDINGS ATTACHMENT

Attachment to ☐ Child Support Information and Order Attachment (form FL-342)
☐ Judgment (Family Law) (form FL-180) ☐ Other *(specify):*

The court makes the following findings required by Family Code sections 4056, 4057, and 4065:

1. **STIPULATION TO NON-GUIDELINE ORDER**
   ☐ The child support agreed to by the parties is ☐ below or ☐ above the statewide child support guidelines. The amount of support that would have been ordered under the guideline formula is: $ ___ per month. The parties have been fully informed of their rights concerning child support. Neither party is acting out of duress or coercion. Neither party is receiving public assistance and no application for public assistance is pending. The needs of the children will be adequately met by this agreed-upon amount of child support. If the order is below the guideline, no change of circumstances will be required to modify this order. If the order is above the guideline, a change of circumstances will be required to modify this order.

OTHER REBUTTAL FACTORS

2. ☐ **Support calculation**

   a. The guideline amount of child support calculated is: $ ___ per month **payable** by ☐ mother ☐ father

   b. The court finds by a preponderance of the evidence that rebuttal factors exist. The rebuttal factors result in an ☐ increase ☐ decrease in child support. The revised amount of support is: $ ___ per month.

   c. The court finds the child support amount revised by these factors to be in the best interest of the child and that application of the formula would be unjust or inappropriate in this case.
   These changes remain in effect ☐ until *(date):* ___
   ☐ until further order

   d. **The factors are:**
      (1) ☐ The sale of the family residence is deferred under Family Code section 3800, and the rental value of the family residence in which the children reside exceeds the mortgage payments, homeowners insurance, and property taxes by: $ ___ per month. (Fam. Code, § 4057(b)(2).)

      (2) ☐ The parent paying support has extraordinarily high income, and the amount determined under the guideline would exceed the needs of the child. (Fam. Code, § 4057(b)(3).)

      (3) ☐ The ☐ mother ☐ father is not contributing to the needs of the children at a level commensurate with that party's custodial time. (Fam. Code, § 4057(b)(4).)

      (4) ☐ Special circumstances exist in this case. The special circumstances are:
         (i) ☐ The parents have different timesharing arrangements for different children. (Fam. Code, § 4057(b)(5)(A).)
         (ii) ☐ The parents have substantially equal custody of the children and one parent has a much lower or higher percentage of income used for housing than the other parent. (Fam. Code, § 4057(b)(5)(B).)
         (iii) ☐ The child has special medical or other needs that require support greater than the formula amount. These needs are (Fam. Code, § 4057(b)(5)(C)) *(specify):*

         (iv) ☐ Other (Fam. Code, § 4057(b)(5)) *(specify):*

Form Adopted for Mandatory Use
Judicial Council of California
FL-342(A) [Rev. January 1, 2003]

NON-GUIDELINE CHILD SUPPORT FINDINGS ATTACHMENT

Family Code, § 4056
www.courtinfo.ca.gov

This page intentionally blank.

FL-343

PETITIONER/PLAINTIFF:	CASE NUMBER:
RESPONDENT/DEFENDANT:	
OTHER PARENT:	

SPOUSAL, PARTNER, OR FAMILY SUPPORT ORDER ATTACHMENT

TO ☐ *Findings and Order After Hearing* ☐ *Judgment* ☐ *Other (specify):*

THE COURT FINDS

1. A printout of a computer calculation of the parties' financial circumstances is attached for all required items not filled out below.

2. **Net income.** The parties' monthly income and deductions are as follows *(complete a, b, or both)*:

	Total gross monthly income	Total monthly deductions	Total hardship deductions	Net monthly disposable income
a. Petitioner: ☐ receiving TANF/CalWORKS				
b. Respondent: ☐ receiving TANF/CalWORKS				

3. **Other factors regarding spousal or partner support**
   a. ☐ The parties were married for *(specify numbers):* _____ years _____ months.
   b. ☐ The parties were registered as domestic partners or the equivalent on *(date):*
   c. ☐ The Family Code section 4320 factors were considered, as listed in Attachment 3c.
   d. ☐ The marital standard of living was *(describe):*

   ☐ See Attachment 3d.
   e. ☐ Other *(specify):*

THE COURT ORDERS

4. a. The ☐ petitioner ☐ respondent must pay to the ☐ petitioner ☐ respondent
   as ☐ temporary ☐ spousal support ☐ family support ☐ partner support
   $ _____ per month, beginning *(date):* _____ , payable through *(specify end date):*

   ☐ payable on the *(specify):* _____ day of each month.
   ☐ Other *(specify):*

   b. ☐ Support must be paid by check, money order, or cash. The support payor's obligation to pay support will terminate on the death, remarriage, or registration of a new domestic partnership of the support payee.

   c. ☐ An earnings assignment for the foregoing support will issue. (**Note:** The payor of spousal, family, or partner support is responsible for the payment of support directly to the recipient until support payments are deducted from the payor's earnings, and for any support not paid by the assignment.)

   d. ☐ Service of the earnings assignment is stayed provided the payor is not more than *(specify number):* _____ days late in the payment of spousal, family, or partner support.

Form Approved for Optional Use
Judicial Council of California
FL-343 [Rev. January 1, 2005]
SPOUSAL, PARTNER, OR FAMILY SUPPORT ORDER ATTACHMENT
(Family Law)
Family Code, §§ 150, 299, 3651,
3653, 3654, 4320, 4330, 4337
www.courtinfo.ca.gov

PETITIONER/PLAINTIFF:	CASE NUMBER:
RESPONDENT/DEFENDANT:	
OTHER PARENT:	

5. ☐ The parties must promptly inform each other of any change of employment, including the employer's name, address, and telephone number.

6. ☐ **NOTICE:** It is the goal of this state that each party must make reasonable good faith efforts to become self-supporting as provided for in Family Code section 4320. The failure to make reasonable good faith efforts may be one of the factors considered by the court as a basis for modifying or terminating support.

7. ☐ This order is for family support. Both parties must complete and file with the court a *Child Support Case Registry Form* (form FL-191) within 10 days of the date of this order. The parents must notify the court of any change of information submitted within 10 days of the change by filing an updated form. Form FL-192, *Notice of Rights and Responsibilities* and *Information Sheet on Changing a Child Support Order,* is attached.

8. ☐ The issue of spousal or partner support for the ☐ petitioner ☐ respondent is reserved for a later determination.

9. ☐ The court terminates jurisdiction over the issue of spousal or partner support for the ☐ petitioner ☐ respondent.

10. ☐ Other *(specify):*

NOTICE: Any party required to pay support must pay interest on overdue amounts at the "legal" rate, which is currently 10 percent.

THIS IS A COURT ORDER

SPOUSAL, PARTNER, OR FAMILY SUPPORT ORDER ATTACHMENT
(Family Law)

FL-344

PETITIONER :	CASE NUMBER:
RESPONDENT:	

PROPERTY ORDER ATTACHMENT
TO FINDINGS AND ORDER AFTER HEARING

THE COURT ORDERS

1. ☐ **Property restraining orders**

   a. The ☐ petitioner ☐ respondent ☐ claimant   is restrained from transferring, encumbering, hypothecating, concealing, or in any way disposing of any property, real or personal, whether community, quasi-community, or separate, except in the usual course of business or for the necessities of life.

   b. The ☐ petitioner ☐ respondent   must notify the other party of any proposed extraordinary expenses at least five business days before incurring such expenses, and make an accounting of such to the court.

   c. The ☐ petitioner ☐ respondent   is restrained from cashing, borrowing against, cancelling, transferring, disposing of, or changing the beneficiaries of any insurance or other coverage, including life, health, automobile, and disability, held for the benefit of the parties or their minor child or children.

   d. The ☐ petitioner ☐ respondent   must not incur any debts or liabilities for which the other may be held responsible, other than in the ordinary course of business or for the necessities of life.

2. ☐ **Possession of property.** The exclusive use, possession, and control of the following property that the parties own or are buying is given as specified:

   Property   Given to

   ☐ See Attachment 2.

3. ☐ **Payment of debts.** Payments on the following debts that come due while this order is in effect must be paid as follows:

Total debt	Amount of payments	Pay to	Paid by
$	$		
$	$		
$	$		
$	$		

   ☐ See Attachment 3.

4. ☐ These are temporary orders only. The court will make final orders at the time of judgment.

5. ☐ Other *(specify):*

Form Adopted for Mandatory Use
Judicial Council of California
FL-344 [Rev. January 1, 2007]

PROPERTY ORDER ATTACHMENT
TO FINDINGS AND ORDER AFTER HEARING
(Family Law)

Family Code, §§ 2045, 6324
www.courtinfo.ca.gov

This page intentionally blank.

FL-195
OMB Control No.: 0970-0154

☐ ORDER/NOTICE TO WITHHOLD INCOME FOR CHILD SUPPORT
☐ NOTICE OF AN ORDER TO WITHHOLD INCOME FOR CHILD SUPPORT

☐ Original   ☐ Amended   ☐ Termination   Date:_____
   State/Tribe/Territory_____
   City/Co./Dist./Reservation_____
☐ Non-governmental entity or individual _____
   Case Number_____

_____	RE : _____
Employer's/Withholder's Name	Employee's/Obligor's Name (Last, First, MI)
_____	_____
Employer's/Withholder's Address	Employee's/Obligor's Social Security Number
_____	_____
_____	Employee's/Obligor's Case Identifier
_____	_____
Employer's/Withholder's Federal EIN Number (if known)	Obligee's Name (Last, First, MI)

ORDER INFORMATION: This document is based on the support or withholding order from _____.
You are required by law to deduct these amounts from the employee's/obligor's income until further notice.
$_____ Per _____ current child support
$_____ Per _____ past-due child support - Arrears greater than12 weeks? ☐ yes ☐ no
$_____ Per _____ current cash medical support
$_____ Per _____ past-due cash medical support
$_____ Per _____ spousal support
$_____ Per _____ past-due spousal support
$_____ Per _____ other (specify) _____
for a total of $_____ per _____to be forwarded to the payee below.
You do not have to vary your pay cycle to be in compliance with the support order. If your pay cycle does not match the
ordered payment cycle, withhold one of the following amounts:
$_____per weekly pay period. $_____per semimonthly pay period (twice a month).
$_____per biweekly pay period (every two weeks).$_____per monthly pay period.

REMITTANCE INFORMATION: When remitting payment, provide the pay date/date of withholding and the case identifier. If
the employee's/obligor's principal place of employment is _____, begin withholding no later than the first pay
period occurring_____ days after the date of _____. Send payment within_working days of the pay date/date of withholding.
 The total withheld amount, including your fee, may not exceed_____% of the employee's/obligor's aggregate disposable
weekly earnings.

If the employee's/obligor's principal place of employment is not _____, for limitations on
withholding, applicable time requirements, and any allowable employer fees, follow the laws and procedures of the
employee's/obligor's principal place of employment (see #3 and #9, ADDITIONAL INFORMATION TO EMPLOYERS AND
OTHER WITHHOLDERS).

Make check payable to: (Payee and Case identifier)_____Send check to: _____. If remitting
payment by EFT/EDI, call _____before first submission. Use this FIPS code:_____:
Bank routing number: _____Bank account number:_____.

If this is an Order/Notice to Withhold:	**If this is a Notice of an Order to Withhold:**
Print Name _____	Print Name_____
Title of Issuing Official_____ mandatory _____	Title (if appropriate)_____
Signature and Date _____	Signature and Date_____
☐ IV-D Agency ☐ Court	☐ Attorney ☐ Individual ☐ Private Entity

☐ Attorney with authority under state law to issue order/notice.

NOTE: Non-IV-D Attorneys, individuals, and non-governmental entities must submit a Notice of an Order to Withhold and
include a copy of the income withholding order unless, under a state's law, an attorney in that state may issue an income
withholding order. In that case, the attorney may submit an Order/Notice to Withhold and include a copy of the state law

IMPORTANT: The person completing this form is advised that the information on this form may be shared with the obligor
authorizing the attorney to issue an income withholding order/notice.

324

FL-195 / OMB Control No.: 0970-0154

ADDITIONAL INFORMATION TO EMPLOYERS AND OTHER WITHHOLDERS

☐ If checked, you are required to provide a copy of this form to your employee/obligor. If your employee works in a state that is different from the state that issued this order, a copy must be provided to your employee/obligor even if the box is not checked.

1. **Priority:** Withholding under this Order or Notice has priority over any other legal process under state law (or tribal law, if applicable) against the same income. If there are federal tax levies in effect, please notify the contact person listed below. (See 10 below.)

2. **Combining Payments:** You may combine withheld amounts from more than one employee's/obligor's income in a single payment to each agency/party requesting withholding. You must, however, separately identify the portion of the single payment that is attributable to each employee/obligor.

3. **Reporting the Paydate/Date of Withholding:** You must report the paydate/date of withholding when sending the payment. The paydate/date of withholding is the date on which the amount was withheld from the employee's wages. You must comply with the law of the state of employee's/obligor's principal place of employment with respect to the time periods within which you must implement the withholding and forward the support payments.

4. **Employee/Obligor with Multiple Support Withholdings:** If there is more than one Order or Notice against this employee/obligor and you are unable to honor all support Orders or Notices due to federal, state, or tribal withholding limits, you must follow the state or tribal law/procedure of the employee's/obligor's principal place of employment. You must honor all Orders or Notices to the greatest extent possible. (See 9 below.)

5. **Termination Notification:** You must promptly notify the Child Support Enforcement (IV-D) Agency and/or the contact person listed below when the employee/obligor no longer works for you. Please provide the information requested and return a complete copy of this Order or Notice to the Child Support Enforcement (IV-D) Agency and/or the contact person listed below. (See 10 below.)

THE EMPLOYEE/OBLIGOR NO LONGER WORKS FOR:_____
EMPLOYEE'S/OBLIGOR'S NAME: _____CASE IDENTIFIER: _____
DATE OF SEPARATION FROM EMPLOYMENT: _____
LAST KNOWN HOME ADDRESS: _____
NEW EMPLOYER/ADDRESS: _____

6. **Lump Sum Payments:** You may be required to report and withhold from lump sum payments such as bonuses, commissions, or severance pay. If you have any questions about lump sum payments, contact the Child Support Enforcement (IV-D) Agency.

7. **Liability :** If you have any doubts about the validity of the Order or Notice, contact the agency or person listed below under 10. If you fail to withhold income as the Order or Notice directs, you are liable for both the accumulated amount you should have withheld from the employee's/obligor's income and any other penalties set by state or tribal law/procedure.

_____
_____

8. **A nti-discrimination:** You are subject to a fine determined under state or tribal law for discharging an employee/obligor from employment, refusing to employ, or taking disciplinary action against any employee/obligor because of a child support withholding.

_____
_____

9. **Withholding Limits:** For state orders, you may not withhold more than the lesser of: 1) the amounts allowed by the Federal Consumer Credit Protection Act (15 U.S.C. § 1673(b)); or 2) the amounts allowed by the state of the employee's/obligor's principal place of employment. The federal limit applies to the aggregate disposable weekly earnings (ADWE). ADWE is the net income left after making mandatory deductions such as: state, federal, local taxes, Social Security taxes, statutory pension contributions, and Medicare taxes. The Federal CCPA limit is 50% of the ADWE for child support and alimony, which is increased by 1) 10% if the employee does not support a second family; and/or 2) 5% if arrears greater than 12 weeks.
For tribal orders, you may not withhold more than the amounts allowed under the law of the issuing tribe. For tribal employers who receive a state order, you may not withhold more than the amounts allowed under the law of the state that issued the order.

Child(ren)'s Names and Additional Information:_____
_____
_____

10. If you or your employee/obligor have any questions, contact_____by telephone at
_____by Fax at _____or by internet at_____.

FL-195 Page 2 of 2

Instructions to complete the Order/Notice to Withhold Income for Child Support or Notice of an Order to Withhold Income for Child Support

The Order/Notice to Withhold Income for Child Support (Order/Notice) or Notice of an Order to Withhold Income for Child Support (Notice) is a standardized form used for income withholding in tribal, intrastate, interstate, and intergovernmental cases. Please note that information provided on this form may be shared with the obligor.   When completing the form, please include the following information.

The following information 1a – 1g refers to the government agency, non-government entity, or individual completing and sending this form to the employer.

1a.   Check whether this is an Order/Notice to Withhold Income for Child Support or a Notice of an Order to Withhold Income for Child Support. Attorneys, individuals, and non-governmental entities must submit a Notice of an Order to Withhold and include a copy of the income withholding order unless, under a state's law, an attorney in that state may issue an income withholding order/notice. In that case, the attorney may submit an Order/Notice to Withhold and include a copy of the state law authorizing the attorney to issue an income withholding order/notice.

1b.   Check the appropriate status of the Order or Notice.

1c.   Date this form is completed and/or signed.

1d.   Name of the state, tribe or territory sending this form. This must be a governmental entity.

1e.   Name of the county, city, district, or reservation sending this Order or Notice, if appropriate. This must be a governmental entity.

1f.   Check and indicate the non-governmental entity or individual sending this Order or Notice. Complete this item only if a non-governmental entity or individual is submitting this Order or Notice.

1g.   Identifying case number used by the entity or individual sending this Order or Notice. In a IV-D case, this must be the IV-D case number.

The following information in 2 and 3 refers to the obligor, obligor's employer, and case identification.

2a.   Employer's/Withholder's name.

2b-c.   Employer's/Withholder's mailing address, city, and state. (This may differ from the Employee's/Obligor's work site.)

2d.   Employer's/Withholder's nine-digit federal employer identification number (if available). Include three-digit location code.

OMB 0970-0154

3a.   Employee's/Obligor's last name, first name, and middle initial.

3b.   Employee's/Obligor's Social Security Number (if known).

3c.   The case identifier used by the order issuing state or tribe for recording payments. (Should be the same as #21.) In a IV-D case, this must be the IV-D case number.

3d.   Custodial Parent's last name, first name, and middle initial (if known).

ORDER INFORMATION - **The following information in 4 -14e refers to the dollar amounts taken directly from the child support order.**

4.   Name of the state or tribe that issued the support order.

5a-b.   Dollar amount to be withheld for payment of current child support, time period that corresponds to the amount in #6a (such as month, week, etc.).

6a-b.   Dollar amount to be withheld for payment of past-due child support, time period that corresponds to the amount in #6a (such as month, week, etc.).

7a-b.   Dollar amount to be withheld for payment of current cash medical support, as appropriate, based on the underlying order, time period that corresponds to the amount in #7a (such as month, week, etc.).

8a-b.   Dollar amount to be withheld for payment of past-due cash medical support, if appropriate, based on the underlying order and the time period that corresponds to the amount in #8a (such as month, week, etc.).

9a-b.   Dollar amount to be withheld for payment of spousal support (alimony), if appropriate, based on the underlying order, time period that corresponds to the amount in #9a (such as month, week, etc.).

10a-b. Dollar amount to be withheld for payment of past-due spousal support (alimony), if appropriate, based on the underlying order, time period that corresponds to the amount in #10a (such as month, week, etc.).

11a-c. Dollar amount to be withheld for payment of miscellaneous obligations, if appropriate, based on the underlying order, time period that corresponds to the amount in #11a (e.g., month, week, etc.), and description of the miscellaneous obligation.

12a.   Total of #5a, #6a, #7a, #8a, #9a, #10a, and # 11a.

12b.   Time period that corresponds to the amount in #12a (e.g., month).

13.   Check this box if arrears greater than 12 weeks.

14a.   Amount an employer should withhold if the employee is paid weekly.

2

14b. Amount an employer should withhold if the employee is paid every two weeks.

14c. Amount an employer should withhold if the employee is paid twice a month.

14d. Amount an employer should withhold if the employee is paid once a month.

REMITTANCE INFORMATION

15. The state, tribe, or territory from which this Order/Notice or Notice of an Order is sent.

16. Number of days in which the withholding must begin pursuant to the issuing state's or tribe's laws/procedures.

17. The effective date of the income withholding.

18. Number of working days within which an employer or other withholder of income must remit amounts withheld pursuant to the issuing state's law.

19. The percentage of income that may be withheld from the employee's/obligor's income. For state orders, you may not withhold more than the lesser of: 1) the amounts allowed by the Federal Consumer Credit Protection Act (15 U.S.C. § 1673(b)); or 2) the amounts allowed by the state of the employee's/obligor's principal place of employment. The federal limit applies to the aggregate disposable weekly earnings (ADWE). ADWE is the net income left after making mandatory deductions such as: state, federal, local taxes, Social Security taxes, statutory pension contributions, and Medicare taxes.

   For tribal orders, you may not withhold more than the amounts allowed under the law of the issuing tribe. For tribal employers who receive a state order, you may not withhold more than the amounts allowed under the law of the state that issued the order.

20. The state, tribe, or territory from which the Order or Notice is sent.

21. Name of the State Disbursement Unit, individual, tribunal/court, or tribal child support enforcement agency specified in the underlying income withholding order to which payments are required to be sent. This form may not indicate a location other than that specified by an entity authorized under state or tribal law to issue an income withholding order. Please include the case identifier used to record payment (should be the same as 3c). In a IV-D case, this must be the IV-D case number.

22. Address of the State Disbursement Unit, tribunal/court, tribal child support enforcement agency, or individual identified in #21. This information is shared with the obligor. Be sure to safeguard confidential addresses.

Complete only for EFT/EDI transmission.

23a. Telephone number of contact to provide EFT/EDI instructions.

3

OMB 0970-0154

23b. Federal Information Process Standard (FIPS) code for transmitting payments through EFT/EDI. The FIPS code is five characters that identify the state, county or tribe. It is seven characters when it identifies the state, county, and a location within the county. It is necessary for centralized collections.

23c. Receiving agency's bank routing number.

23d. Receiving agency's bank account number.

IV-D agencies, courts, and attorneys (with authority to issue an income withholding order/notice) sending an Order/Notice to Withhold Income for Child Support must complete 24a-e.

24a. Print name of the government official authorizing this Order or Notice to Withhold.

24b. Print title of the government official authorizing this Order or Notice to Withhold.

24c. Signature of Government Official authorizing this Order/Notice to Withhold and date of signature. This line may be optional only if the Withholding Order/Notice includes the name and title of a government official (line 24a, 24b) and a signature of the official (line 24c) is not required by state or tribal law. Provide a signature if required by state or tribal law.

24d. Check the appropriate box to indicate whether a child support enforcement agency (IV-D) or court is authorizing this Order or Notice for withholding.

24e. Check the box if you are an attorney with authority to issue an order or notice under state law.

Attorneys, individuals, and private entities sending a Notice of an Order to Withhold Income for Child Support complete 25a-d.

25a. Print name of the individual or entity sending this Notice.

25b. Print title of the individual sending this Notice, if appropriate

25c. Signature of the individual sending this Notice and date of signature.

25d. Please check the appropriate box to indicate whether you are an attorney, individual, or private entity sending this Notice of an Order.

OMB 0970-0154

The following information refers to federal, state, or tribal laws that apply to issuing an income withholding order/notice or notice of an order to the employer. Any state or tribal specific information may be included in space provided.

26. Check the box if the state or tribal law requires the employer to provide a copy of the Order or Notice to the employee.

27. Use this space to provide additional information on the penalty and/or citation for an employer who fails to comply with the Order or Notice. The law of the obligor's principal place of employment governs the penalty.

28. Use this space to provide additional information on the penalty and/or citation for an employer, who discharges, refuses to employ, or disciplines an employee/obligor as a result of the Order or Notice. The law of the obligor's principal place of employment governs the penalty.

29. Use this space to provide the child(ren)'s names listed in the support order and/or additional information regarding this income withholding Order or Notice of an Order.

Please provide the following contact information to the employer. Employers may need additional information to process the Order or Notice.

30a. Name of the contact person sending the Order or Notice of an Order that an employer and/or employee/obligor may call for information regarding the Order or Notice of an Order.

30b. Telephone number for the contact person whose name appears in #30a.

30c. Fax number for the person whose name appears in #30a.

30d. Internet address for the person whose name appears in #30a.

If the employer is a Federal Government agency, the following instructions apply.

■ Serve the Order or Notice of an Order upon the governmental agent listed in 5 CFR part 581, appendix A.

■ Sufficient identifying information must be provided in order for the obligor to be identified. It is, therefore, recommended that the following information, if known and if applicable, be provided:

■ (1) full name of the obligor; (2) date of birth; (3) employment number, Department of Veterans Affairs claim number, or civil service retirement claim number; (4) component of the government entity for which the obligor works, and the official duty station or worksite; and (5) status of the obligor, e.g., employee, former employee, or annuitant.

■ You may withhold from a variety of incomes and forms of payment, including voluntary separation incentive payments (buy-out payments), incentive pay, and cash awards. For a

OMB 0970-0154

more complete list see 5 CFR 581.103.

****

The Paperwork Reduction Act of 1995

This information collection is conducted in accordance with 45 CFR 303.100 of the child support enforcement program. Standard forms are designed to provide uniformity and standardization for interstate case processing. Public reporting burden for this collection of information is estimated to average one hour per response. The responses to this collection are mandatory in accordance with 45 CFR 303.7. This information is subject to State and Federal confidentiality requirements; however, the information will be filed with the tribunal and/or agency in the responding State and may, depending on State law, be disclosed to other parties. An agency may not conduct or sponsor, and a person is not required to respond to, a collection of information unless it displays a currently valid OMB control number.

OMB 0970-0154

1a ☐ **ORDER/NOTICE TO WITHHOLD INCOME FOR CHILD SUPPORT**
☐ **NOTICE OF AN ORDER TO WITHHOLD INCOME FOR CHILD SUPPORT**

☐Original ☐Amended ☐Termination **#1b** Date: ___**#1c**___
☐State/Tribe/Territory_____ **#1d**_____
  City/Co./Dist./Reservation_____ **#1e**_____
☐Non-governmental entity or Individual ____ **#1f**_____
  Case Number_____ **#1g**_____

_____**#2a**_____ Employer's/Withholder's Name	RE:_____**#3a**_____ Employee's/Obligor's Name (Last, First, MI)
_____**#2b**_____ Employer's/Withholder's Address	_____**#3b**_____ Employee's/Obligor's Social Security Number
_____**#2c**_____	_____**#3c**_____ Employee's/Obligor's Case Identifier
_____**#2d**_____ Employer's/Withholder's Federal EIN Number (if known)	_____**#3d**_____ Obligee's Name (Last, First, MI)

ORDER INFORMATION: This document is based on the support or withholding order from _____▮▮▮▮▮_____.
You are required by law to deduct these amounts from the employee's/obligor's income until further notice.

$____**# 5a**____ Per ____**# 5b**_ current child support **#13**
$____**# 6a**____ Per ____**# 6b**_ past-due child support - Arrears greater than12 weeks? ☐yes ☐no
$____**# 7a**____ Per ____**# 7b**_ current cash medical support
$____**# 8a**____ Per ____**# 8b**_ past-due cash medical support
$____**# 9a**____ Per ____**# 9b**_ spousal support
$____**#10a**____ Per ____**#10b**_ past-due spousal support
$____**#11a**____ Per ____**#11b**_ other (specify) _____**#11c**_____
for a total of $_____**#12a**_____ per _____**#12b**_____to be forwarded to the payee below.
You do not have to vary your pay cycle to be in compliance with the support order. If your pay cycle does not match the
ordered payment cycle, withhold one of the following amounts:
$_**# 14a**_per weekly pay period. $_**# 14c**_per semimonthly pay period (twice a month).
$\_**# 14b**\_per biweekly pay period (every two weeks).$_**# 14d**__per monthly pay period.

REMITTANCE INFORMATION: When remitting payment, provide the pay date/date of withholding and the case identifier. If
the employee's/obligor's principal place of employment is ____**#15**_____, begin withholding no later than the first pay period
occurring_**#16**_ days after the date of __**#17**__. Send payment within **#18** working days of the pay date/date of withholding.
The total withheld amount, including your fee, may not exceed _**#19**_ % of the employee's/obligor's aggregate disposable
weekly earnings.

If the employee's/obligor's principal place of employment is not _____**#20**_____, for limitations on
withholding, applicable time requirements, and any allowable employer fees, follow the laws and procedures of the
employee's/obligor's principal place of employment (see #3 and #9, ADDITIONAL INFORMATION TO EMPLOYERS AND
OTHER WITHHOLDERS).

Make check payable to:_____**#21**(Payee and Case identifier)_____Send check to:_____**#22**_____.
If remitting payment by EFT/EDI, call __**#23a**_____before first submission. Use this FIPS code: **#23b**__:
Bank routing number: _____**#23c**_____Bank account number:_**#23d**_____.

If this is an Order/Notice to Withhold:	**If this is a Notice of an Order to Withhold:**
24a Print Name _____	**25a** Print Name_____
24b Title of Issuing Official_____▮▮▮▮____	**25b** Title (if appropriate)_____
24c Signature and Date__ (if required by state or tribal law)	**25c** Signature and Date_____
24d ☐ IV-D Agency ☐Court	**25d** ☐ Attorney ☐Individual ☐Private Entity
24e ☐ Attorney with authority under state law to issue order/notice.	

NOTE: Non-IV-D Attorneys, individuals, and non-governmental entities must submit a Notice of an Order to Withhold and
include a copy of the income withholding order unless, under a state's law, an attorney in that state may issue an income
withholding order. In that case, the attorney may submit an Order/Notice to Withhold and include a copy of the state law

IMPORTANT: The person completing this form is advised that the information on this form may be shared with the obligor.

OMB 0970-0154

authorizing the attorney to issue an income withholding order/notice.

ADDITIONAL INFORMATION TO EMPLOYERS AND OTHER WITHHOLDERS

#26 ☐ If checked, you are required to provide a copy of this form to your employee/obligor. If your employee works in a state that is different from the state that issued this order, a copy must be provided to your employee/obligor even if the box is not checked.

1. **Priority:** Withholding under this Order or Notice has priority over any other legal process under state law (or tribal law, if applicable) against the same income. If there are federal tax levies in effect, please notify the contact person listed below. (See 10 below.)

2. **Combining Payments:** You may combine withheld amounts from more than one employee's/obligor's income in a single payment to each agency/party requesting withholding. You must, however, separately identify the portion of the single payment that is attributable to each employee/obligor.

3. **Reporting the Paydate/Date of Withholding:** You must report the paydate/date of withholding when sending the payment. The paydate/date of withholding is the date on which the amount was withheld from the employee's wages. You must comply with the law of the state of employee's/obligor's principal place of employment with respect to the time periods within which you must implement the withholding and forward the support payments.

4. **Employee/Obligor with Multiple Support Withholdings:** If there is more than one Order or Notice against this employee/obligor and you are unable to honor all support Orders or Notices due to federal, state, or tribal withholding limits, you must follow the state or tribal law/procedure of the employee's/obligor's principal place of employment. You must honor all Orders or Notices to the greatest extent possible. (See 9 below.)

5. **Termination Notification:** You must promptly notify the Child Support Enforcement (IV-D) Agency and/or the contact person listed below when the employee/obligor no longer works for you. Please provide the information requested and return a complete copy of this Order or Notice to the Child Support Enforcement (IV-D) Agency and/or the contact person listed below. (See 10 below.)

   THE EMPLOYEE/OBLIGOR NO LONGER WORKS FOR:_____
   EMPLOYEE'S/OBLIGOR'S NAME: _____CASE IDENTIFIER: _____
   DATE OF SEPARATION FROM EMPLOYMENT: _____
   LAST KNOWN HOME ADDRESS: _____
   NEW EMPLOYER/ADDRESS: _____

6. **Lump Sum Payments:** You may be required to report and withhold from lump sum payments such as bonuses, commissions, or severance pay. If you have any questions about lump sum payments, contact the Child Support Enforcement (IV-D) Agency.

7. **Liability:** If you have any doubts about the validity of the Order or Notice, contact the agency or person listed below under 10. If you fail to withhold income as the Order or Notice directs, you are liable for both the accumulated amount you should have withheld from the employee's/obligor's income and any other penalties set by state or tribal law/procedure.
   #27_____
   _____

8. **Anti-discrimination:** You are subject to a fine determined under state or tribal law for discharging an employee/obligor from employment, refusing to employ, or taking disciplinary action against any employee/obligor because of a child support withholding.
   #28_____
   _____

9. **Withholding Limits:** For state orders, you may not withhold more than the lesser of: 1) the amounts allowed by the Federal Consumer Credit Protection Act (15 U.S.C. § 1673(b)); or 2) the amounts allowed by the state of the employee's/obligor's principal place of employment. The federal limit applies to the aggregate disposable weekly earnings (ADWE). ADWE is the net income left after making mandatory deductions such as: state, federal, local taxes, Social Security taxes, statutory pension contributions, and Medicare taxes. The Federal CCPA limit is 50% of the ADWE for child support and alimony, which is increased by 1) 10% if the employee does not support a second family; and/or 2) 5% if arrears greater than 12 weeks.
   For tribal orders, you may not withhold more than the amounts allowed under the law of the issuing tribe. For tribal employers who receive a state order, you may not withhold more than the amounts allowed under the law of the state that issued the order.

   Child(ren)'s Names and Additional Information:___ **#29** _____
   _____

10. If you or your employee/obligor have any questions, contact____ **#30a** _____by telephone at
    ____ **#30b** _____by Fax at _____ **#30c** ___or by internet at_____ **#30d** _____.

FL-450

ATTORNEY OR PARTY WITHOUT ATTORNEY *(Name, State Bar number, and address)*:	*FOR COURT USE ONLY*

TELEPHONE NO.:   FAX NO. *(Optional)*:

E-MAIL ADDRESS *(Optional)*:

ATTORNEY FOR *(Name)*:

SUPERIOR COURT OF CALIFORNIA, COUNTY OF

STREET ADDRESS:

MAILING ADDRESS:

CITY AND ZIP CODE:

BRANCH NAME:

PETITIONER/PLAINTIFF:

RESPONDENT/DEFENDANT:

OTHER PARENT:

REQUEST FOR HEARING REGARDING EARNINGS ASSIGNMENT	CASE NUMBER:

NOTICE: Complete and file this form with the court clerk to request a hearing *only* if you object to the *Order/Notice to Withhold Income for Child Support* (form FL-195/OMB0970-0154) or *Earnings Assignment Order for Spousal or Partner Support* (form FL-435). This form may not be used to modify your current child support amount. (See page 2 of form FL-192, *Information Sheet on Changing a Child Support Order*.) Page 3 of this form is instructional only and does not need to be delivered to the court.

1. A hearing on this application will be held as follows *(see instructions for getting a hearing date on page 3)*:

   a. Date: Time: ☐ Dept.:   ☐ Div.:   ☐ Room:

   b. The address of the court is: ☐ same as noted above ☐ other *(specify)*:

2. ☐ I request that service of the *Earnings Assignment Order for Spousal or Partner Support* (form FL-435) or *Order/Notice to Withhold Income for Child Support* (form FL-195/OMB0970-0154) be quashed (set aside) because

   a. ☐ I am not the obligor named in the earnings assignment.

   b. ☐ There is good cause to recall the earnings assignment because **all** of the following conditions exist:

      (1) Recalling the earnings assignment would be in the best interest of the children for whom I am ordered to pay support *(state reasons)*:

      (2) I have paid court-ordered support fully and on time for the last 12 months without either an earnings assignment or another mandatory collection process.

      (3) I do not owe any arrearage (back support).

      (4) Service of the earnings assignment would cause extraordinary hardship for me, as follows *(state reasons; you must prove these reasons at any hearing on this application by clear and convincing evidence)*:

   c. ☐ The other parent and I have a written agreement that allows the support order to be paid by an alternative method. A copy of the agreement is attached. **(NOTE: If the support obligation is paid to the local child support agency, this agreement must be signed by a representative of that agency.)**

Page 1 of 3

REQUEST FOR HEARING REGARDING EARNINGS ASSIGNMENT
(Family Law—Governmental—UIFSA)

Family Code, § 5246
www.courtinfo.ca.gov

PETITIONER/PLAINTIFF:	CASE NUMBER:
RESPONDENT/DEFENDANT:	
OTHER PARENT:	

3. ☐ I request that the earnings assignment be modified because

    a. ☐ the total amount of arrearages claimed as owing is incorrect. (*Check one or more of the following reasons.*)

        (1) ☐ I did not receive credit for all of the payments I have made. (*Check (a), (b), or both.*)

            (a) ☐ I have attached my statement of the payment history, which includes a monthly breakdown of amounts ordered and amounts paid.

            (b) ☐ I made the following payments that were not credited (*for each payment, specify the date, the amount, and the name of the person or agency paid*):

        (2) ☐ Child support was terminated (*specify name of child, child's date of birth, date of termination, and reason support was terminated*):

        (3) ☐ Other (*specify*):

    b. ☐ the monthly payment specified in the earnings assignment is more than half of my total net income each month from all sources.

    c. ☐ the monthly arrearage payment stated in the earnings assignment creates an undue hardship because (*describe the hardship and state the amount you are able to pay on your arrearage*):

    (NOTE: If you want to change the amount of money being deducted for arrearage because it creates a hardship, please attach a completed *Financial Statement (Simplified)* (form FL-155) or *Income and Expense Declaration* (form FL-150).)

I declare under penalty of perjury under the laws of the State of California that the foregoing is true and correct.

Date:

▶

_____   _____
(TYPE OR PRINT NAME OF PERSON REQUESTING HEARING)   (SIGNATURE OF PERSON REQUESTING HEARING)

CLERK'S CERTIFICATE OF MAILING

I certify that I am not a party to this action and that a true copy of the *Request for Hearing Regarding Earnings Assignment* (form FL-450) was mailed, with postage fully prepaid, in a sealed envelope addressed as shown below, and that the request was mailed at (*place*):   on (*date*):

Date:

        Clerk, by _____ , Deputy

     REQUEST FOR HEARING REGARDING EARNINGS ASSIGNMENT
(Family Law—Governmental—UIFSA)

INFORMATION SHEET AND INSTRUCTIONS
FOR REQUEST FOR HEARING REGARDING EARNINGS ASSIGNMENT
(Do *not* deliver this information sheet to the court clerk.)

Please follow these instructions to complete the *Request for Hearing Regarding Earnings Assignment* (form FL-450) if you do not have an attorney representing you. Your attorney, if you have one, should complete this form. You must file the completed *Request for Hearing* form and its attachments with the court clerk **within 10 days** after the date your employer gave you a copy of *Earnings Assignment Order for Spousal or Partner Support* (form FL-435) or an *Order/Notice to Withhold Income for Child Support* (form FL-195/OMB0970-0154). The address of the court clerk is the same as the one shown for the superior court on the earnings assignment order. You may have to pay a filing fee. If you cannot afford to pay the filing fee, the court may waive it, but you will have to fill out some forms first. For more information about the filing fee and waiver of the filing fee, contact the court clerk or the family law facilitator in your county.

(TYPE OR PRINT IN INK)

Front page, first box, top of form, left side: Print your name, address, and telephone number in this box if they are not already there.

Item 1. **a–b.** You must contact the court clerk's office and ask that a hearing date be set for this motion. The court clerk will give you the information you need to complete this section.

Item 2. Check this box if you want the court to stop the local child support agency or the other parent from collecting any support from your earnings. If you check this box, you must check the box for either a, b, or c beneath it.

    a. Check this box if you are not the person required to pay support in the earnings assignment.

    b. Check this box if you believe that there is "good cause" to recall the earnings assignment. **Note:** The court must find that **all** of the conditions listed in item 2b exist in order for good cause to apply.

    c. Check this box if you and the other parent have a written agreement that allows you to pay the support another way. **You must attach a copy of the agreement,** which must be signed by both the other parent and a representative of the local child support agency if payments are made to a county office.

Item 3. Check this box if you want to change the earnings assignment. If you check this box, you must check the box for either a, b, or c beneath it.

    a. Check this box if the total arrearages listed in item 9 on the earnings assignment order are wrong. If you check this box, you must check one or more of (1), (2), and (3). You must attach the original of your statement of arrearages. Keep one copy for yourself.

        (1) Check this box if you believe the amount of arrearages listed on the earnings assignment order does not give you credit for all the payments you have made. If you check this box, you must check one or both of the boxes beneath it.

            (a) Check this box if you are attaching your own statement of arrearages. This statement must include a monthly listing of what you were ordered to pay and what you actually paid.

            (b) Check this box if you wish to list any payments that you believe were not included in the arrearages amount. For each payment you must list the date you paid it, the amount paid, and the person or agency (such as the local child support agency) to whom you made the payment. Bring to the hearing proof of any payment that is in dispute.

        (2) Check this box if the child support for any of the children in the case has been terminated (ended). If you check this box, you must list the following information for each child:

            • The name and birthdate of each child.

            • The date the child support order was terminated.

            • The reason child support was terminated.

        (3) Check this box if there is another reason you believe the amount of arrearages is incorrect. You must explain the reasons in detail.

    b. Check this box if the total monthly payment shown in item 1 of the earnings assignment order is more than half of your monthly net income.

    c. Check this box if the total monthly payment shown in item 1 of the earnings assignment order causes you a serious hardship. You must write the reasons for the hardship in this space.

You must date this *Request for Hearing* form, print your name, and sign the form under penalty of perjury. You must also complete the certificate of mailing at the bottom of page 2 of the form by printing the name and address of the other parties in brackets and providing a stamped envelope addressed to each of the parties. When you sign this *Request for Hearing* form, you are stating that the information you have provided is true and correct. After you file the request, the court clerk will notify you by mail of the date, time, and location of the hearing.

You must file your request within 10 days of receiving the *Earnings Assignment Order for Spousal or Partner Support* or the *Order/Notice to Withhold Income for Child Support* from your employer. You may file your request in person at the clerk's office or mail it to the clerk. In either event, it must be received by the clerk within the 10-day period.

If you need additional assistance with this form, contact an attorney or the family law facilitator in your county. Your family law facilitator can help you, for free, with any questions you have about the above information. For more information on finding a lawyer or family law facilitator, see the California Courts Online Self-Help Center at *www.courtinfo.ca.gov/selfhelp/*.

NOTICE: Use form FL-450 to request a hearing only if you object to the *Order/Notice to Withhold Income for Child Support* (form FL-195/OMB0970-0154) or *Earnings Assignment Order for Spousal or Partner Support* (form FL-435). This form will *not* modify your current support amount. (See page 2 of form FL-192, *Information Sheet on Changing a Child Support Order*.)

REQUEST FOR HEARING REGARDING EARNINGS ASSIGNMENT
(Family Law—Governmental—UIFSA)

This page intentionally blank.

State of California
Secretary of State

FILE NO: _____

This Space For Filing Use Only

DECLARATION OF DOMESTIC PARTNERSHIP
(Please read instructions on reverse side before completing form.)

We the undersigned, do declare that we meet the requirements of Family Code section 297, as follows:

- Both persons have a common residence.
- Neither person is married to someone else or is a member of another domestic partnership with someone else that has not been terminated, dissolved, or adjudged a nullity.
- Both persons are not related by blood in a way that would prevent them from being married to each other in this state.
- Both persons are at least 18 years of age.
- Both persons are members of the same sex, **OR** One or both of the persons of opposite sex are over the age of 62 and meet the eligibility criteria under Title II of the Social Security Act as defined in 42 U.S.C. section 402(a) for old-age insurance benefits or Title XVI of the Social Security Act as defined in 42 U.S.C. section 1381 for aged individuals.
- Both persons are capable of consenting to the domestic partnership.
- Both persons consent to the jurisdiction of the Superior Courts of California for the purpose of a proceeding to obtain a judgment of dissolution or nullity of the domestic partnership or for legal separation of partners in the domestic partnership, or for any other proceeding related to the partners' rights and obligations, even if one or both partners ceases to be a resident of, or to maintain a domicile in, this state.

The representations are true and correct, and contain no material omissions of fact to the best of our knowledge and belief.

_____   _____
Signature   (Last)   (First)   (Middle)

_____   _____
Signature   (Last)   (First)   (Middle)

_____   _____
Mailing Address   City   State   Zip Code

_____
E-Mail Address(es) (optional)

NOTARIZATION IS REQUIRED
State of California
County of _____

On _____, before me, _____ Notary Public, personally appeared _____,
personally known to me (or proved to me on the basis of satisfactory evidence) to be the person(s) whose name(s) is/are subscribed to the within instrument and acknowledged to me that he/she/they executed the same in his/her/their authorized capacity(ies), and that by his/her/their signature(s) on the instrument the person(s), or the entity upon behalf of which the person(s) acted, executed the instrument.
WITNESS my hand and official seal.

_____
Signature of Notary Public

[PLACE NOTARY PUBLIC SEAL HERE]

INSTRUCTIONS FOR COMPLETING THE
DECLARATION OF DOMESTIC PARTNERSHIP (FORM NP/SF DP-1)

For easier completion, this form is available on the Secretary of State's website at http://www.sos.ca.gov/dpregistry/ and can be viewed, filled in and printed from your computer. If you are not completing this form online, please type or legibly print in black or blue ink. This form should not be altered.

Statutory filing provisions are found in California Family Code sections 297 and 298. All statutory references are to the California Family Code, unless otherwise stated.

The Declaration of Domestic Partnership form may be used to establish a domestic partnership of two persons meeting the requirements of Section 297 (as stated on the front of the form). A copy of the declaration and a Certificate of Registration of Domestic Partnership will be returned to the partners after the declaration is filed. Note: Filing an intentionally and materially false Declaration of Domestic Partnership shall be punishable as a misdemeanor. (Section 298(c).)

Complete the Declaration of Domestic Partnership (Form NP/SF DP-1) as follows:

- Both persons must sign and affix their signatures to the same Declaration of Domestic Partnership form.

- Both persons must print their names legibly. The names must be printed in the order requested: Last name, First name, Middle name. If there is a suffix, i.e. Jr., Sr., etc., include this as part of the last name.

- A complete mailing address is required (address, city, state, zip code). Print legibly. Do not abbreviate city names.

- The signatures of both persons must be notarized with a certificate of acknowledgment.

The completed form can be mailed to Secretary of State, Domestic Partners Registry, P.O. Box 942877 Sacramento, CA 94277-0001 OR delivered in person to the Sacramento office, 1500 11th Street, 2nd Floor Sacramento, CA 95814 or to any of the regional offices located in Fresno, Los Angeles, San Diego, and San Francisco. Note: The regional offices are only able to process documents delivered in person. Please refer to the Secretary of State's website at http://www.sos.ca.gov/dpregistry/ for regional office locations and addresses.

FEES: The fee for filing Form NP/SF DP-1 is $10.00. For same-sex partners, an additional $23.00 fee must be paid at the time of filing the form, for a total of $33.00. There is an additional $15.00 special handling fee for processing a document delivered in person to the Sacramento office or any of the regional offices located in Fresno, Los Angeles, San Diego, and San Francisco. Checks or money orders should be made payable to the Secretary of State.

Payments for documents submitted:

- by mail to Sacramento can be made by check or money order.

- over-the-counter in Sacramento can be made by check, money order, cash, or credit card (Visa or MasterCard).

- over-the-counter in any of the four regional offices can be made by check, money order or credit card (Visa or MasterCard). Regional offices are not able to accept cash.

The additional $23.00 fee will be used to develop and support a training curriculum specific to lesbian, gay, bisexual, and transgender domestic abuse support service providers who serve that community in regard to domestic violence, and to provide brochures specific to lesbian, gay, bisexual, and transgender domestic abuse. Brochures developed by the Department of Health Services will be available upon request from the Secretary of State, as funding allows. (Sections 298, 298.5 and 358.)

State of California
Secretary of State

FILE NO: _____

_____

(Office Use Only)

NOTICE OF TERMINATION OF DOMESTIC PARTNERSHIP
(Family Code section 299)

Instructions:

1. Complete and send to:
   Secretary of State
   P.O. Box 942877
   Sacramento, CA 94277-0001
   (916) 653-3984

2. There is no fee for filing this Notice of Termination

We, the undersigned, do declare that:

We are terminating our domestic partnership. We have read and understand the brochure prepared by the Secretary of State describing the requirements, nature, and effect of terminating a domestic partnership. We also declare that all of the conditions exist as specified in Section 299(a) of the Family Code.

Secretary of State File Number (if known): _____ .

_____   _____
Signature of Partner   Printed Name (Last)   (First)   (Middle)

_____   _____
Signature of Partner   Printed Name (Last)   (First)   (Middle)

NOTARIZATION IS REQUIRED
State of California
County of _____

On _____ , before me, _____ , personally

appeared _____

_____

personally known to me (or proved to me on the basis of satisfactory evidence) to be the person(s) whose name(s) is/are subscribed to the within instrument and acknowledged to me that he/she/they executed the same in his/her/their authorized capacity(ies), and that by his/her/their signature(s) on the instrument the person(s) or the entity upon behalf of which the person(s) acted, executed the instrument.
WITNESS my hand and official seal.

_____
Signature of Notary Public   [PLACE NOTARY SEAL HERE]

RETURN TO (Enter the name and the address of the person to whom a copy of the filed document should be returned.)

NAME   ⌈   ⌉

ADDRESS

CITY/STATE/ZIP ⌊   ⌋

This page intentionally blank.

FILE NO._____

State of California
Secretary of State

REVOCATION OF TERMINATION OF DOMESTIC PARTNERSHIP
(Family Code section 299)

(Office Use Only)

Instructions:

1. Complete and mail to:

   Secretary of State
   P.O. Box 942877
   Sacramento, CA 94277-0001
   (916) 653-3984

2. There is no fee for filing this Revocation of Termination of Domestic Partnership.

I, the undersigned, do declare that:

I am revoking the termination of domestic partnership, notice of which was filed with the Secretary of

State on _____. This revocation is being filed within six months of the date the
            (month/day/year)

Notice of Termination was filed with the Secretary of State. I have sent the other party a copy of this

notice of revocation by first-class mail, postage prepaid, at the other party's last known address.

Signature	Printed Name (Last)	(First)	(Middle)

Partner's Name (Last)	(First)	(Middle)

RETURN TO (Enter the name and the address of the person to whom a copy of the filed document should be returned.)

NAME ⌐   ⌐

ADDRESS

CITY/STATE/ZIP L   L

SEC/STATE NP/SF DP-3 (Rev 03/2005)

This page intentionally blank.

Form **8332**
(Rev. January 2006)

Department of the Treasury
Internal Revenue Service

**Release of Claim to Exemption
for Child of Divorced or Separated Parents**

▶ Attach to noncustodial parent's return each year exemption is claimed.

OMB No. 1545-0074

Attachment
Sequence No. **115**

Name of noncustodial parent claiming exemption

Noncustodial parent's
social security number (SSN) ▶

Part I   Release of Claim to Exemption for Current Year

I agree not to claim an exemption for _____

Name(s) of child (or children)

for the tax year 20 _____ .

_____   _____   _____
Signature of custodial parent releasing claim to exemption   Custodial parent's SSN   Date

Note. If you choose not to claim an exemption for this child (or children) for future tax years, also complete Part II.

Part II   Release of Claim to Exemption for Future Years (If completed, see **Noncustodial parent** on page 2.)

I agree not to claim an exemption for _____

Name(s) of child (or children)

for the tax year(s)_____ .
        (Specify. See instructions.)

_____   _____   _____
Signature of custodial parent releasing claim to exemption   Custodial parent's SSN   Date

General Instructions

Purpose of form. If you are a custodial parent, you can use this form to release your claim to a dependency exemption for your child. The release of the dependency exemption will also release to the noncustodial parent the child tax credit and the additional child tax credit (if either applies). Complete this form (or a similar statement containing the same information required by this form) and give it to the noncustodial parent who will claim the child's exemption. The noncustodial parent must attach this form or a similar statement to his or her tax return each year the exemption is claimed.

You are the custodial parent if you had custody of the child for the greater part of the year. You are the noncustodial parent if you had custody for a shorter period of time or did not have custody at all.

Exemption for a dependent child. A dependent is either a qualifying child or a qualifying relative. In most cases, a child of divorced or separated parents will qualify as a dependent of the custodial parent under the rules for a qualifying child. However, the noncustodial parent may be able to claim the child's exemption if the *Special rule for children of divorced or separated parents* on this page applies.

For the definition of a qualifying child and a qualifying relative, see your tax return instruction booklet.

Post-1984 decree or agreement. If the divorce decree or separation agreement went into effect after 1984, the noncustodial parent can attach certain

pages from the decree or agreement instead of Form 8332. To be able to do this, the decree or agreement must state all three of the following.

1. The noncustodial parent can claim the child as a dependent without regard to any condition (such as payment of support).

2. The other parent will not claim the child as a dependent.

3. The years for which the claim is released.

The noncustodial parent must attach all of the following pages from the decree or agreement.

● Cover page (include the other parent's SSN on that page).

● The pages that include all of the information identified in (1) through (3) above.

● Signature page with the other parent's signature and date of agreement.

 The noncustodial parent must attach the required information even if it was filed with a return in an earlier year.

Special rule for children of divorced or separated parents. A child is treated as a qualifying child or a qualifying relative of the noncustodial parent if all of the following apply.

1. The child received over half of his or her support for the year from one or both of the parents (see the *Exception* on this page). Public assistance payments, such as Temporary Assistance for Needy Families (TANF), are not support provided by the parents.

2. The child was in the custody of one or both of the parents for more than half of the year.

3. Either of the following applies.

a. The custodial parent agrees not to claim the child's exemption by signing this form or a similar statement. If the decree or agreement went into effect after 1984, see *Post-1984 decree or agreement* on this page.

b. A pre-1985 decree of divorce or separate maintenance or written separation agreement states that the noncustodial parent can claim the child as a dependent. But the noncustodial parent must provide at least $600 for the child's support during the year. This rule does not apply if the decree or agreement was changed after 1984 to say that the noncustodial parent cannot claim the child as a dependent.

For this rule to apply, the parents must be one of the following.

● Divorced or legally separated under a decree of divorce or separate maintenance.

● Separated under a written separation agreement.

● Living apart at all times during the last 6 months of the year.

If this rule applies, and the other dependency tests in your tax return instruction booklet are also met, the noncustodial parent can claim the child's exemption.

Exception. If the support of the child is determined under a multiple support agreement, this special rule does not apply and this form should not be used.

For Paperwork Reduction Act Notice, see back of form.   Cat. No. 13910F   Form **8332** (Rev. 1-2006)

344

 TIP *Special rules may apply for people who had to relocate because of Hurricane Katrina, Rita, or Wilma. See Pub. 4492, Information for Taxpayers Affected by Hurricanes Katrina, Rita, and Wilma, for details.*

Specific Instructions

Custodial parent. You may agree to release your claim to the child's exemption for the current tax year or for future years, or both.

● Complete Part I if you agree to release your claim to the child's exemption for the current tax year.

● Complete Part II if you agree to release your claim to the child's exemption for any or all future years. If you do, write the specific future year(s) or "all future years" in the space provided in Part II.

 TIP *To help ensure future support, you may not want to release your claim to the child's exemption for future years.*

Noncustodial parent. Attach this form or similar statement to your tax return for each year you claim the child's exemption. You can claim the exemption only if the other dependency tests in your tax return instruction booklet are met.

 TIP *If the custodial parent released his or her claim to the child's exemption for any future year, you must attach a copy of this form or similar statement to your tax return for each future year that you claim the exemption. Keep a copy for your records.*

Paperwork Reduction Act Notice. We ask for the information on this form to carry out the Internal Revenue laws of the United States. You are required to give us the information. We need it to ensure that you are complying with these laws and to allow us to figure and collect the right amount of tax.

You are not required to provide the information requested on a form that is subject to the Paperwork Reduction Act unless the form displays a valid OMB control number. Books or records relating to a form or its instructions must be retained as long as their contents may become material in the administration of any Internal Revenue law. Generally, tax returns and return information are confidential, as required by Internal Revenue Code section 6103.

The average time and expenses required to complete and file this form will vary depending on individual circumstances. For the estimated averages, see the instructions for your income tax return.

If you have suggestions for making this form simpler, we would be happy to hear from you. See the instructions for your income tax return.

PETITIONER:	CASE NUMBER:
RESPONDENT:	

ADVISEMENT AND WAIVER OF RIGHTS RE: ESTABLISHMENT OF PARENTAL RELATIONSHIP

RIGHT TO BE REPRESENTED BY A LAWYER. I understand that I have the right to be represented by a lawyer of my own choice at my own expense. If I cannot afford a lawyer, I can contact the Lawyer Referral Association of the local bar association or the Family Law Facilitator for assistance.

RIGHT TO A TRIAL. I understand that I have a right to have a judge determine whether I am the parent of the children named in this action.

RIGHT TO CONFRONT AND CROSS-EXAMINE WITNESSES. I understand that in a trial I have the right to confront and cross-examine the witnesses against me and to present evidence and witnesses in my own defense.

RIGHT TO HAVE PARENTAGE TESTS. I understand that, where the law permits, I have the right to have the court order parentage tests. The court will decide who pays for the tests. The court could order that I pay none, some, or all of the costs of the tests.

OBLIGATIONS. I understand that if I admit that I am the parent of the children in this action that those children will be my children for legal purposes.

WAIVER. I understand that I am admitting that I am the parent of the children named in the stipulation and am giving up the rights stated above (except the right to an attorney if I have an attorney).

CHILD SUPPORT. I understand that I will have the duty to contribute to the support of the children named in this action and that this duty of support will continue for each child until the obligation is terminated by law.

CRIMINAL NON-SUPPORT. I understand that if I willfully fail to support the children, criminal proceedings may be initiated against me.

UNDERSTANDING.

   ☐ I have read and understand the *Judgment (Uniform Parentage—Custody and Support)* (form FL-250) and this *Advisement and Waiver of Rights*.
   ☐ I understand the translation.

> IF I AM REPRESENTED BY AN ATTORNEY, I ACKNOWLEDGE THAT MY ATTORNEY HAS READ AND EXPLAINED TO ME THE CONTENTS OF THE STIPULATION, RECITALS, AND WAIVERS, AND I ACKNOWLEDGE THAT I UNDERSTAND THEM.

▶

_____   _____
(TYPE OR PRINT NAME)   (SIGNATURE OF DECLARANT)

INTERPRETER'S DECLARATION

The ☐ Petitioner ☐ Respondent is unable to read or understand the *Judgment (Uniform Parentage—Custody and Support)* (form FL-250) and this *Advisement and Waiver of Rights* because:

   ☐ his/her primary language is *(specify)*:
   ☐ other *(specify)*:

I certify under penalty of perjury under the laws of the State of California that I have, to the best of my ability, read or translated for the ☐ Petitioner ☐ Respondent the *Judgment (Uniform Parentage—Custody and Support)* (form FL-250) and this *Advisement and Waiver of Rights.* ☐ Petitioner ☐ Respondent said he or she understood the *Judgment (Uniform Parentage—Custody and Support)* (form FL-250) and this *Advisement and Waiver of Rights* before signing them.

▶

_____   _____
(TYPE OR PRINT NAME)   (SIGNATURE OF INTERPRETER)

Page 1 of 1

Approved for Optional Use
Judicial Council of California
[Rev. January 1, 2003]

**ADVISEMENT AND WAIVER OF RIGHTS RE:
ESTABLISHMENT OF PARENTAL RELATIONSHIP**
(Uniform Parentage)

Family Code, § 7600 et seq.
www.courtinfo.ca.gov.

This page intentionally blank.

Index

E

F

H

I